The Bioarchaeology of Continental Croatia

An analysis of human skeletal remains from the prehistoric to post-medieval periods

Mario Šlaus

BAR International Series 1021

2002

Published in 2016 by
BAR Publishing, Oxford

BAR International Series 1021

The Bioarchaeology of Continental Croatia

© M Šlaus and the Publisher 2002

Typesetting & layout: Darko Jerko

ISBN 9781841714028 paperback
ISBN 9781407324043 e-format
DOI https://doi.org/10.30861/9781841714028
A catalogue record for this book is available from the British Library

BAR Publishing is the trading name of British Archaeological Reports (Oxford) Ltd.
British Archaeological Reports was first incorporated in 1974 to publish the BAR
Series, International and British. In 1992 Hadrian Books Ltd became part of the BAR
group. This volume was originally published by Archaeopress in conjunction with
British Archaeological Reports (Oxford) Ltd / Hadrian Books Ltd, the Series principal
publisher, in 2002. This present volume is published by BAR Publishing, 2016.

BAR
PUBLISHING

BAR titles are available from:

BAR Publishing
122 Banbury Rd, Oxford, OX2 7BP, UK
EMAIL   info@barpublishing.com
PHONE +44 (0)1865 310431
FAX   +44 (0)1865 316916
www.barpublishing.com

ACKNOWLEDGMENTS

This book could not have been written without the help and support of numerous individuals to whom I express my deepest gratitude. Chief among them are the archaeologists who - despite the previously prevailing, virtually nonexistent interest in the analysis of skeletal material - recovered, stored, and ultimately made available to me the skeletal series and relevant archaeological data from the sites they excavated. These people are: M. Šmalcelj, prof., who besides recovering the skeletal series from Privlaka and Đelekovec taught countless generations of archaeologists the importance of preserving skeletal remains from archaeological sites, K. Simoni, prof., Dr. Ž. Demo, Prof. Dr. A. Durman, M. Dalić, prof., M. Dizdar, M.Sc., Dr. B. Migotti, H. Göricke-Lukić, M.Sc., S. Filipović, prof., K. Filipec, M.Sc., I. Pavlović, prof., T. Pintarić, prof., Z. Hitrec, prof., Dr. Z. Marić, and G. Jakovljević, M.Sc..

Dr. Douglas Owsley from the Division of Physical Anthropology of the Smithsonian Institution, Washington, D.C. has been, and still is, a good friend and mentor. Although not directly involved in the making of this book, his previous guidance and example have been an important influence.

I would also like to thank Dana Kollmann, M.Sc. from the Department of Anthropology, American University, Washington, D.C., who supplied the photographs for this book.

CONTENTS

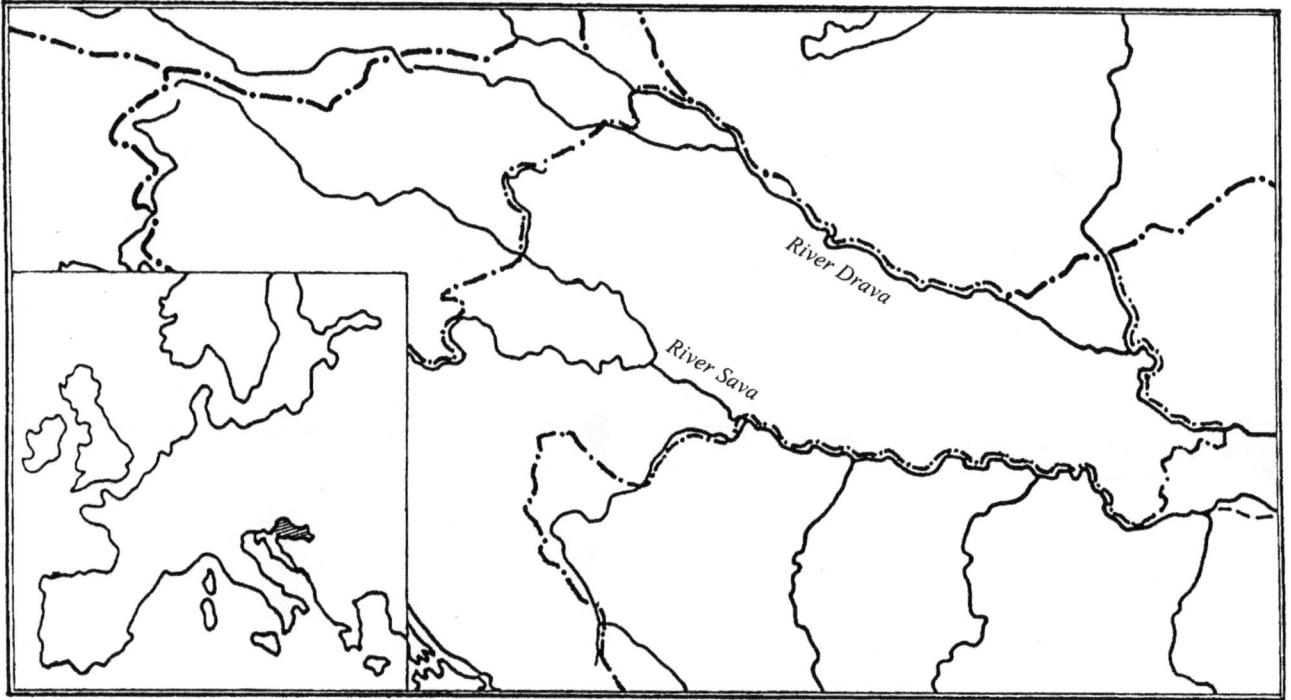

River Drava

River Sava

Location Map

1. INTRODUCTION

1.1. HISTORY OF BIOARCHAEOLOGICAL RESEARCH

The first report of a physical anthropology investigation by a Croatian osteologist was published in 1951 (Ivaniček, 1951). In this pioneering work Ivaniček reports on the sex, age and metric characteristics of 299 skeletons from the medieval town of Ptuj in neighboring Slovenia which was at that time, together with Croatia and four other republics, part of Yugoslavia. Although of evident quality, this report failed to generate interest and results of the next physical anthropology investigations were published in the late sixties. These investigations, carried out by Pilarić (1967, 1968, 1969), and later Pilarić and Schwidetzky (1987), focused on cranial typology and classification in an attempt to explain the origins and migrations of early medieval Croat populations. With the recovery of larger samples, and with new analytical methods and theoretical approaches which were developed in the seventies, the study of human skeletal remains recovered from archaeological sites changed and expanded dramatically. In this respect physical anthropology in Croatia mirrored the changes through which European and American physical anthropology were going through. With regard to craniofacial morphology, population origins and biological distances, this transition required a shift from typological thinking to a process-oriented approach focused on microevolutionary problems and an emphasis on the use of multivariate statistical procedures. A shift towards a more multidisciplinary approach led to the development of bioarchaeology, the analysis of human skeletons in an archaeological and environmental context. In this research design skeletal data are incorporated in the construction of ecological models of human adaptation. Osteologists with an interest in various parameters of population biology, demographic structure and dynamics, and biocultural behavior, not only evaluate archaeologically derived hypotheses by comparing them with the results of osteological analyses, but also propose hypotheses founded in the biological data that can be tested in archaeological contexts. The results of such research are of basic concern not only to osteologists but also to archaeologists who, in the past, frequently relegated osteological reports to appendixes.

These advances in osteological research take full advantage of newly developed analytical techniques and benefit greatly from the use of computerized data bases. In Croatia, this approach to osteological analyses was spearheaded by Boljunčić (1991, 1993 1997a and 1997b), Šarić-Bužančić (1999), and Šlaus (1993, 1994, 1996, 1997a, 1997b, 1998a, 1998b, 1999, 2000a, and 2000b).

This book presents the results of a decade of studying skeletal archaeological collections from continental Croatia. Results of the analyses of 786 skeletons from 21 archaeological sites are presented by site and synthesized temporally into five groups: the Prehistoric period, the Antique period, the Early medieval period, the Late medieval period, and the Historic period. The purpose of this book is to report on skeletal data from an, in this respect, still under-represent part of the world, and to summarize information pertaining to demography and specific disease classifications. From these compilations, inferences on demographic trends, disease and the quality of life from prehistoric to historic times in continental Croatia may be drawn.

The last chapter deals with cranial variation in medieval populations from continental Croatia and the way in which such data can be used to explain apparent inconsistencies between historical sources and the biological data.

Geographically, the area analyzed in this book is the continental part of the Republic of Croatia. This encompasses the area between the rivers Drava to the north and Danube to the east, the southern boundary is defined by the north-eastern slopes of the Velebit mountain range, while the western boundary is Croatia's border with Slovenia. Data were collected from skeletal series from 21 archaeological sites. The geographical locations of these sites are shown in Figure 1. Table 1 provides information on the datation of the sites and the number of human skeletons recovered. As can be seen in Figure 1 and Table 1, some of the sites included in the

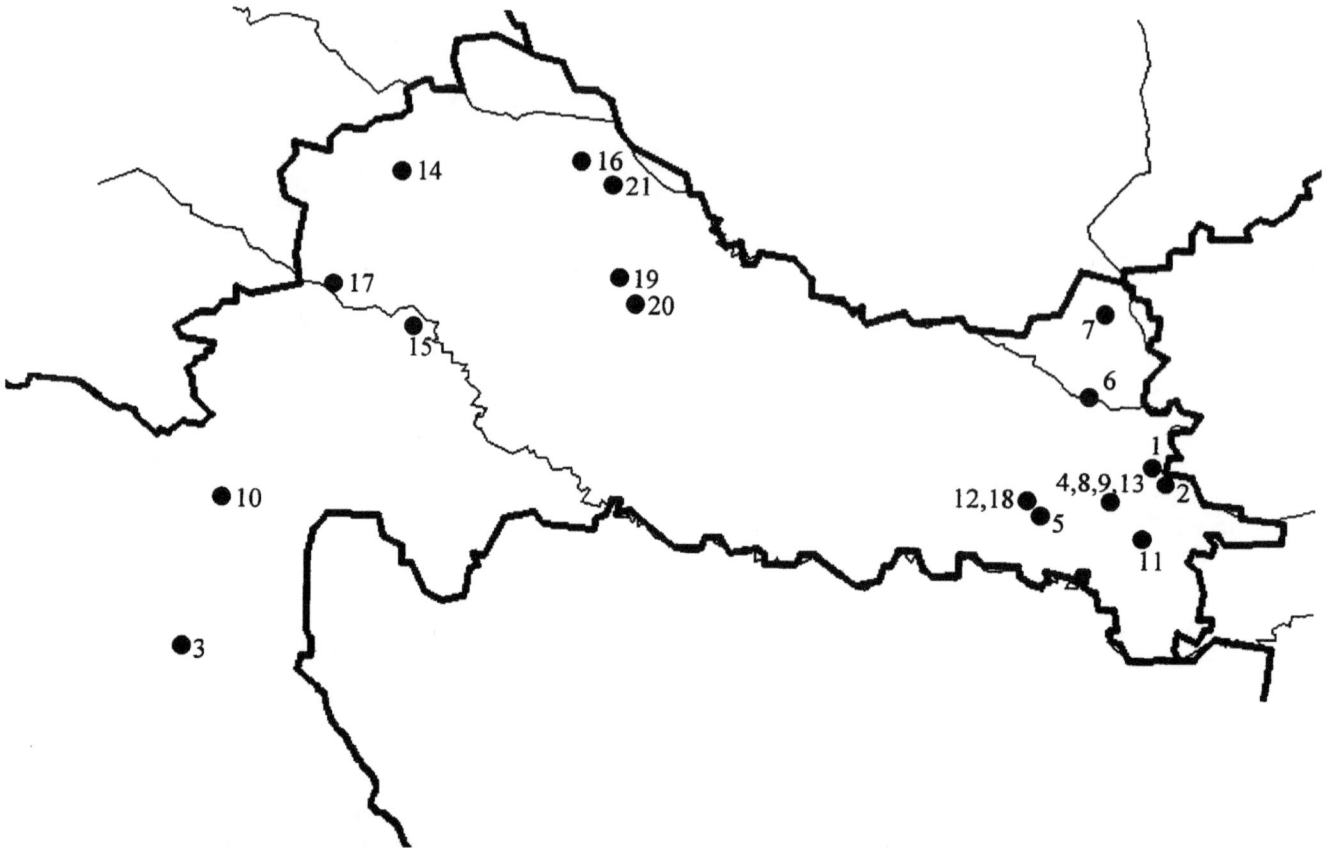

Figure 1. The geographical locations of the analyzed sites. *Prehistoric sites:* 1. Vukovar-High School, 2. Vukovar-Vučedol, 3. Bezdanjača, 4. Vinkovci NaMa; *Antique sites:*5. Štrbinci, 6. Eastern necropolis of Mursa (Osijek), 7. Zmajevac, 8. Vinkovci; *Early medieval sites:* 9. Vinkovci, 10. Jopićeva špilja, 11. Privlaka; *Late medieval sites:* 12. Đakovo, 13. Vinkovci, 14. Lobor, 15. Ščitarjevo, 16. Đelekovec, 17. Stenjevac; *Historic sites:* 18. Đakovo, 19. Tomaš, 20. Nova Rača, 21. Kamengrad.

analysis exhibit evidence of temporal continuity in the sense that they are represented by multiple skeletal series from succeeding time periods or cultures. Vukovar is, for instance, represented by two prehistoric skeletal series, one dated to the Neolithic Stračevo culture, and one to the Eneolithic Vučedol culture. Đakovo is also represented by two skeletal series, one from the Late medieval period, and one from the Historic period. Vinkovci (Roman *Cibalae*) exhibits the greatest temporal continuity in terms of inhabitation. This site is represented by four skeletal series from succeeding time periods, beginning with a skeletal series from the Iron Age Hallstatt culture, followed by a romanized Antique series from *Cibalae*, an Early medieval Gepid sample, and a Late medieval series affiliated with the Bijelo brdo culture.

As expected, the prehistoric series exhibits the largest temporal variation and contains the smallest number of skeletons. Furthermore, because of the absence of defined cemeteries, poor bone preservation, and specific burial practices such as secondary inhumation, this series is under-represented in comparison to others in some areas of dental and skeletal baseline counts. However, at present these are all of the data available for analysis from this time period in continental Croatia. The other series are more evenly balanced in terms of the numbers of recovered skeletons and their states of preservation.

1.2. DETERMINATION OF SEX, AGE AND BONE INVENTORY

Accurate determinations of sex, age and precise bone element baseline counts are essential for sample comparisons between different skeletal series. Cross-population interpretations of mortality trends and morbidity patterns are based on sound demographic profiles established through careful consideration of applicable up-to-date morphological, metric, and multivariate criteria.

The criteria selected for determination of sex include pelvic (Phenice, 1969) and cranial morphology (Krogman and Iscan, 1986). These criteria generally provide accurate results. From a sample of skeletons of known sex, Meindl et al. (1985) report a 3% error rate when both the pelvis and skull were evaluated. When these elements were missing, sex was determined by recently developed discriminant functions for sexing adult femora (Šlaus, 1997b). These functions have an accuracy rate of between 87% to 95%. No attempt was made to estimate the sex of subadult individuals.

Adult age at death was estimated using as many methods as possible, including ectocranial suture fusion (Meindl and

Table 1: Datation and number of human skeletons recovered from the sites included in analysis

Site	Datation	Number of skeletons
Prehistory		
Vukovar-High School	5000 BC	5
Vukovar-Vučedol	2900 BC	12
Bezdanjača	1300-1100 BC	41
Vinkovci-"NAMA"	450-300 BC	11
Antique		
Štrbinci	300-400 AD	26
Osijek	300-400 AD	28
Zmajevac	300-400 AD	37
Vinkovci	300-400 AD	34
Early medieval		
Vinkovci-Gepid	500-550 AD	34
Jopić	700-800 AD	1
Privlaka	700-800 AD	181
Late medieval		
Đakovo phase I	1050-1242 AD	31
Vinkovci	1050-1300 AD	17
Lobor	1000-1100 AD	11
Ščitarjevo	1000-1300 AD	13
Đelekovec	1000-1300 AD	19
Stenjevac	900-1200 AD	84
Historic		
Đakovo phase II	1300-1536 AD	42
Tomaš	1500-1600 AD	20
Nova Rača	1300-1700 AD	104
Kamengrad	1350-1500 AD	35

Lovejoy, 1985), pubic symphysis morphology (Brooks and Suchey, 1990; Gilbert and McKern, 1973; McKern and Stewart, 1957; Todd, 1920, 1921), auricular surface morphology (Lovejoy et al., 1985), and sternal rib end changes (Iscan et al., 1984, 1985). In subadults, age at death was estimated using epiphyseal fusion, diaphyseal lengths, and dental eruption criteria (McKern and Stewart, 1957; Bass, 1987; Fazekas and Kósa, 1978; Moorrees et al., 1963).

Detailed bone inventories were obtained for each skeleton. The coding format used in this procedure is designed for computer analysis and provides a comprehensive inventory of the entire skeleton. This detailed format is essential for paleopathological analysis. In general, it is seldom adequate to base the frequency of pathological observations on the total number of individuals present in a skeletal series. This approach, although perhaps ideal, is impractical because of the vagaries of skeletal preservation and recovery. While some skeletons may be well preserved and nearly complete, as are for instance most of the skeletons from the Historic period Nova Rača series, usually only partial skeletons are recovered. Specific cultural practices such as secondary inhumations, in which for instance only the skull and femurs are buried, can also cause erroneous frequency tabulations. Given this variation in cultural practices, bone preservation, and recovery, it is essential to list the elements present in any skeletal collection being investigated. Such a system enables precise bone counts by side including proximal and distal joint surfaces for all major long bones. In this manner when evaluating, for instance, arthritic changes in the distal humerus, it is possible to tabulate the number of complete and partial distal humeral epiphyses by side, sex and age.

All skeletal elements were, therefore, coded for their presence and completeness (i.e., complete or partial). A bone was scored as complete if more than 50% of the bone was preserved. As described, completeness does not reflect total bone preservation but identifies the number of elements that are nearly complete and can be scored for the presence or absence of pathological features.

Detailed dental inventories were also completed for each skeleton. All teeth were coded for their presence as: present, lost antemortem, lost postmortem, partially erupted or unerupted. The presence of carious lesions was noted and scored according to location as: occlusal, buccal, lingual, interproximal, or root (at the cementoenamel junction). The presence of alveolar abscesses was also scored when present.

1.3. CODING FORMAT FOR BONE LESIONS

Bone pathological features were scored using a hierarchical approach that coded lesions descriptively according to the predominant osteoclastic or osteoblastic response as: 1) bone loss, 2) bone increase, or 3) bone loss and bone increase. This general classification refers to the major changes possible in living bone. Following this determination, a second more precise designation was recorded using descriptors that defined the nature of the lesion. For example, pathologies identified as representing bone loss were classified within several subcategories, such as 1) bone loss owing to resorptive (lytic) lesion, 2) bone loss owing to porosity (pinpoint to coalesced), 3) bone loss owing to osteoporosis or osteopenia, or 4) bone loss caused by benign cortical defect. All lesions were further coded for: 1) severity (i.e., mild, moderate, severe), 2) state (i.e., active, healing), 3) extent of involvement (i.e., localized, widespread), and 4) specific location on the bone. Changes caused by degenerative bone disease were scored for presence, location and severity of hypertrophic bone formation (marginal, lipping, osteophytes), porosity, and eburnation (Ortner and Putschar, 1981; Steinbock, 1976).

Traumatic injuries (fractures) were coded separately using a similarly detailed descriptive computer coding format. Skull fractures involving the frontal, occipital, parietals, and temporals were coded for shape, presence of radiating fractures, size and presence of healing. Fractures involving the zygoma, maxillae, and mandible were coded for presence and state.

The inventory and pathology coding procedures used in this investigation are a modified version of those developed by Owsley (Owsley et al., 1987; Owsley et al., 1991).

While all pathological changes noted in the analyzed skeletal material are reported on, not all are summarized. The specific disease categories summarized for all sites, and all composite temporal series are: dental pathology - including caries and alveolar bone disease, subadult stress indicators - including dental enamel hypoplasia and cribra orbitalia, infectious disease - as evidenced by the presence of periostitis and osteomyelitis, trauma, and physical stress - including osteoarthritis on major joints and the spinal column, and the presence of Schmorl's depressions in vertebral bodies. These categories were chosen for two reasons. First, the pathological conditions comprising these categories are relatively common and leave relatively unambiguous traces in the skeleton. Second, when taken together, these categories create a composite profile of general health and quality of life.

Dental pathology data are tabulated for alveolar bone disease and caries. Dental caries is a complex infectious disease of the external surface of the tooth. Various bacteria, primarily *Streptococcus* spp., produce decalcifying acids, which, if left unchecked, cause dissolution of the enamel and dentin (Bhaskar, 1981). Physiological and possibly external environmental factors may be related to caries incidence (Hildebolt et al., 1988). In a study of lower Great Lakes populations Schneider (1986) reports that zinc, copper and iron when present in enamel have a cariostatic effect whereas nickel has a cariogenic effect. Results such as these suggest that diet may play a multifaceted role in the production of carious lesions. Alveolar bone disease is for the purpose of this report defined as the presence of periodontal or periapical abscesses and antemortem tooth loss.

Dental enamel hypoplasia or chronological aplasia is generally defined as any macroscopic defect in the enamel surface (Pindborg, 1970, Sarnat and Schour, 1941, 1942). Hypoplastic defects can range from minor depressions in the enamel surface, with no dentin exposure, to a complete disruption of the enamel. These defects appear as bandlike depressions (linear enamel hypoplasia) or as pits. They result from a disturbance of the enamel development in the growing deciduous or permanent tooth bud (phase of amelogenesis). The causes of the hypoplastic defects are commonly attributed to a variety of factors including physiological stresses such as malnutrition, infectious disease, psychological or physical trauma, or other metabolic disruptions (Goodman et al., 1980; Goodman and Rose, 1991; Kreshover, 1960). Hypoplasias remain visible until the affected enamel is worn away through dental attrition, providing a nearly permanent record of developmental arrest during infancy and early childhood.

While the development of enamel hypoplastic defects cannot be attributed to a specific disease or episode in the life of a deceased individual, studies of living children document the association between higher frequencies of hypoplastic defects and poor nutrition and low socioeconomic status (Goodman et al., 1991, 1992).

Data on enamel hypoplasias were collected on the permanent maxillary central incisors and canines, and on the permanent mandibular canines. The selection of these tooth categories for study was dictated by the following considerations: 1) central incisors and canines are considered to be more susceptible to stress than other teeth (Goodman and Armelagos, 1985; Goodman and Rose, 1990); 2) canines have a long developmental period, from around four months to 6 years (Gustafson and Koch, 1974); and 3) incisors and canines in general display a relatively small amount of dental calculus which obscures enamel in other teeth. Only macroscopic, linear enamel defects - transverse grooves or rows of pits on the crown surface - are counted in these data. Other enamel defects such as circular pits in deciduous dentition, hyperplastic defects, and zones of discoloration were observed in the dental remains, but are not treated in this study. Hypoplasia frequencies are tabulated by individual. Because some of the skeletal series are poorly preserved and the recovered individuals are incomplete even in their dental remains, it can be argued that counting all teeth, instead of only one antimere per individual, may create a bias towards well preserved individuals as those with more teeth contribute more to the data set than those with only the right or left preserved. Therefore, to avoid any possibility of artificially altering frequencies, enamel hypoplasia data are presented by considering only one tooth from each tooth category per individual. Enamel defects were counted on teeth from the right side of the mouth, with teeth from the left side being substituted if the one on the right was missing.

Cribra orbitalia is recognized by the presence of sievelike lesions or pitting on the orbital roof. The etiology of this lesion is not fully established, and several diseases have been implicated (El-Najjar, 1976; Mensforth et al. 1978). Of these, iron deficiency anemia is the most often attributed cause (Stuart-Macadam, 1985).

Skeletal evidence for infectious disease was determined by the presence of periostitis and osteomyelitis. Periostitis involves inflammation of the periosteum as evidenced by the deposition of new bone on the outer surface of the affected element (Mann and Murphy, 1990; Ortner and Putschar, 1981, Steinbock, 1976). Osteomyelitis, which results from an acute or chronic infection, affects both the marrow and the bone cortex. Inflammation accompanies the infection and causes bone remodeling and expansion (thickening of the cortex), often with a draining sinus (Mann and Murphy, 1990; Ortner and Putschar, 1981, Steinbock, 1976). The primary causes of these conditions are difficult to determine. Especially in the case of periostitis, many factors (for example trauma, hematogenous infection originating in another part of the body, venous insufficiency, and scurvy) contribute to localized or widespread dissemination throughout the skeleton.

Skeletal evidence for trauma was determined by the presence of fractures, dislocations involving joints out of articulation or alignment as a result of force, and enthesophytes. The latter include bone spurs, heterotopic bone formations, and traumatic myositis ossificans. They form in response to torn ligaments or muscles, and other types of injury and biomechanical stress that result in calcification of inflamed tissue.

Several skeletal features were used to evaluate physical stress. These features are: degenerative osteoarthritis in major joints, vertebral degenerative changes, and the occurrence and frequency of Schmorl's depressions in vertebral bodies.

Degenerative osteoarthritis is characterized by the progressive formation of osteophytes around the edges of an articular joint surface. In advanced cases the normally smooth articular surface develops ossific nodules, porosis or eburnation. These changes are associated with the wear and tear of everyday activities and are distinguished from traumatic arthritis which is caused by disruption of the biomechanical functioning of a joint. Degenerative changes in spinal columns were assessed in the vertebral bodies (osteophytosis and osteoporosis of centra) and the articular surfaces of the posterior elements (osteoarthritis of facets).

Schmorl's depressions are lesions which result from herniation and displacement of intervertebral disc tissue into the adjacent vertebral body. The presence of Schmorl's depressions can be idiopathic, or related to a variety of reasons including among others certain diseases and congenital factors that produce a weakening of the subchondral bone and a disruption of the cartilaginous end-plate, and strong compression caused by traumatic injury. However, the most common cause of Schmorl's depressions according to Schmorl and Junghanns (1971) are degenerative changes associated with ordinary stress on the vertebral column. "The origin, progression and symptoms of vertebral disk prolapse ... are influenced decisively by everyday demands of life. Fatigue damage,

similar to fatigue fractures in the bone, can be produced in disk tissue when the demand surpasses the functional ability" (Schmorl and Junghanns, 1971: 175).

Some of the described diseases, for instance dental disease and degenerative osteoarthritis, are age-dependent (i.e., increase with advanced age). Therefore, when tabulating the data, age was controlled by dividing the sample into two broad categories: young adults, defined as individuals aged between 16-35 years, and old adults, defined as individuals older than 36 years.

2. BIOARCHAEOLOGY OF THE PREHISTORIC PERIOD

The prehistoric period includes a skeletal series from the first identified classical agricultural and pottery based Neolithic culture in continental Croatia, as well as series from Eneolithic, Bronze Age, and Iron Age cultures. This period covers the largest temporal span encompassing the period from approximately 5300 BC to 400 BC. The period is represented by four skeletal series: the Vukovar High School skeletal series dated to the Neolithic Starčevo culture, the Vukovar Vučedol skeletal series dated to the Eneolithic Vučedol culture, the Bezdanjača skeletal series dated to the Middle and Late Bronze age periods, and the Vinkovci "NaMa" skeletal series dated to the late Hallstatt period. The geographical distribution of the sites is shown in Figure 2.

As previously mentioned, the prehistoric series is characterized by under-representation in some areas of dental and skeletal baseline counts. The reason for this is twofold. Firstly, at present, there is an absence of defined cemeteries belonging to the Neolithic and Eneolithic cultures from continental Croatia. In both the Neolithic Starčevo, and the Eneolithic Vučedol cultures skeletal remains were recovered either as individual burials, or in small possibly family units in the vicinity of subterranean dwellings (Starčevo culture), or in abandoned cellars or pits in recognized settlements (Vučedol culture). The second reason is the practice of secondary inhumation in the Bronze Age series from Bezdanjača. This large series consists only of crania with, or in some cases without, adjoining mandibles. The most recorded disease categories in the composite prehistoric series are therefore, of necessity, dental disease and cribra orbitalia.

Figure 2. The geographical locations of the Prehistoric sites: 1. Vukovar-High School, 2. Vukovar-Vučedol, 3. Bezdanjača, 4.Vinkovci NaMa

2.1. THE VUKOVAR HIGH SCHOOL SKELETAL SERIES

The Vukovar High School skeletal series is a small series consisting of five, well preserved human skeletons. The remains were recovered in 1999 from the basement of the Vukovar High School. The High School was completely demolished during the 1991 conflict between Croatia and Yugoslavia, and extensive reconstruction was being carried out. During the course of this reconstruction, five skeletons were uncovered at a depth of approximately 1 m below ground level in the basement of the High School. One of the five recovered skeletons belonged to an adult male, one to an adult female, and three to subadults. All of the skeletons were placed on their sides, tightly flexed with their legs drawn up to their body (i.e., in a fetal position). Two of the subadult skeletons were placed facing each other with their foreheads touching. Bone preservation was excellent. Pottery from the burial site belonging to the Stračevo cultural complex dated the remains to approximately 5000 BC (Dalić, personal communication)

The Stračevo culture is the first clearly identified agricultural and pottery based Neolithic culture in continental Croatia. Sites belonging to this culture are located in the eastern part of continental Croatia between the rivers Drava and Sava, from Eastern Slavonia and Baranja in the east, to the town of Bjelovar in the west. The most important sites are: Sarvaš near Osijek, Vučedol near Vukovar, Zadubravlje near Slavonski Brod and Stara Rača near Bjelovar. Settlements of the Starčevo culture were located on elevated river banks or on natural rises near streams, small rivers or marshes. The

dwellings were exclusively subterranean (Dimitrijević et. al. 1998).

The age and sex distribution of the Vukovar Starčevo skeletal series is presented in Table 2.

Dental disease frequencies are low in this series. Only one tooth socket exhibits evidence of alveolar bone disease (one case of antemortem tooth loss recorded in the adult female). None of the 46 subadult and 23 adult teeth recovered show evidence of caries.

Dental data does, however, indicate the presence of subadult stress. Deep hypoplastic lines are visible on both subadult central maxillary incisors, on one of the two subadult maxillary canines, and on one recovered subadult canine.

The presence of cribra orbitalia also indicates subadult stress. Both older subadults exhibit bilateral cribra orbitalia, active and severe in expression in the subadult aged from 12.5-13.5 years, and healed and mild in the subadult aged from 11.5-12.5 years.

There is no evidence of infectious disease or trauma in the series. Both adults exhibit mild osteophyte development on the posterior calcanei, at the insertion of the Achilles tendon.

Physical stress frequencies are low in the series. The adult male shows mild osteoarthritis in the form of osteophyte development along the margins of the left glenoid cavity. None of the 11 preserved adult vertebrae show evidence of degenerative disease, and none of the 7 present thoracic and lumbar vertebrae exhibit Schmorl's defects.

Table 2:   Age and sex distribution in the Vukovar-High School skeletal series

Age category	Subadult N[1]	Subadult %[2]	Female N	Female %	Male N	Male %	Total N	Total %
Birth -1	1	33.3					1	20.0
2- 5	0						0	
6-10	0						0	
11-15	2	66.7					2	40.0
16-20			0		0		0	
21-25			0		0		0	
26-30			0		0		0	
31-35			0		0		0	
36-40			0		1	100.0	1	20.0
41-45			1	100.0	0		1	20.0
46-50			0		0		0	
51-55			0		0		0	
56-60			0		0		0	
60+			0		0		0	
Total	3	100.0	1	100.0	1	100.0	5	100.0

[1] N = number of individuals dying.
[2] % = % of individuals dying.

2.2. THE VUKOVAR VUČEDOL SKELETAL SERIES

The Vukovar Vučedol skeletal series contains the remains of 12 individuals. The majority of the osteological material was recovered in 1985 during systematic excavations of the Vučedol site (Durman, 2000). Eight of the 12 recovered individuals were found in one abandoned storage pit (known as pit number 6, grave number 3) and were immediately, because of the sex distribution - one male, six females and one subadult, the center of attention. The remaining individuals were recovered from grave number 1 - which contained the remains of two individuals, grave 2 - which contained one undisturbed burial, and grave 3/112 which contained the remains of one individual who may have belonged to an earlier eneolithic culture, the Baden culture. Radiocarbon dating of associated organic material dates the recovered skeletons to approximately 2900 BC (Durman and Obelić, 1989).

The Vučedol culture is the most important Eneolithic culture in continental Croatia. It is named after the eponymous site located on the right bank of the Danube, not far from Vukovar. At the height of it's development the Vučedol culture spread across a large part of Central and Southeastern Europe, from Prague to the north to southern Bosnia in the south, and from the Rumanian Banat in the east to the southeastern Alpine region in the west. The Vučedol culture probably originated in the Slavonian-Syrmian region, in a time marked by major ethnic changes caused by the migration of eastern steppe peoples (the migration of the Indo-Europeans). Settlements of the Vučedol culture reflect this uncertainty and are generally located on raised loess terraces along rivers or on the slopes of hilly zones. The settlements were fortified either by improving steep slopes, or with palisades and moats (Dimitrijević et al. 1998). Similar to the Stračevo culture, no defined cemeteries have been discovered. All of the recovered individuals were found in settlements and may represent socially prominent individuals, and/or may reflect specific cult practices.

The age and sex distribution of the Vukovar Vučedol skeletal series is presented in Table 3. Because of the sex distribution in pit 6, most of the recovered individuals (9/12) are females.

Dental disease frequencies are summarized in Tables 4 and 5. The one recovered subadult exhibits no evidence of alveolar bone disease, but does show a relatively high frequency of caries (4/20 teeth or 20%). Alveolar bone disease frequencies in adult females are low (5/215 tooth sockets or 2.3%). Caries frequencies are slightly higher (in 13/178 observed teeth or 7.3%). Typically, most of the carious lesions (10/13) were recorded in the two older females. The two adult males show higher frequencies of

Table 3: Age and sex distribution in the Vukovar-Vučedol series

Age category	Subadult N[1]	%[2]	Female N	%	Male N	%	Total N	%
Birth -1	0						0	
2- 5	0						0	
6-10	1	100.0					1	8.3
11-15	0						0	
16-20			2	22.2	1	50.0	3	25.0
21-25			4	44.5	0		4	33.5
26-30			0		0		0	
31-35			1	11.1	0		1	8.3
36-40			0		0		0	
41-45			1	11.1	0		1	8.3
46-50			1	11.1	0		1	8.3
51-55			0		1	50.0	1	8.3
56-60			0		0		0	
60+			0		0		0	
Total	1	100.0	9	100.0	2	100.0	12	100.0

Mean age at death[3]   x = 28.00   x = 35.50

sd = 10.89   sd = 24.75

[1] N = number of individuals dying.

[2] % = % of individuals dying.

[3] Mean age at death is calculated using median values of each age category (for example, 23 for the age category 21-25), and 65 for the age category 60+.

TABLE 4: Frequency of alveolar bone disease in the Vukovar-Vučedol series

Age category	Subadult A[1]/O[2] %[3]		Female A/O %		Male A/O %	
Young adult[4]			2/152	1.3	0/24	0.0
Old adult			3/63	4.8	8/29	27.6
Total	0/23	0.0	5/215	2.3	8/53	15.1

[1] A = number of tooth sockets with periodontal or periapical abscess, or antemortem tooth loss.
[2] O = number of tooth sockets observed.
[3] % = % of tooth sockets with periodontal or periapical abscess, or antemortem tooth loss.
[4] Young adult = individuals aged between 16 to 35 years; Old adult = individuals older than 36 years.

TABLE 5: Frequency of carious lesions in the Vukovar-Vučedol series

Age category	Subadult A[1]/O[2] %[3]		Female A/O %		Male A/O %	
Young adult[4]			3/123	2.4	0/21	0.0
Old adult			10/55	18.2	1/15	6.7
Total	4/20	20.0	13/178	7.3	1/36	2.8

[1] A = number of teeth with carious lesions.
[2] O = number of teeth observed.
[3] % = % of teeth with carious lesions.
[4] Young adult = individuals aged between 16 to 35 years; Old adult = individuals older than 36 years.

TABLE 6: Hypoplasia frequencies by individual in the Vukovar-Vučedol series

Tooth	N[1]	NwLEH	%wLEH
Maxillary I1[2]	6	3	50.0
Maxillary C	7	2	28.6
Mandibular C	9	3	33.3

[1] N = number of teeth observed; NwLEH = number of teeth with one or more LEH; %wLEH = % of N with one or more LEH.
[2] I = incisor; C = canine.

alveolar bone disease (8/53 tooth sockets or 15.1%), but lower caries frequencies (1/36 or 2.8%). In both subadults and adults, the majority of the observed caries are located interproximally (in 11/18 lesions or 61.1%). Females also exhibited six cases of root caries while the only caries recorded in an adult male is located occlusally.

Enamel hypoplasia frequencies are summarized in Tables 6 and 7. Hypoplasias are most frequent in central maxillary incisors (50.0 %), followed by mandibular canines (33.3%) and maxillary canines (28.6%). The only recovered subadult exhibits no evidence of hypoplastic defects.

Cribra orbitalia is observed in 1 of the 10 crania with intact orbits (Table 8). The lesion is present in the subadult and was bilateral, severe in expression, and active at time of death.

Three individuals exhibit skeletal evidence for infectious disease. The subadult with cribra orbitalia also exhibits generalized, severe, and active endocranial periostitis, most pronounced on the frontal, parietal and occipital bones, possibly reflecting a systemic bacterial infection. The older of the two recovered males exhibits healed periostitis on the medial side of the distal third of the diaphysis of the left tibia. The lesion is localized and has a small area of dense sclerotic bone in the middle. It appears to have been caused by some type of trauma. One female also exhibits periostitis; bilateral, healed and mild in expression on the medial sides of the middle thirds of the tibiae.

The skeletal series from Vukovar-Vučedol is characterized by a high incidence of healed fractures. As all of the observed fractures are present in individuals from pit 6, grave 3 (one male, six females and one subadult), and the majority of the fractures are located on the skull vault, some researchers (Durman, 2000) have speculated that they may be related to cult activities or some type of initiation ceremony. Skeletal data alone cannot conclusively prove or disprove this hypothesis. The frequency and patterning of the lesions is, however, unique, and certainly compatible with cult activities. However, one should also bear in mind that other types of fractures, besides cranial, are present in the series (two rib fractures and one tibial fracture), and that, as already stated, the period during which the Vučedol culture existed is characterized by migration and instability.

TABLE 7: Hypoplasia frequencies in the Vukovar-Vučedol series for subadults and adults

Tooth	Subadults Nw/N[1]	%wLEH[2]	All adults Nw/N	%wLEH	Females Nw/N	%wLEH	Males Nw/N	%wLEH
Maxillary I1[3]	0/1	0.0	3/5	60.0	3/4	75.0	0/1	0.0
Maxillary C	0/0	0.0	2/7	28.6	2/6	33.3	0/1	0.0
Mandibular C	0/1	0.0	3/8	37.5	2/6	33.3	1/2	50.0

[1] Nw = number of individuals with one or more LEH; N = number of individuals observed.
[2] %wLEH = % of N with one or more LEH.
[3] I = incisors; C = canines.

TABLE 8: Frequency of occurrence of cribra orbitalia in the Vukovar-Vučedol series

| Age/sex | Cribra orbitalia | | | Active lesions | |
	O^1	$A1^2$	%	$A2^3$	% of A1
0 - 0.9	0	0	0.0	0	0.0
1 - 3.9	0	0	0.0	0	0.0
4 - 9.9	1	1	100.0	1	100.0
10 - 14.9	0	0	0.0	0	0.0
All subadults	1	1	100.0	1	100.0
Adult females	7	0	0.0	0	0.0
Adult males	2	0	0.0	0	0.0
All adults	9	0	0.0	0	0.0

[1] O = number of frontal bones observed.

[2] A1 = number of frontal bones in which at least one orbit shows evidence of cribra orbitalia.

[3] A2 = number of frontal bones in which cribra orbitalia is active at time of death.

Of the eight individuals recovered from pit 6, all but one, the only subadult in the series, exhibit skeletal evidence of healed fractures. A total of 14 healed fractures are present in the remaining 7 individuals. Most individuals exhibit more than one healed fracture. The highest incidence is recorded in the only adult male who has two healed cranial fractures and two healed rib fractures (on the 6. and 7. right ribs, one above the other, both approximately 63 mm from the head of the rib). Two females (individuals 3/2 and 3/6) have only one fracture, individual 3/2 a healed depression fracture on the frontal bone, and individual 3/6 a healed depression fracture on the lateral proximal joint surface of the right tibia.

Six individuals (five females and one male) exhibit healed cranial fractures. In all cases the fractures are well healed, relatively shallow depression fractures, roughly circular or elliptic in diameter, with a slightly porous floor and rounded margins. None of the fractures penetrated the inner table of the skull vault, and none show evidence of fracture lines or signs of subsequent infection. The skulls were not available for photography as they were on tour as part of a museum exhibition of the Vučedol culture. Excellent photographs are, however, available in Teschler-Nicola and Berner (1994), and Durman (2000). What differentiates this skeletal series from other series with high incidences of cranial trauma is the patterning of the fractures. Five of the six individuals with cranial fractures have two fractures on the cranial vault. In all of these cases one of the fractures is located on the frontal bone while the other is placed posterior to the first fracture on one of the parietals, generally in the immediate vicinity, or on the sagittal suture. No fractures are noted on the occipital bone. In all five individuals with two cranial fractures the anterior fracture is smaller in diameter (diameters are 11 mm for female individual 3/5, 7 mm for female 3/3, 5 mm for female 3/1, 6 mm for female 3/8 and 10 mm for male 3/4) than the posterior fracture (diameters 13 mm, 11 mm, 10 mm, 11 mm and 11 mm respectively). The posterior fractures also tend to be slightly deeper than the anterior ones. Distances between the fractures are of interest. In three of the five individuals with

two cranial fractures (females 3/1, 3/5 and 3/8) the distance between the two fractures is identical. This distance, as measured from the deepest points of the depressions, is 54 mm. In female 3/3 this distance is slightly larger - 62 mm, while in the only male the distance is 140 mm. It seems unlikely that separate and non-related incidences of cranial trauma in three individuals could result in the same pattern and distance between two depression fractures. It is therefore likely that individuals with two fractures either sustained the injuries at the same time, possibly by some type of tool or weapon unknown to us, or, indeed, participated in some common cult or initiation ceremony. Continued anthropological and archaeological research, as well as comparison with other prehistoric skeletal series, are necessary to illuminate the cause of these fractures.

The Vučedol culture existed in a period of instability caused by the migration of the Indo-Europeans. The uniform practice of fortifying settlements is clear evidence of the insecurity of the times. Use of the horse in warfare, either for riding or for pulling war chariots, may have contributed to this insecurity. The presence of horses has been documented in other Eneolithic cultures (for instance the Baden culture), but there is no archaeological evidence for their presence in this capacity in Vučedol. It is, therefore, interesting to note that the adult male from pit 6 (individual 3/4) exhibits bilateral, hypertrophied adductor tubercules on the medial sides of the distal femurs. Hypertrophy of the adductor tubercules has been linked with horseback riding. In extreme cases the tubercule hypertrophies to such a degree that it is referred to as "riders bone" (Smokvina 1959).

The male from pit 6 also exhibits spondylolysis of the fifth lumbar vertebrae. Spondylolysis is a separation of the vertebral body from the vertebral arch, usually in the region of the pars interarticularis. Although the presence of certain anatomical variations in individuals affected by the condition suggest a genetic predisposition to it (Cyron et al. 1976), a triggering mechanism in the form of sustained stress or trauma is usually required for fracturing to occur (Merbs, 1983, 1989). Most commonly the fifth lumbar is affected, but the fourth and third may also show this trait.

Physical stress frequencies in the series are summarized in Tables 9-11. Degenerative osteoarthritis frequencies are highest in the shoulder (Table 9). All of the reported cases reflect mild or moderate degrees of osteoarthritis.

The total frequency of vertebral osteoarthritis in females is 10.6% (Table 10). Greatest involvement occurs in the lumbar region of the spine, followed by the cervical and thoracic regions. The two recovered males show no evidence of vertebral degenerative disease and no evidence of Schmorl's depressions (Table 11).

The distribution and frequency of Schmorl's depressions in the female sample shows a 9.1% total frequency with greater involvement in the thoracic region and a considerably higher frequency of Schmorl's depressions in older adults. In the female thoracic spine this difference is statistically significant ($\chi^2 = 7.64$; $P < 0.01$).

TABLE 9: Frequency of occurrence of osteoarthritis at major joints in the Vukovar-Vučedol series

	Shoulder A^1/O^2	%	Elbow A/O	%	Hip A/O	%	Knee A/O	%
Female								
Young adult[3]	1/6	16.7	0/6	0.0	0/6	0.0	0/6	0.0
Old adult	1/2	50.0	1/2	50.0	1/2	50.0	1/2	50.0
Total	2/8	25.0	1/8	12.5	1/8	12.5	1/8	12.5
Male								
Young adult	0/1	0.0	0/1	0.0	0/1	0.0	0/1	0.0
Old adult	1/1	100.0	0/1	0.0	1/1	100.0	1/1	100.0
Total	1/2	50.0	0/2	0.0	1/2	50.0	1/2	50.0

[1] A = number of joints affected with osteoarthritis. Osteoarthritis was scored as present if at least one joint element showed evidence of osteoarthritic change.
[2] O = number of joints observed. A joint was scored as present if at least one joint element was completely present, or if two or three elements were partially present.
[3] Young adult = individuals aged between 16 to 35 years; Old adult = individuals older than 36 years.

TABLE 10: Frequency of occurrence of vertebral osteoarthritis in the Vukovar-Vučedol series

	Cervical A^1/O^2	%	Thoracic A/O	%	Lumbar A/O	%	Total A/O	%
Female								
Young adult[3]	0/27	0.0	0/53	0.0	2/23	8.7	2/103	1.9
Old adult	4/14	28.6	6/24	25.0	4/10	40.0	14/48	29.2
Total	4/41	9.8	6/77	7.8	6/33	18.2	16/151	10.6
Male								
Young adult	0/4	0.0	0/12	0.0	0/5	0.0	0/21	0.0
Old adult	0/7	0.0	0/12	0.0	0/5	0.0	0/24	0.0
Total	0/11	0.0	0/24	0.0	0/10	0.0	0/45	0.0

[1] A = number of vertebrae affected with osteoarthritis or osteophytosis.
[2] O = number of vertebrae observed.
[3] Young adult = individuals aged between 16 to 35 years; Old adult = individuals older than 36 years.

TABLE 11: Frequency of occurrence of Schmorl's depressions in the Vukovar-Vučedol series

	Thoracic A^1/O^2	%	Lumbar A/O	%	Total A/O	%
Female						
Young adult[3]	1/53	1.9	1/23	4.3	2/76	2.6
Old adult	7/24	29.2	1/10	10.0	8/34	23.5
Total	8/77	10.4	2/33	6.1	10/110	9.1
Male						
Young adult	0/12	0.0	0/5	0.0	0/17	0.0
Old adult	0/12	0.0	0/5	0.0	0/17	0.0
Total	0/24	0.0	0/10	0.0	0/34	0.0

[1] A = number of vertebrae with Schmorl's depressions.
[2] O = number of vertebrae observed.
[3] Young adult = individuals aged between 16 to 35 years; Old adult = individuals older than 36 years.

2.3. THE BEZDANJAČA CAVE SKELETAL SERIES

The Bezdanjača skeletal series is the largest prehistoric series. It contains the remains of 41 individuals. This large series was recovered from the Bezdanjača cave on the northeastern slopes of the Velebit mountain range. All of the recovered individuals were interred as secondary burials. The most common element interred was the skull. A small amount of postcranial bones were also recovered but because they could not be associated with specific skulls, and could not be precisely aged or sexed (the recovered bones include 3 femurs, 2 humeri, 2 ulnae and 3 calcanei), these remains are not included in analysis. Based on material artifacts, individuals recovered from the Bezdanjača cave are dated from the 14th to the 12th century B.C., or to the Middle and Late Bronze Age periods (Drechler-Bižić, 1979; Dimitrijević et al., 1998).

TABLE 12: Age and sex distribution in the Bezdanjača series

Age category	Subadult N[1]	%[2]	Female N	%	Male N	%	Total N	%
Birth -1	0						0	
2- 5	0						0	
6-10	7	87.5					7	17.1
11-15	1	12.5					1	2.5
16-20			2	22.2	1	4.2	3	7.3
21-25			1	11.1	5	20.8	6	14.6
26-30			0		0		0	
31-35			3	33.4	7	29.2	10	24.4
36-40			1	11.1	3	12.5	4	9.7
41-45			1	11.1	3	12.5	4	9.7
46-50			0		0		0	
51-55			1	11.1	4	16.6	5	12.2
56-60			0		0		0	
60+			0		1	4.2	1	2.5
Total	8	100.0	9	100.0	24	100.0	41	100.0

Mean age at death[3]   x = 32.44   x = 36.83
                        sd = 11.58   sd = 12.11

[1] N = number of individuals dying.

[2] % = % of individuals dying.

[3] Mean age at death is calculated using median values of each age category (for example, 23 for the age category 21-25), and 65 for the age category 60+.

The age and sex distribution of the series is presented in Table 12. The series is characterized by a biased distribution with a preponderance of adult males. Subadults, particularly infants, are underrepresented in the series as are adult females (the male female ratio is 100 : 22). Peak mortality for both males and females is between 31-35 years (33.4% of females and 29.2% of males died during this interval). The average age at death for adult females is 32.4 years (SD = 10.9), for adult males 36.8 years (SD = 11.8).

Dental disease frequencies are summarized in Tables 13 and 14. Alveolar bone disease is not present in subadults. In adults, alveolar bone disease is higher in males (19.5%) than in females (10.9%) with a relatively low frequency (17.3%) overall. Males and females exhibit considerably higher frequencies of alveolar bone disease in the old adult age category. This difference is statistically significant for both females ($\chi^2 = 7.1$, $P < 0.01$) and males ($\chi^2 = 42.3$, $P < 0.01$). The higher frequency of alveolar bone disease in males may

TABLE 13: Frequency of alveolar bone disease in the Bezdanjača series

Age category	Subadult A[1]/O[2]	%[3]	Female A/O	%	Male A/O	%
Young adult[4]			3/80	3.75	7/192	3.6
Old adult			11/48	22.9	64/172	37.2
Total	0/86	0.0	14/128	10.9	71/364	19.5

[1] A = number of tooth sockets with periodontal or periapical abscess, or antemortem tooth loss.

[2] O = number of tooth sockets observed.

[3] % = % of tooth sockets with periodontal or periapical abscess, or antemortem tooth loss.

[4] Young adult = individuals aged between 16 to 35 years; Old adult = individuals older than 36 years.

TABLE 14: Frequency of carious lesions in the Bezdanjača series

Age category	Subadult A[1]/O[2]	%[3]	Female A/O	%	Male A/O	%
Young adult[4]			0/34	0.0	5/87	5.7
Old adult			6/26	23.1	5/49	10.2
Total	2/36	5.5	6/60	10.0	10/136	7.3

[1] A = number of teeth with carious lesions.

[2] O = number of teeth observed.

[3] % = % of teeth with carious lesions.

[4] Young adult = individuals aged between 16 to 35 years; Old adult = individuals older than 36 years.

be related to the longer average male life span. Caries frequencies are, again, low in subadults (5.5%), and relatively low in adults (8.2%), with females exhibiting slightly higher frequencies (10%) than males (7.3%). Most of the carious lesions are slight in severity (defined as the presence of a pit or slight fissure) and located interproximally (10/18 or 55.5% of all lesions). Also present are occlusal (3/18), root (4/18), and buccal (1/18) caries.

Enamel hypoplasia frequencies are summarized in Tables 15 and 16. Hypoplasias are most frequent in mandibular canines (40.0 %), followed by maxillary canines (33.3 %). No central maxillary incisors were available for analysis.

TABLE 15: Hypoplasia frequencies by individual in the Bezdanjača series

Tooth	N^1	NwLEH	%wLEH
Maxillary I1[2]	0	0	0.0
Maxillary C	9	3	33.3
Mandibular C	5	2	40.0

[1] N = number of teeth observed; NwLEH = number of teeth with one or more LEH; %wLEH = % of N with one or more LEH.
[2] I = incisor; C = canine.

TABLE 17: Frequency of occurrence of cribra orbitalia in the Bezdanjača series

| Age/sex | Cribra orbitalia | | | Active lesions | |
	O^1	$A1^2$	%	$A2^3$	% of A1
0 - 0.9	0	0	0.0	0	0.0
1 - 3.9	0	0	0.0	0	0.0
4 - 9.9	7	3	100.0	2	66.7
10 - 14.9	1	1	100.0	0	0.0
All subadults	8	4	50.0	2	50.0
Adult females	8	2	25.0	0	0.0
Adult males	22	6	27.3	0	0.0
All adults	30	8	26.7	0	0.0

[1] O = number of frontal bones observed.
[2] A1 = number of frontal bones in which at least one orbit shows evidence of cribra orbitalia.
[3] A2 = number of frontal bones in which cribra orbitalia is active at time of death.

TABLE 16: Hypoplasia frequencies in the Bezdanjača series for subadults and adults

| Tooth | Subadults | | All adults | | Females | | Males | |
	Nw/N^1	$%wLEH^2$	Nw/N	%wLEH	Nw/N	%wLEH	Nw/N	%wLEH
Maxillary I1[3]	0/0	0.0	0/0	0.0	0/0	0.0	0/0	0.0
Maxillary C	0/1	0.0	2/6	33.3	0/3	0.0	2/3	66.7
Mandibular C	0/0	0.0	2/4	50.0	2/3	66.7	0/1	0.0

[1] Nw = number of individuals with one or more LEH; N = number of individuals observed.
[2] %wLEH = % of N with one or more LEH.
[3] I = incisors; C = canines.

Cribra orbitalia frequencies are presented in Table 17. The lesion is observed in 12 of the 38 (31.6 %) crania with intact orbits. Subadults exhibit a higher overall frequency (50.0%) than adults (26.7%). In half of the subadult sample the lesion was active at time of death.

There is no evidence of infectious disease in the series.

Cranial trauma is present in two females (2/9 or 22.2% of the female sample) and two males (2/24 or 8.3%). In three cases (one female and two males) the fractures are healed depression fractures with smooth floors and rounded margins. The fractures did not penetrate the inner table of the skull and show no evidence of infection. The cranial fracture in the frontal bone of female 39 A (Figures 3 and 4) is a well healed fracture displaying the remodeled residual of an old penetrating injury. The wound healed with a bone fragment in a displaced position leaving an opening in the skull. The degree of healing and absence of any sign of

infection indicate the injury occurred many months before death.

As this series contains only skulls, data for physical stress could not be gathered.

2.4. THE VINKOVCI NAMA IRON AGE SKELETAL SERIES

The Vinkovci "NaMa" skeletal series contains the remains of 11 individuals. These remains were recovered in 1976 during rescue excavations at the construction site of the "NaMa" department store in Vinkovci. The remains were recovered from a small Hallstatt cemetery which, besides human remains, contained three horse burials. The graves are dated from the second half of the fifth century to the first half of the fourth century B.C. (Majnarić-Pandžić, 2000).

Figure 3. Cranial trauma in an adult female from Bezdanjača.

Until recently (1999), the recovered remains had been stored in numerous paper bags without corresponding grave numbers or other relevant information. To further complicate the situation one skeleton was typically dispersed into two, three, or in one case even four different paper bags. Before any sort of analysis could, therefore, be attempted it was necessary to "reindividualize" the skeletons and to correlate skeletons with specific grave units.

The "reindividualization" process was carried out on the basis of compatibility in sex, age, general skeletal morphology, taphonomic characteristics and muscle crest development. The age and sex distribution (4 males, 3 females and 4 subadults) in the sample facilitated this endeavor. The "reindividualized" skeletons were correlated to specific grave units on the basis of: 1) the presence and location of oxidation marks on specific bones - these marks were correlated to the presence and location of metal grave goods as noted in the field diary, 2) the presence of other grave goods - for instance glass pearls of the type found in one grave unit were found in one cranium and, 3) "in situ" measured femoral lengths also noted in the field diary.

The "reindividualized" sample contains the remains of 11 individuals. The sex and age distribution of the series is presented in Table 18. The series is characterized by relative

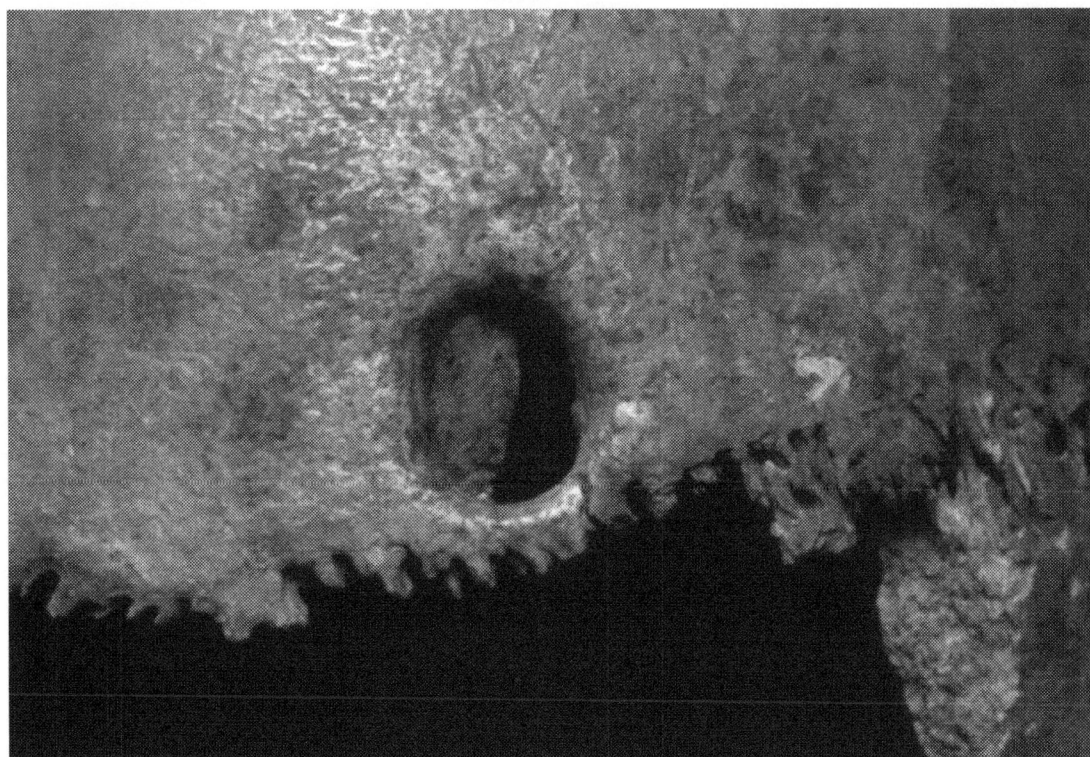

Figure 4. Detailed view of the fracture. The wound healed with a small fragment of bone displaced leaving an opening in the skull.

TABLE 18: Age and sex distribution in the Vinkovci NaMa Iron Age series

Age category	Subadult N[1]	%[2]	Female N	%	Male N	%	Total N	%
Birth -1	1	25.0					1	9.1
2- 5	3	75.0					3	27.2
6-10	0						0	
11-15	0						0	
16-20			0		0		0	
21-25			0		0		0	
26-30			0		0		0	
31-35			2	66.7	0		2	18.2
36-40			0		0		0	
41-45			0		2	50.0	2	18.2
46-50			1	33.3	0		1	9.1
51-55			0		1	25.0	1	9.1
56-60			0		0		0	
60+			0		1	25.0	1	9.1
Total	4	100.0	3	100.0	4	100.0	11	100.0
Mean age at death[3]			x = 38.00		x = 51.00			
			sd = 8.66		sd = 10.45			

[1] N = number of individuals dying.

[2] % = % of individuals dying.

[3] Mean age at death is calculated using median values of each age category (for example, 23 for the age category 21-25), and 65 for the age category 60+.

TABLE 19: Frequency of alveolar bone disease in the Vinkovci NaMa Iron Age series

Age category	Subadult A[1]/O[2]	%[3]	Female A/O	%	Male A/O	%
Young adult[4]			3/57	5.2	0/0	0.0
Old adult			0/0	0.0	30/69	43.5
Total	0/33	0.0	3/57	5.2	30/69	43.5

[1] A = number of tooth sockets with periodontal or periapical abscess, or antemortem tooth loss.

[2] O = number of tooth sockets observed.

[3] % = % of tooth sockets with periodontal or periapical abscess, or antemortem tooth loss.

[4] Young adult = individuals aged between 16 to 35 years; Old adult = individuals older than 36 years.

TABLE 20: Frequency of carious lesions in the Vinkovci NaMa Iron Age series

Age category	Subadult A[1]/O[2]	%[3]	Female A/O	%	Male A/O	%
Young adult[4]			4/39	10.3	0/0	0.0
Old adult			0/3	0.0	4/27	14.8
Total	0/21	0.0	4/42	9.5	4/27	14.8

[1] A = number of teeth with carious lesions.

[2] O = number of teeth observed.

[3] % = % of teeth with carious lesions.

[4] Young adult = individuals aged between 16 to 35 years; Old adult = individuals older than 36 years.

longevity. The mean age at death for adult males is 51.0 years (SD = 9.0), for adult females 38.0 years (SD = 7.1).

Alveolar bone disease frequencies are summarized in Table 19. In this small series males exhibit considerably higher frequencies of alveolar bone disease (43.5%) than females (5.2%). This difference is statistically significant ($\chi^2 = 13.0$, P < 0.01). Males also exhibit higher frequencies of carious lesions (Table 20), although in this case the difference is not statistically significant. In both males and females the observed carious lesions are slight to moderate in expression (ranging from a small pit or fissure on the surface of the tooth to more than a pit, but less than half of the surface destroyed). All of the carious lesions observed in males are located interproximally. In females, 3 of the 4 recorded lesions are located bucally, while one is located interproximally.

Only 3 maxillary central incisors, 3 maxillary canines and 3 mandibular canines were available for analyzing hypoplasia frequencies. Of these, one incisor (from an adult male) and one mandibular canine (from an adult female) exhibit hypoplastic defects.

Cribra orbitalia is present in one of two subadult crania with intact orbits (moderate in expression and active at time of death), and in 1 of 5 adult crania (an adult male, the lesion was healed at time of death).

Two individuals exhibit skeletal evidence of infectious disease. One subadult exhibits bilateral, generalized, severe periostitis, active at time of death on the tibiae. One female exhibits mild, localized, healed periostitis on the distal third of the diaphysis of the left tibia.

Two individuals also exhibit skeletal evidence of trauma. One male exhibits an old, well healed transverse fracture, 26 mm long, on the frontal bone approximately 45 mm superior of nasion. The fracture did not penetrate the inner table of the skull and the smooth margins of the fracture indicate that the trauma occurred many months before death. One female has a compression fracture of the superior end plate of the first lumbar vertebra which resulted in moderate kyphosis.

Physical stress frequencies are low in this series. Osteoarthritis is not present in any of the major joints in adults from this series. The frequencies of vertebral osteoarthritis are very low, and confined to females (Table 21). None of the thoracic or lumbar vertebrae in the series exhibits Schmorl's defects.

TABLE 21: Frequency of occurrence of vertebral osteoarthritis in the Vinkovci NaMa Iron Age series

	Cervical A[1]/O[2]	%	Thoracic A/O	%	Lumbar A/O	%	Total A/O	%
Female								
Young adult[3]	1/5	20.0	0/22	0.0	0/9	0.0	1/36	2.8
Old adult	0/0	0.0	0/0	0.0	0/0	0.0	0/0	0.0
Total	1/5	20.0	0/22	0.0	0/9	0.0	1/36	2.8
Male								
Young adult	0/0	0.0	0/0	0.0	0/0	0.0	0/0	0.0
Old adult	0/14	0.0	0/21	0.0	0/10	0.0	0/45	0.0
Total	0/14	0.0	0/21	0.0	0/10	0.0	0/45	0.0

[1] A = number of vertebrae affected with osteoarthritis or osteophytosis.

[2] O = number of vertebrae observed.

[3] Young adult = individuals aged between 16 to 35 years; Old adult = individuals older than 36 years.

2.5. CHARACTERISTICS OF THE COMPOSITE PREHISTORIC SERIES

The composite prehistoric series is comprised of four prehistoric series - the Vukovar High School Neolithic, Vukovar Vučedol Eneolithic, Bezdanjača Bronze Age and Vinkovci "NaMa" Hallstatt series. This is the smallest of the five composite series reported on in this book, and as previously discussed, covers the largest temporal span, from approximately 5300 BC to 400 BC.

The age and sex distribution of the series is presented in Table 22. The series is characterized by an underrepresentation of subadults and an uneven distribution of males and females. Subadults comprise only 23.2% (16/69) of the total sample. In the youngest age categories (birth to 5 years), where subadult mortality is typically highest, the subadult sample is represented by only 5 individuals (7.3% of the total sample).

In the adult sample males (31) outnumber females (22) yielding a sex ratio of 100:71. The average age at death of

TABLE 22: Age and sex distribution in the Prehistoric composite series

Age category	Subadult N[1]	%[2]	Female N	%	Male N	%	Total N	%
Birth -1	2	12.6					2	2.9
2- 5	3	18.7					3	4.4
6-10	8	50.0					8	11.6
11-15	3	18.7					3	4.4
16-20			4	18.2	2	6.4	6	8.7
21-25			5	22.8	5	16.2	10	14.5
26-30			0		0		0	
31-35			6	27.3	7	22.6	13	18.8
36-40			1	4.5	4	12.9	5	7.2
41-45			3	13.6	5	16.2	8	11.6
46-50			2	9.1	0		2	2.9
51-55			1	4.5	6	19.3	7	10.1
56-60			0		0		0	
60+			0		2	6.4	2	2.9
Total	16	100.0	22	100.0	31	100.0	69	100.0
Mean age at death[3]			x = 31.86		x = 38.61			
			sd = 10.75		sd = 12.73			

[1] N = number of individuals dying.

[2] % = % of individuals dying.

[3] Mean age at death is calculated using median values of each age category (for example, 23 for the age category 21-25), and 65 for the age category 60+.

adults over 15 years is 38.6 years for males and 31.9 years for females. This 6.7 years difference is reflected in differential mortality profiles for males and females. While both males and females exhibit peak mortality between 31-35 years (27.3% of females and 22.6% of males died while in this age category), females clearly seem to be at greater risk during young adulthood. Female mortality between 16-25 years (40.9%) is considerably higher than male (22.6%). Similarly, a large percentage of adult males (54.8%) live longer than 35 years, while the same is true for only 31.8 % of females. The undernumeration of subadults and the uneven distribution of adult males and females is most likely the result of several factors including the absence of defined cemeteries, specific cultural practices such as secondary inhumation, and random variation in small samples.

The frequencies of alveolar bone disease and carious lesions in the composite prehistoric series are summarized in Tables 23 and 24. The correlation of these pathologies with each other, and their age-dependence (i.e. increasing with advancing age) requires careful consideration. The general observation that alveolar bone disease is more common in males could be attributed to a longer average male life span. Additional analyses were therefore conducted, controlling for age in broad categories (young adult and old adult).

Alveolar bone disease (defined by the presence of periodontal or periapical abscesses and antemortem tooth loss) is not present in subadults, and is higher in males (21.1%) than in females (5.7%), with a low adult frequency

(14.3%) overall. The difference between the adult male total and the adult female total is statistically significant (χ^2=32.5, P< .01). Controlling for age, the frequency of alveolar bone disease in young adults is very similar (3.2% in males and 2.8% in females). Significant differences are, however, present in the old adult age category where males exhibit a 33.9% frequency of alveolar bone disease compared to 12.9% in females. These frequencies are significantly different (χ^2 =10.3, P < .01). The combination of similar frequencies of alveolar bone disease in the young adult age category, with significantly different frequencies in the old adult age category, implies that the higher frequency of alveolar bone disease noted in males is related to the longer average male life span.

The overall frequency of carious lesions in the prehistoric composite series is 7.0%. The subadult frequency is 4.9% (6/123). Adult male and female frequencies are similarly low, 6.8% for males and 8.2% for females. Females in the old adult age category exhibit higher frequencies of carious lesions than males (19.0% compared to 8.8%) but this difference is not significant.

Both males and females display the same modal category for severity of carious lesions. A four scale grading system was used to evaluate the severity of carious lesions: grade 1 - a pit or slight fissure, grade 2 - more than a pit but less than half of the surface destroyed, grade 3 - more than half of the surface destroyed but not the complete crown, and grade 4 - complete destruction of the tooth crown. The modal category for severity of lesion is grade 1 in both males and females, in both the young adult and old adult age categories.

The distribution of carious lesions in both sexes is also similar. Carious lesions are most frequently located interproximally (in 73.3% of all carious lesions in males and in 43.5% of all carious lesions in females). In males this is followed by occlusal (20%) and root caries (6.7%), and in females by root (39.1%), buccal (13.0%) and occlusal (4.4%) caries.

The overall frequencies of dental pathologies are low in this series. Analyses by controlling for age suggest the sex differences in frequencies of dental pathologies are primarily related to the greater longevity of males in the sample.

Enamel hypoplasia frequencies are summarized in Tables 25-27. Hypoplasias are most frequent in the maxillary central incisors - 54.5%, followed by mandibular canines - 42.1%, and maxillary canines - 33.3%.

TABLE 23: Frequency of alveolar bone disease in the Prehistoric composite series

Age category	Subadult A[1]/O[2]	%[3]	Female A/O	%	Male A/O	%
Young adult[4]			8/289	2.8	7/216	3.2
Old adult			15/116	12.9	102/301	33.9
Total	0/193	0.0	23/405	5.7	109/517	21.1

[1] A = number of tooth sockets with periodontal or periapical abscess, or antemortem tooth loss.
[2] O = number of tooth sockets observed.
[3] % = % of tooth sockets with periodontal or periapical abscess, or antemortem tooth loss.
[4] Young adult = individuals aged between 16 to 35 years; Old adult = individuals older than 36 years.

TABLE 24: Frequency of carious lesions in the Prehistoric composite series

Age category	Subadult A[1]/O[2]	%[3]	Female A/O	%	Male A/O	%
Young adult[4]			7/196	3.6	5/108	4.6
Old adult			16/84	19.0	10/114	8.8
Total	6/123	4.9	23/280	8.2	15/222	6.8

[1] A = number of teeth with carious lesions.
[2] O = number of teeth observed.
[3] % = % of teeth with carious lesions.
[4] Young adult = individuals aged between 16 to 35 years; Old adult = individuals older than 36 years.

TABLE 25: Hypoplasia frequencies by individual in the Prehistoric composite series

Tooth	N[1]	NwLEH	%wLEH
Maxillary I1[2]	11	6	54.5
Maxillary C	21	7	33.3
Mandibular C	19	8	42.1

[1] N = number of teeth observed; NwLEH = number of teeth with one or more LEH; %wLEH = % of N with one or more LEH.
[2] I = incisor; C = canine.

TABLE 26: Hypoplasia frequencies in the Prehistoric composite series for subadults and adults

Tooth	Subadults		All adults		Females		Males	
	Nw/N[1]	%wLEH[2]	Nw/N	%wLEH	Nw/N	%wLEH	Nw/N	%wLEH
Maxillary I1[3]	2/3	66.6	4/8	50.0	3/6	50.0	1/2	50.0
Maxillary C	1/2	50.0	6/19	31.6	2/11	18.2	4/8	50.0
Mandibular C	1/2	50.0	7/17	41.1	5/11	45.4	2/6	33.3

[1] Nw = number of individuals with one or more LEH; N = number of individuals observed.
[2] %wLEH = % of N with one or more LEH.
[3] I = incisors; C = canines.

TABLE 27: Mean number of hypoplasias in incisors and canines in the Prehistoric composite series

Tooth	Subadults			All adults			Females			Males		
	Mean	N	S.D.	Mean	N	S.D.	Mean	N	S.D.	Mean	N	S.D.
Maxillary I1[1]	0.66	3	0.58	0.50	8	0.50	0.50	6	0.50	0.50	2	0.50
Maxillary C	0.50	2	0.71	0.47	19	0.75	0.27	11	0.62	0.75	8	0.83
Mandibular C	0.50	2	0.71	0.65	17	0.84	0.64	11	0.77	0.67	6	0.94

[1] I = incisors; C = canines.

Subadults are poorly represented in the analyzed sample. Only 7 teeth are available for analysis (3 central maxillary incisors, 2 maxillary, and 2 mandibular canines). Four teeth (two incisors, one maxillary, and one mandibular canine) exhibit hypoplastic defects.

A breakdown of the adult sample by sex (Table 26) shows that adult males and females exhibit similar frequencies of hypoplastic teeth. The frequency is identical (50.0%) in central maxillary incisors, higher in males for maxillary canines (50.0% compared to 18.2% in females), and slightly higher in females for mandibular canines (45.4% compared to 33.3%).

TABLE 28: Frequency of occurrence of cribra orbitalia in the Prehistoric composite series

Age/sex	Cribra orbitalia			Active lesions	
	O[1]	A1[2]	%	A2[3]	% of A1
0 - 0.9	1	0	0.0	0	0.0
1 - 3.9	1	1	100.0	1	100.0
4 - 9.9	9	4	44.4	3	75.0
10 - 14.9	3	3	100.0	1	33.3
All subadults	14	8	57.1	5	62.5
Adult females	18	2	11.1	0	0.0
Adult males	28	7	25.0	0	0.0
All adults	46	9	19.6	0	0.0

[1] O = number of frontal bones observed.
[2] A1 = number of frontal bones in which at least one orbit shows evidence of cribra orbitalia.
[3] A2 = number of frontal bones in which cribra orbitalia is active at time of death.

The mean number of hypoplasias per tooth shows, however, that males may have been experiencing greater subadult stress. When the number of defects in each tooth with hypoplasias is averaged for the different groups in the sample (Table 27), males have an equal (maxillary central incisors) or greater (maxillary canines and mandibular canines) number of defects per tooth than females. The mean number of defects in subadults and adults is similar.

Cribra orbitalia frequencies are summarized in Table 28. In the prehistoric composite series the expression of this condition ranges from very slight pitting to severe sievelike lesions with considerable diplotic expansion.

Cribra orbitalia is observed in 17 of the 60 crania (28.3%) with intact orbits. The overall subadult frequency is 57.1%. In adults the lesion has a frequency of 19.6%. The higher lesion frequency associated with infancy and childhood is consistent with the pattern observed in other skeletal series (Cybulski, 1977; El-Najjar, 1976; Stuart-Macadam, 1985; Mittler and VanGerven, 1994). Further support for the age association of the lesion is seen when a distinction is made between active and healing lesions. In subadults 62.5% of the lesions are active at time of death. After the age of 15, all lesions show some degree of healing.

Sex differences in healing lesion frequencies are not statistically significant. However, male lesion frequencies (25.0%) are considerably higher than female (11.1%) frequencies. Together with the enamel hypoplasia data, this may be indicative of greater subadult stress in males.

The underlying iron deficiency causing cribra orbitalia appears to have a huge effect on mortality patterns. There is a significant difference in mean ages at death between adults who show evidence of cribra orbitalia, and adults with no evidence of the lesion. Adults with healing cribra orbitalia lesions (n=9; mean age at death=30.66 years), on average live 7.46 years shorter than adults who show no evidence of the lesion (n=37; mean age at death=38.13 years).

Skeletal evidence of infectious disease is present in both subadults and adults. Because of the different preservation of the recovered remains, periostitis frequencies are calculated not "by individual", but by bone.

TABLE 29: Frequency of occurrence of active periosteal lesions in the Prehistoric composite series

| | **Periosteal lesions** | | |
Sex	A1[1]	A2[2]	% of A1
Subadults	10	6	60.0
Adult females	3	0	0.0
Adult males	1	0	0.0
All adults	4	0	0.0
Total	14	6	42.9

[1] A1 = number of bones with periostitis.
[2] A2 = number of bones with periostitis active at time of death.

In comparison to adults, subadults show less resistance to infectious disease. Endocranial periostitis is present on 4 of the 46 recovered subadult cranial vault bones (8.7%). None of the adult cranial vault bones exhibit this condition. Periostitis on the tibia is present in 2 of the 9 recovered subadult tibiae, and on 4 of the 38 recovered adult tibiae (10.5%). Furthermore, while most of the subadult lesions show no evidence of healing, none of the adult lesions were active at time of death (Table 29). No cases of osteomyelitis are noted in the series.

The prehistoric composite series is characterized by a high frequency of healed fractures. The types of fractures identified include depressed lesions on the cranial vault, long bone fractures, rib fractures and vertebral compression fractures. Fractures of the cranium, particularly of the frontal bone (present in 7/18 adult females and 4/28 adult males with preserved frontal bones) are the most commonly recorded fractures, followed by parietal fractures (4/36 female, and 1/52 male parietals) rib fractures (2/45 male, 0/113 female ribs), vertebral fractures (1/176 female, 0/94 male vertebrae), and tibial fractures (1/24 female, and 0/14 male tibiae). There are no fractures of the upper limb or on the clavicles.

The proportionately high rate of cranial fractures suggests participation in violent activities conducive to head injury. Seven of the 18 complete adult female skulls (38.9%) exhibit at least one cranial fracture, and 4 (22.2%) exhibit two fractures. In the male sample, 4/27 (14.8%) complete skulls exhibit cranial fractures. Although fractures of the skull vault can occur as a result of a fall, a blow to the head by, for instance, a stone or club, is more often the cause. Of interest are the differential rates of cranial fractures in males and females. Although not statistically significant, female frequencies are considerably higher than male. Even if the Vukovar Vučedol series is removed from the data base (as there is some evidence that the cranial fractures in this series may be related to cult activities or an initiation ceremony), female cranial fracture frequencies (18.2%) are higher than male (12.0%). With a caveat for small sample size, this is consistent with patterns of domestic violence and assault. Further systematic analyses of prehistoric skeletal series from continental Croatia are necessary to evaluate if the observed male and female frequencies of cranial fractures are the result of random variation in a small sample, or a realistic reflection of the incidence of cranial trauma in prehistoric populations from Croatia.

Enthesophytes are recorded on one of the 22 recovered female femurs (from the Vukovar Vučedol series - a small bone spur on the inferior side of the lesser trochanter of the left femur, probably trauma induced), and on 5/18 female and 4/6 male calcanei, (at the insertion site of the Achilles tendon). There is no skeletal evidence for dislocation in the series. Spondylolysis is present in one fifth lumbar vertebra (a male from the Vukovar Vučedol series), or in 1/14 adults (9 females and 5 males) with complete lumbar spines.

Osteoarthritis frequencies in the series are summarized in Table 30. All of the cases reported reflect mild or moderate degrees of osteoarthritis, there are no cases of eburnation in the series. Of the four major joints in the skeleton, osteoarthritis is most frequently recorded in the shoulder. Osteoarthritis is more common in males than in females, and more common in the old adult than the young adult

TABLE 30: Frequency of occurrence of osteoarthritis at major joints in the Prehistoric composite series

| | **Shoulder** | | **Elbow** | | **Hip** | | **Knee** | |
	A[1]/O[2]	%	A/O	%	A/O	%	A/O	%
Female								
Young adult[3]	1/8	12.5	0/8	0.0	0/8	0.0	0/8	0.0
Old adult	1/3	33.3	1/4	25.0	1/4	25.0	1/4	25.0
Total	2/11	18.1	1/12	8.3	1/12	8.3	1/12	8.3
Male								
Young adult	0/1	0.0	0/1	0.0	0/1	0.0	0/1	0.0
Old adult	3/3	100.0	0/4	0.0	1/6	16.7	3/6	50.0
Total	2/4	50.0	0/5	0.0	1/7	14.3	1/7	14.3

[1] A = number of joints affected with osteoarthritis. Osteoarthritis was scored as present if at least one joint element showed evidence of osteoarthritic change.
[2] O = number of joints observed. A joint was scored as present if at least one joint element was completely present, or if two or three elements were partially present.
[3] Young adult = individuals aged between 16 to 35 years; Old adult = individuals older than 36 years.

TABLE 31: Frequency of occurrence of vertebral osteoarthritis in the Prehistoric composite series

	Cervical		Thoracic		Lumbar		Total	
	A[1]/O[2]	%	A/O	%	A/O	%	A/O	%
Female								
Young adult[3]	1/32	3.1	0/75	0.0	2/32	6.2	3/139	2.2
Old adult	4/14	28.6	6/24	25.0	4/10	40.0	14/48	29.2
Total	5/46	10.9	6/99	6.1	6/42	14.3	17/187	9.1
Male								
Young adult	0/4	0.0	0/12	0.0	0/5	0.0	0/21	0.0
Old adult	0/25	0.0	0/36	0.0	0/19	0.0	0/80	0.0
Total	0/29	0.0	0/48	0.0	0/24	0.0	0/101	0.0

[1] A = number of vertebrae affected with osteoarthritis or osteophytosis.
[2] O = number of vertebrae observed.
[3] Young adult = individuals aged between 16 to 35 years; Old adult = individuals older than 36 years.

age group demonstrating the age-dependence of this pathology.

The overall frequency of vertebral osteoarthritis in the series is low (17/288 or 5.9%). Comparing the different regions of the spine (Table 31), greatest involvement occurs in the lumbar region (6/166; 9.1%), followed by the cervical (5/71; 7.0%) and thoracic (6/147; 4.1%) regions. None of the male vertebrae in the series exhibits osteoarthritis. The difference between male and female frequencies is statistically significant ($\chi^2 = 7.4$; P < .01).

TABLE 32: Frequency of occurrence of Schmorl's depressions in the Prehistoric composite series

	Thoracic		Lumbar		Total	
	A[1]/O[2]	%	A/O	%	A/O	%
Female						
Young adult[3]	1/75	1.3	1/32	3.1	2/107	1.9
Old adult	7/24	29.2	1/10	10.0	8/34	23.5
Total	8/99	8.1	2/42	4.8	10/141	7.1
Male						
Young adult	0/12	0.0	0/5	0.0	0/17	0.0
Old adult	0/36	0.0	0/19	0.0	0/55	0.0
Total	0/48	0.0	0/24	0.0	0/72	0.0

[1] A = number of vertebrae with Schmorl's depressions.
[2] O = number of vertebrae observed.
[3] Young adult = individuals aged between 16 to 35 years; Old adult = individuals older than 36 years.

The frequencies of Schmorl's depressions in the series are summarized in Table 32. The overall frequency of Schmorl's depressions in the sample is 4.7% (10/213). Schmorl's depressions are more common in thoracic (8/147; 5.4%) than in lumbar (2/66; 3.0%) vertebrae and are, similar to vertebral osteoarthritis, only present in females. The difference between total male and female frequencies in the series is marginally not significant ($\chi^2 = 3.56$; P < .06).

The absence of Schmorl's depressions and vertebral osteoarthritis in male spinal columns is surprising. The age-dependence of vertebral osteoarthritis is well documented and as males in the series have a longer average life-span than females, it would be reasonable to expect similar, or slightly higher, frequencies of degenerative change in male spinal columns. Further analyses are needed to evaluate if the observed differences are a realistic reflection of spinal column stress in males, or the result of random variation in a small sample.

3. BIOARCHAEOLOGY OF THE ANTIQUE PERIOD

Within the administrative framework of the Roman Empire, continental Croatia encompassed the southern parts of two Roman provinces; Upper and Lower Pannonia (*Pannonia Superior* and *Inferior*). This division remained until the end of the third century AD when the emperor Diocletian divided Pannonian into four provinces: *Prima*, *Valeria*, *Savia* and *Secunda*. Continental Croatia encompassed all of *Savia* and part of *Secunda*. This area bordered with *Noricum* (Slovenia) on the west, with *Pannonia Prima* and *Valeria* (Hungary) on the north, and with *Dalmatia* (Central and Southern Croatia and Bosnia and Herzegovina) on the south.

Continental Croatia offered good natural resources and developed rapidly during the period of stability which characterized the first two centuries of Roman rule. The area is rich in water and fertile soils, has a mild climate, and offered natural riches for exploitation. Roman quarries are known from Medvednica near Zagreb and from the Kordun region south of Karlovac. Rich clay deposits enabled an extensive and varied production of pottery vessels. Metallurgy was also developed, particularly in Sisak (*Siscia*), where ore was brought from the Bosnian mines (Gregl, 1997). The strategic importance of the region in terms of transportation is evident from the presence of itinerary (main) roads, such as the *Emona-Siscia-Sirmium*, *Poetovia-Siscia*, *Senia-Siscia* and others. The importance of the river routes is indicated by the fact that the headquarters of the river flotilla were located in *Siscia*. The major reason for such an extensively developed transportation network probably lies in the fact that the shortest overland routes from the central part of the Empire to the eastern provinces were laid out and constructed through Pannonia, along the Sava and Drava rivers (Gregl, 1997). These routes were important not only because of trade, but also (for instance the *Itinerarium Hierosolymitanum* which stretched along the Drava river) because they transported pilgrims from western parts of the Empire to the holy places in the Near East (Migotti, 1997).

The antique period is represented by four skeletal series. The series were recovered from Štrbinci (*Certisia*), Vinkovci (*Cibalae*), Osijek (*Mursa*), and Zmajevac. The geographical position of the sites is shown in Figure 5. As can be seen, all of the sites are located in the eastern part of continental Croatia. All of the sites are dated to the 4th century AD. The absence of skeletal material from earlier periods of Roman rule can be attributed to differences in burial practices. Cremation was the favored disposal rite in Republican Rome and remained so until the 2nd century AD when inhumation replaced it. The transition appears to have been fairly swift in Rome, occurring between about 120 and 190 AD (Philpott, 1991). In the provinces it's spread was more gradual but by the mid 3rd century AD inhumation had become common (Cambi, 1988).

under their leader Odoacar, settled in continental Croatia as Roman allies (pushing out the Gepids), and held this territory until the destruction of the Gothic kingdom by the Byzantine Emperor Justinian in the middle of the sixth century.

3.1. THE ŠTRBINCI SKELETAL SERIES

The Štrbinci site is located approximately 3 km southeast of the town of Đakovo. It covers an area of about 63 hectares. The site was previously known in archaeological literature for it's prehistoric artifacts and Roman finds. At present, there is a considerable amount of evidence (archaeological, numismatic and epigraphic) linking the site with the Roman town *Certissia* (Migotti, 1998). Recovered material artifacts including pottery, jewelry, and coins date the skeletal remains to the 4th century AD.

The series contains the remains of 26 individuals. They were recovered in two campaigns carried out in 1993 and 1999 (Gregl, 1994; Perinić, 1999). The majority of the remains were recovered from single primary inhumations. Only one grave contained two individuals, a young adult woman and a poorly preserved subadult. The series is characterized by excellent bone preservation.

The age and sex distribution of the series is presented in Table 33. The series is characterized by an underrepresentation of subadults from the youngest (0-1 year) age category, and an even distribution of males and females. Subadults comprise 34.6% (9/26) of the total

Figure 5. The geographical locations of the Antique sites: 1. Štrbinci, 2. Eastern Necropolis of Mursa (Osijek), 3. Zmajevac, 4. Vinkovci.

The 4th century AD in continental Croatia is characterized by political instability. Like other frontier provinces, continental Croatia was subjected to civil war and barbarian intrusions as a result of socio-economic and political crises in the Roman Empire. At the end of the 4th century (378/9) Western Goths plundered Mursa on their way to Dalmatia and Aquileia. Roman rule remained, however, in force, and the new population was accepted as allies - *foederati*. The first appearance of the Huns in continental Croatia also occurred in the second half of the 4th century when the emperor Theodosius, with their help, defeated his rival Maxim in 388, probably somewhere in the area between the Danube and Sava rivers. By the mid fifth century, most of continental Croatia was under Hun rule. This rule was, however, short-lived and lasted until 454. After the decline of Hun power, and the fall of the Western Roman Empire (476) Germanic tribes, previously subject to the Huns, began functioning independently. Among these were the Eastern Goths who,

sample. Peak mortality for females is between 31-35 years (50.0% of females died during this interval). Males show no clear peak mortality period. Females, however, appear to be at greater risk during young adulthood. Only 37.5% of adult females live longer than 35 years, compared to 55.6% of males. The average age at death for adult females is 35.5 years (SD = 5.34), for adult males 39.3 years (SD = 14.7).

The frequencies of alveolar bone disease and carious lesions are summarized in Tables 34 and 35. Alveolar bone disease is rare in subadults (1.9%). Males exhibit slightly higher frequencies (4.1%) than females (3.4%), but the overall adult frequency is low (14/372, 3.8%).

Adult caries frequencies are slightly higher; 5.9% in females, 12.5% in males, and 10.0% overall. Subadults exhibit no carious lesions. Controlling for age, young males and females exhibit similar frequencies of lesions (2.6% females, 5.8%

TABLE 33: Age and sex distribution in theŠtrbinci series

Age category	Subadult N[1]	%[2]	Female N	%	Male N	%	Total N	%
Birth -1	1	11.1					1	3.8
2- 5	3	33.3					3	11.6
6-10	3	33.3					3	11.6
11-15	2	22.3					2	7.7
16-20			0		0		0	
21-25			0		2	22.2	2	7.7
26-30			1	12.5	2	22.2	3	11.6
31-35			4	50.0	0		4	15.4
36-40			1	12.5	0		1	3.8
41-45			2	25.0	2	22.2	4	15.4
46-50			0		1	11.2	1	3.8
51-55			0		1	11.1	1	3.8
56-60			0		0		0	
60+			0		1	11.1	1	3.8
Total	9	100.0	8	100.0	9	100.0	26	100.0

Mean age at death[3]   x = 35.50   x = 39.33

sd = 5.34   sd = 14.73

[1] N = number of individuals dying.
[2] % = % of individuals dying.
[3] Mean age at death is calculated using median values of each age category (for example, 23 for the age category 21-25), and 65 for the age category 60+.

TABLE 34: Frequency of alveolar bone disease in the Štrbinci series

Age category	Subadult A[1]/O[2]	%[3]	Female A/O	%	Male A/O	%
Young adult[4]			0/83	0.0	1/126	0.8
Old adult			6/94	6.4	7/69	10.1
Total	1/52	1.9	6/177	3.4	8/195	4.1

[1] A = number of tooth sockets with periodontal or periapical abscess, or antemortem tooth loss.
[2] O = number of tooth sockets observed.
[3] % = % of tooth sockets with periodontal or periapical abscess, or antemortem tooth loss.
[4] Young adult = individuals aged between 16 to 35 years; Old adult = individuals older than 36 years.

TABLE 35: Frequency of carious lesions in the Štrbinci series

Age category	Subadult A[1]/O[2]	%[3]	Female A/O	%	Male A/O	%
Young adult[4]			2/77	2.6	7/120	5.8
Old adult			6/58	10.3	20/96	20.8
Total	0/60	0.0	8/135	5.9	27/216	12.5

[1] A = number of teeth with carious lesions.
[2] O = number of teeth observed.
[3] % = % of teeth with carious lesions.
[4] Young adult = individuals aged between 16 to 35 years; Old adult = individuals older than 36 years.

males), while old adult males exhibit twice as many carious lesions as old adult females (20.8% in males compared to 10.3% in females). This difference is not, however, statistically significant and as frequencies in the young adult age category are similar, probably reflects a slightly higher average male life-span

Both males and females display the same modal category - grade 2 (the lesion is more than a pit but less than half of the crown surface destroyed), for severity of carious lesion.The distribution of carious lesions in both sexes is also similar. Carious lesions are most frequently located interproximally (in 21/27 or 77.8% of all carious lesions in males, and in 5/8 of all carious lesions in females). In males the only other location for carious lesions is on the root of the tooth (in 6/27 or 22.2%), while in females lesions are recorded on the buccal surface (in 2/8 lesions) and on the root (1/8 lesions) of the tooth.

Enamel hypoplasia frequencies are summarized in Tables 36-38. Hypoplasias are most frequent in the maxillary canines - 76.9%, followed by

TABLE 36: Hypoplasia frequencies by individual in the Štrbinci series

Tooth	N[1]	NwLEH	%wLEH
Maxillary I1[2]	9	5	55.5
Maxillary C	13	10	76.9
Mandibular C	14	8	57.1

[1] N = number of teeth observed; NwLEH = number of teeth with one or more LEH; %wLEH = % of N with one or more LEH.
[2] I = incisor; C = canine.

mandibular canines - 57.1% and maxillary central incisors - 55.5%.

Subadults are poorly represented in the analyzed sample. Only 9 teeth were available for analysis (3 central maxillary incisors, 3 maxillary and 3 mandibular canines). Most of these teeth, however, exhibit deep hypoplastic defects (Table 37) with the highest frequency (3/3) recorded in maxillary canines. Adult frequencies are slightly lower than subadult with the highest frequency recorded, once again, in maxillary canines (7/10). A breakdown of the adult sample by sex shows that adult males and females exhibit similar frequencies of hypoplastic teeth.

The mean number of hypoplasias per tooth (Table 38) shows a slightly higher number of hypoplastic defects in subadults for maxillary and mandibualr canines. Male and female values are similar.

TABLE 37: Hypoplasia frequencies in the Štrbinci series for subadults and adults

Tooth	Subadults		All adults		Females		Males	
	Nw/N[1]	%wLEH[2]	Nw/N	%wLEH	Nw/N	%wLEH	Nw/N	%wLEH
Maxillary I1[3]	2/3	66.7	3/6	50.0	0/1	0.0	3/5	60.0
Maxillary C	3/3	100.0	7/10	70.0	2/4	50.0	5/6	83.3
Mandibular C	2/3	66.7	6/11	54.5	3/5	60.0	3/6	50.0

[1] Nw = number of individuals with one or more LEH; N = number of individuals observed.
[2] %wLEH = % of N with one or more LEH.
[3] I = incisors; C = canines.

TABLE 38: Mean number of hypoplasias in incisors and canines in the Štrbinci series

Tooth	Subadults			All adults			Females			Males		
	Mean	N	S.D.	Mean	N	S.D.	Mean	N	S.D.	Mean	N	S.D.
MaxillaryI1[1]	0.67	3	0.58	0.67	6	0.82	0.00	1	0.00	0.80	5	0.83
Maxillary C	1.00	3	0.00	0.80	10	0.63	0.75	4	0.96	0.83	6	0.40
Mandibular C	1.00	3	1.00	0.82	11	0.87	0.80	5	0.83	0.83	6	0.98

[1] I = incisors; C = canines.

TABLE 39: Frequency of occurrence of cribra orbitalia in the Štrbinci series

Age/sex	Cribra orbitalia			Active lesions	
	O[1]	A1[2]	%	A2[3]	% of A1
0 - 0.9	1	0	0.0	0	0.0
1 - 3.9	1	1	100.0	1	100.0
4 - 9.9	0	0	0.0	0	0.0
10 - 14.9	0	0	0.0	0	0.0
All subadults	2	1	50.0	1	100.0
Adult females	5	0	0.0	0	0.0
Adult males	9	2	22.2	0	0.0
All adults	14	2	14.3	0	0.0

[1] O = number of frontal bones observed.
[2] A1 = number of frontal bones in which at least one orbit shows evidence of cribra orbitalia.
[3] A2 = number of frontal bones in which cribra orbitalia is active at time of death.

Cribra orbitalia frequencies are summarized in Table 39. Only two subadult frontal bones with intact orbits were available for analysis one of which exhibits active, severe cribra orbitalia. Two males (2/9 males with preserved orbits) also show healing cribra orbitalia lesions. None of the 5 females with intact orbits exhibits this condition.

Periostitis is noted on the endocranial surface of the cranial vault and on the tibiae. One subadult exhibits healed periostitis on the endocranial surface of the right parietal and occipital bone (1/4 recovered intact subadult cranial vaults). None of the 13 adult (6 female and 7 male) cranial vaults exhibits this condition. Periostitis on the medial surfaces of the tibiae is noted in 6/9 recovered subadult tibiae and in 3/31 (9.7%)

adult tibiae (0/18 male and 3/13 or 23.1% of female tibiae). In comparison to adults, subadults show less resistance to infectious disease. Four of the six recorded cases of tibial periostitis are active at time of death, while all adult cases are healed. No cases of osteomyelitis are noted in the series.

Two healed fractures, both recorded in adult males, are noted in the series. One is a healed depression fracture on the left parietal bone (1/7 intact male cranial vaults), and one is a healed fracture of the second right rib. The cranial fracture did not penetrate the inner table of the skull and exhibits a smooth floor with rounded margins.

Enthesophytes are common in the series and are recorded on the patellae and calcanei. Both sexes show similar frequencies. Enthesophytes are recorded on 4/17 (23.5%) male calcanei, 2/6 female calcanei, and on 2/10 recovered male patellae, and 2/8 female patellae.

The series is characterized by relatively high frequencies of benign cortical defects. These defects appear as elongated depressions or pits with smooth cortical margins and generally porous floors at ligamentous or tendinous attachment sites. They are normal variants in growing bone were they reflect rapid bone remodeling and pulling stresses in the immature skeleton. Their presence in fully developed adults may reflect repeated chronic physical stress related to muscular exertion (Mann and Murphy, 1990; Owsley et al., 1991). In the Štrbinci skeletal series their presence is noted in subadults and adults. In subadults, two cases of rhomboid fossae are noted on medial clavicles (in 2/7 recovered subadult clavicles).The rhomboid fossa is located on the inferior surface of the medial clavicle and is the attachment site for the costoclavicular ligament. Both cases are deep, with sharply defined cortical margins and porous centers. In adults, cortical defects are noted only in males and are present in 2/15 (13.3%) recovered male humerii (at the insertion sites of the pectoralis major muscle), 2/14 (14.3%) radii (at the insertion site of the biceps brachii muscle), and on 5/15 (33.3%) recovered clavicles (rhomboid fossae).

The series is also characterized by a high incidence of developmental anomalies. Congenital anomalies are recorded in 3 males and 1 subadult and include dental and skeletal disorders. The following anomalies are noted. One adult male exhibits a small facial (globulomaxillary) cyst. The cyst has a diameter of approximately 2 mm and is located on the left maxilla, between the second incisor and the canine. This individual also exhibits marked mandible ramus asymmetry - the right mandibular ramus is 12 mm higher than the left. While differences in mandible ramus heights are common, such a large difference may reflect localized growth disturbance. This individual also exhibits several dental abnormalities. The second left maxillary incisor is rotated 90° in the anterior direction, the maxillary first left premolar is rotated and placed in the position of the canine while the canine is located anterior to the first and second left premolars. The right second maxillary molar and premolar are congenitally absent. A second male exhibits scoliosis of the upper thoracic spine. The condition is apparent in the vertebrae, which show asymmetrical ("twisted") vertebral bodies and spinous processes, and in the sternum and first two ribs which exhibit different curvature. This individual also exhibits talocalcaneal coalition on the left foot, and a small supernumerary tooth between the central maxillary incisors. The third male exhibits a palato-gingival groove on the left maxillary second incisor. One subadult exhibits 13 thoracic vertebrae.

Osteoarthritis frequencies in the series are summarized in Table 40. The overall frequencies are low with no significant

TABLE 41: Frequency of occurrence of vertebral osteoarthritis in the Štrbinci series

	Cervical A^1/O^2	%	Thoracic A/O	%	Lumbar A/O	%	Total A/O	%
Female								
Young adult[3]	0/0	0.0	0/18	0.0	0/5	0.0	0/23	0.0
Old adult	0/17	0.0	4/32	12.5	0/15	0.0	4/64	6.3
Total	0/17	0.0	4/50	8.0	0/20	0.0	4/87	4.6
Male								
Young adult	0/28	0.0	0/47	0.0	0/20	0.0	0/95	0.0
Old adult	4/15	26.7	5/24	20.8	1/10	10.0	10/49	20.4
Total	4/43	9.3	5/71	7.0	1/30	3.3	10/144	6.9

[1] A = number of vertebrae affected with osteoarthritis or osteophytosis.
[2] O = number of vertebrae observed.
[3] Young adult = individuals aged between 16 to 35 years; Old adult = individuals older than 36 years.

TABLE 42: Frequency of occurrence of Schmorl's depressions in the Štrbinci series

	Thoracic A^1/O^2	%	Lumbar A/O	%	Total A/O	%
Female						
Young adult[3]	0/18	0.0	0/5	0.0	0/23	0.0
Old adult	5/32	15.6	5/15	33.3	10/47	21.3
Total	5/50	10.0	5/20	25.0	10/70	14.3
Male						
Young adult	0/47	0.0	2/20	10.0	2/67	3.0
Old adult	3/24	12.5	0/10	0.0	3/34	8.8
Total	3/71	4.2	2/30	6.7	5/101	4.9

[1] A = number of vertebrae with Schmorl's depressions.
[2] O = number of vertebrae observed.
[3] Young adult = individuals aged between 16 to 35 years; Old adult = individuals older than 36 years.

TABLE 40: Frequency of occurrence of osteoarthritis at major joints in the Štrbinci series

	Shoulder A^1/O^2	%	Elbow A/O	%	Hip A/O	%	Knee A/O	%
Female								
Young adult[3]	0/2	0.0	0/2	0.0	0/4	0.0	0/3	0.0
Old adult	1/3	33.3	0/3	0.0	0/3	0.0	1/3	33.3
Total	1/5	20.0	0/5	0.0	0/7	0.0	1/6	16.7
Male								
Young adult	1/4	25.0	0/4	0.0	0/4	0.0	1/4	25.0
Old adult	0/3	0.0	1/4	25.0	0/4	0.0	0/5	0.0
Total	1/7	14.3	1/8	12.5	0/8	0.0	1/9	11.1

[1] A = number of joints affected with osteoarthritis. Osteoarthritis was scored as present if at least one joint element showed evidence of osteoarthritic change.
[2] O = number of joints observed. A joint was scored as present if at least one joint element was completely present, or if two or three elements were partially present.
[3] Young adult = individuals aged between 16 to 35 years; Old adult = individuals older than 36 years.

differences in frequencies between the sexes. All of the cases reported reflect mild or moderate degrees of osteoarthritis. Of the four major joints in the skeleton, osteoarthritis is most frequently recorded in the shoulder.

The overall frequency of vertebral osteoarthritis in the series is low (14/231 or 6.1%). Comparing the different regions of the spine (Table 41), greatest involvement occurs in the thoracic spine (9/121; 7.4%), followed by the cervical (4/60; 6.7%) and lumbar (1/50; 2.0%) regions. Male and female frequencies are similar.

The frequencies of Schmorl's depressions in the series are summarized in Table 42. The overall frequency of Schmorl's depressions in the sample is 8.8% (15/171). Schmorl's depressions are more common in lumbar (7/50; 14%) than in thoracic (8/121; 6.6%) vertebrae. Females exhibit higher frequencies of Schmorl's defects in both segments of the spine but these differences are not statistically significant.

3.2. THE EASTERN NECROPOLIS OF MURSA SKELETAL SERIES

This series contains the remains of 28 individuals recovered in 1988 during rescue excavations in Osijek (Roman *Mursa*). The recovered individuals were buried in the Eastern necropolis of *Mursa* which was, according to Roman custom, located along the peripheral roads on the outskirts of town. Recovered artifacts date the use of the cemetery to the 4th

TABLE 43: Age and sex distribution in the Eastern necropolis of Mursa series

Age category	Subadult N[1]	%[2]	Female N	%	Male N	%	Total N	%
Birth -1	2	28.6					2	7.1
2- 5	1	14.3					1	3.6
6-10	0						0	
11-15	4	57.1					4	14.3
16-20			1	8.3	3	33.3	4	14.3
21-25			3	25.0	1	11.1	4	14.3
26-30			3	25.0	0		3	10.7
31-35			0		2	22.3	2	7.1
36-40			0		1	11.1	1	3.6
41-45			1	8.3	0		1	3.6
46-50			1	8.3	0		1	3.6
51-55			2	16.8	0		2	7.1
56-60			0		1	11.1	1	3.6
60+			1	8.3	1	11.1	2	7.1
Total	7	100.0	12	100.0	9	100.0	28	100.0

Mean age at death[3] x = 36.08 x = 33.77
 sd = 15.47 sd = 17.47

[1] N = number of individuals dying.
[2] % = % of individuals dying.
[3] Mean age at death is calculated using median values of each age category (for example, 23 for the age category 21-25), and 65 for the age category 60+.

century AD (Göricke-Lukić, 2000). Skeletal material was recovered from 13 individual graves, one grave which contained the remains of two individuals, one which contained three individuals, and one which contained the remains of ten individuals (Göricke-Lukić, 1999). Bone preservation was very good, as was the completeness of the recovered skeletons.

The age and sex distribution of the skeletons is presented in Table 43. The series contains 7 subadults (25% of the total sample) and 21 adults. Peak female mortality is between 21-30 years, peak male mortality between 16-20 years. This difference is reflected in mean ages at death. The average

TABLE 44: Frequency of alveolar bone disease in the Eastern necropolis of Mursa series

Age category	Subadult A[1]/O[2]	%[3]	Female A/O	%	Male A/O	%
Young adult[4]			2/124	1.6	3/122	2.4
Old adult			31/135	23.0	10/90	11.1
Total	0/71	0.0	33/259	12.7	13/212	6.1

[1] A = number of tooth sockets with periodontal or periapical abscess, or antemortem tooth loss.
[2] O = number of tooth sockets observed.
[3] % = % of tooth sockets with periodontal or periapical abscess, or antemortem tooth loss.
[4] Young adult = individuals aged between 16 to 35 years; Old adult = individuals older than 36 years.

age at death for adult females is 36.1 years (SD = 15.5), for adult males 33.8 years (SD = 17.5).

Dental disease frequencies are summarized in Tables 44 and 45. Subadults exhibit no evidence of alveolar bone disease. Female frequencies (12.7%) are higher than male (6.1%). This difference is statistically significant ($\chi^2 = 4.12$; $P < 0.05$). Controlling for age, young adult males and females exhibit similar frequencies of alveolar bone disease (2.4% and 1.6% respectively) while females in the old adult age category exhibit more than twice as many episodes of alveolar bone disease as males (23.0% compared to 11.1%).

Caries frequencies are also higher in females than in males (15.0% compared to 10.7%), although in this case the difference is not statistically significant. Females in the old adult age category, once again, exhibit more than twice as many caries as males. In both sexes the majority of the observed caries are located interproximally (in 22/30 lesions or 73.3% in females, and in 8/20 lesions or 40.0% in males). Males also exhibit high frequencies of occlusal (7/20 or 35.0%) and

TABLE 45: Frequency of carious lesions in the Eastern necropolis of Mursa series

Age category	Subadult A[1]/O[2]	%[3]	Female A/O	%	Male A/O	%
Young adult[4]			4/108	3.7	11/110	10.0
Old adult			26/92	28.3	9/76	11.8
Total	1/65	1.5	30/200	15.0	20/186	10.7

[1] A = number of teeth with carious lesions.
[2] O = number of teeth observed.
[3] % = % of teeth with carious lesions.
[4] Young adult = individuals aged between 16 to 35 years; Old adult = individuals older than 36 years.

buccal caries (5/20 or 25.0%). In the female sample 5 cases of occlusal (16.7%) and 3 cases of buccal caries (10.0%) are noted. The modal category for severity of lesions in females is grade 2, in males grade 1.

TABLE 46: Hypoplasia frequencies by individual in the Eastern necropolis of Mursa series

Tooth	N^1	NwLEH	%wLEH
Maxillary I1[2]	14	2	14.3
Maxillary C	17	4	23.5
Mandibular C	17	5	29.4

[1] N = number of teeth observed; NwLEH = number of teeth with one or more LEH; %wLEH = % of N with one or more LEH.

[2] I = incisor; C = canine.

Enamel hypoplasia frequencies are summarized in Tables 46 and 47. Hypoplasias are most frequent in mandibular canines (29.4 %), followed by maxillary canines (23.5%) and maxillary central incisors (14.3%). Subadults are poorly represented in the sample with only 6 teeth (2 maxillary central incisors, 2 maxillary and 2 mandibular canines) available for analysis. Most of these (4/6), however, exhibit deep hypoplastic defects. In adults, hypoplastic defects are most often noted on the mandibular canines (4/15 or 26.7%). Adult males and females exhibit similar frequencies of hypoplastic defects in all teeth categories analyzed.

TABLE 48: Frequency of occurrence of cribra orbitalia in the Eastern necropolis of Mursa series

Age/sex	Cribra orbitalia			Active lesions	
	O^1	$A1^2$	%	$A2^3$	% of A1
0 - 0.9	1	0	0.0	0	0.0
1 - 3.9	1	0	0.0	0	0.0
4 - 9.9	0	0	0.0	0	0.0
10 - 14.9	2	0	0.0	0	0.0
All subadults	4	0	0.0	0	0.0
Adult females	10	0	0.0	0	0.0
Adult males	8	2	25.0	0	0.0
All adults	18	2	11.1	0	0.0

[1] O = number of frontal bones observed.

[2] A1 = number of frontal bones in which at least one orbit shows evidence of cribra orbitalia.

[3] A2 = number of frontal bones in which cribra orbitalia is active at time of death.

infection. Neither penetrated the inner table of the skull. One female exhibits a typical "parry" fracture on the midshaft of the right ulna. The fracture is healed with no angulation or shortening but with a pronounced callus. Rib fractures are noted in one subadult, 2 females and one male. The females and subadult each exhibit one rib fracture, while the adult male exhibits healed fractures on 7 right and 2 left ribs. This

TABLE 47: Hypoplasia frequencies in the Eastern necropolis of Mursa series for subadults and adults

Tooth	Subadults		All adults		Females		Males	
	Nw/N^1	$\%wLEH^2$	Nw/N	%wLEH	Nw/N	%wLEH	Nw/N	%wLEH
Maxillary I1[3]	1/2	50.0	1/12	8.3	0/5	0.0	1/7	14.3
Maxillary C	2/2	100.0	2/15	13.3	1/8	12.5	1/7	14.3
Mandibular C	1/2	50.0	4/15	26.7	2/8	25.0	2/7	28.6

[1] Nw = number of individuals with one or more LEH; N = number of individuals observed.

[2] %wLEH = % of N with one or more LEH.

[3] I = incisors; C = canines.

Cribra orbitalia is not noted in any of the 4 subadults with intact orbits. It's presence is observed in 2 males (Table 48). In both cases the lesions were slight and healed at time of death.

Two individuals exhibit skeletal evidence for infectious disease. Both are subadults and both exhibit bilateral, severe and active tibial periostitis along the complete diaphyses of the tibiae (Figure 6), possibly reflecting a systemic bacterial infection.

Healed fractures are present in subadults and adults. The fractures are located on the skull vault, ribs, vertebra, ulna and tibia. Cranial fractures are present in one subadult (1/4 preserved subadult crania) and one male (1/8 preserved male) crania. In both cases the fractures are well healed depression fractures with smooth margins and no evidence of subsequent

individual also exhibits a healed depression fracture of the proximal lateral surface of the right tibia (Figure 7), and a superior end plate compression fracture of the first lumbar vertebra which resulted in marked kyphosis.

The same individual, an adult male aged between 55-60 years, also exhibits spondylolysis of the fifth lumbar vertebra, possibly accompanied with spondylolisthesis. The arch is completely free of the body of the vertebra (Figure 8), with the break occurring at the pars interarticularis. The broken margins of the bone exhibit considerable remodeling indicating that the break was long standing. Anterior slippage of the vertebra is suggested by changes on the superior surface of the sacrum. The superior surface of the first sacral vertebra exhibits a well defined slightly curved furrow, similar in appearance to an old fracture line (Figure 9). This furrow corresponds to the posterior margin of the

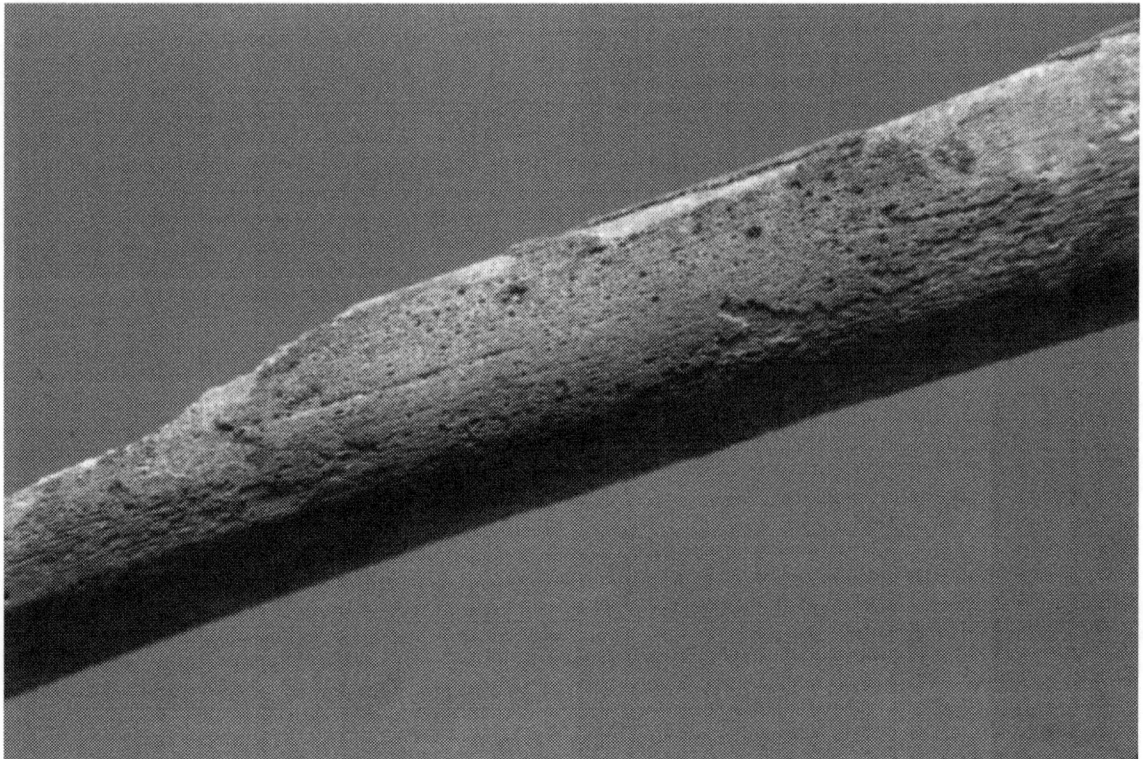

Figure 6. Severe, generalized, active periostitis on the left tibia of a subadult from Mursa.

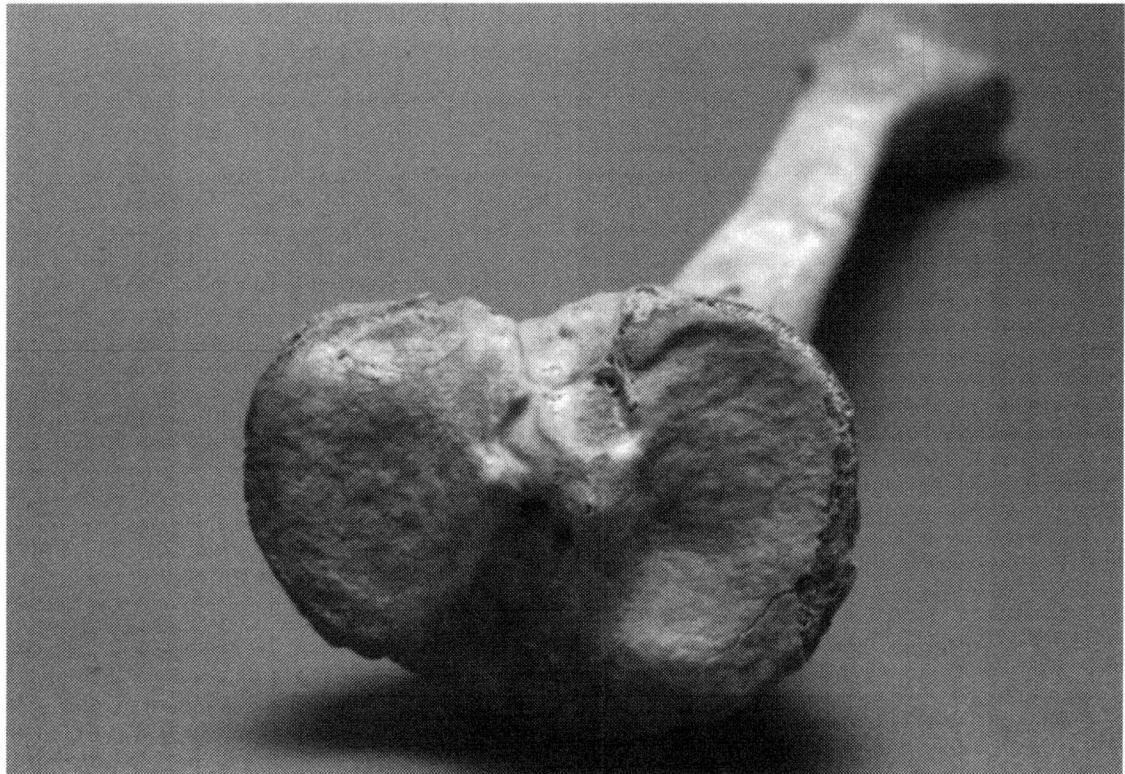

Figure 7. Healed fracture of the proximal, lateral surface of the right tibia in an adult male from Mursa.

inferior end plate of the fifth lumbar vertebra. When the furrow and the posterior margin of the fifth lumbar vertebra are articulated, the remodeled inferior and posterior margins of the fifth lumbar vertebrae articulate well with the superior sacrum. In this position the body of the vertebra projects approximately 14 mm anterior of the anterior margin of the sacrum (Figure 10). The anterior surface of the lumbar vertebra exhibits healed periosteal reactive bone, possibly the result of periosteal activation due to anterior slippage of the vertebra.

Figure 8. Fifth lumbar vertebra of the same individual articulated with the sacrum.
The vertebra exhibits spondylolisis at the pars interarticularis.

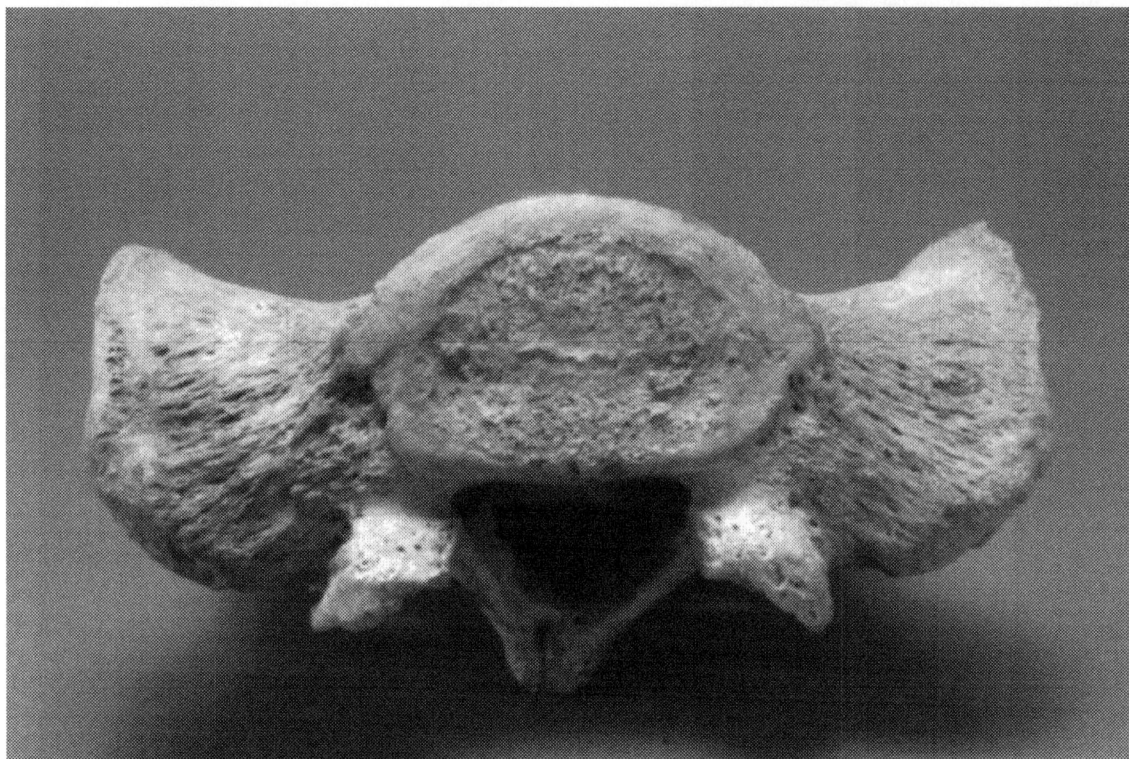

Figure 9. Sacrum of the same individual. Note well defined,
slightly curved furrow on the superior surface of the first sacral vertebra.

A possible fibrous cortical defect is noted in the metaphysis of the left distal femur in an adolescent male. The individual, aged between 15.5-16.5 years, exhibits a well defined solitary lesion with scalloped margins on the lateral side of the distal femoral metaphysis (Figure 11). The lesion measures 21 mm in length and 9 mm in width. Fibrous cortical defects are common lesions in the skeleton. They are located on the metaphysial cortex of the long bones, most commonly in the distal femur. The smaller lesions frequently fill in with bone and disappear by 30 years of

Figure 10. The posterior margin of the fifth lumbar vertebra articulated with the furrow. In this position the remodeled broken posterior margins of the vertebra articulate well with the superior sacrum. The vertebra projects approximately 14 mm in front of the anterior margin of the sacrum.

Figure 11. Possible fibrous cortical defect on the distal, posterior left femur of an adolescent male from Mursa.

age, while larger lesions may persist, migrate into the diaphysis with bone growth, and produce pathological fractures in adulthood (Ortner and Putschar, 1981; Aufderheide and Rodrigez-Martin, 1998).

Osteoarthritis frequencies in females are highest in the elbow and knee (Table 49). Males exhibit identical frequencies in

all major joints except the hip. All of the reported cases reflect mild or moderate degrees of osteoarthritis.

The total female vertebral osteoarthritis frequency is 6.1% (Table 50), with greatest involvement in the cervical region of the spine, followed by the thoracic and lumbar. Males exhibit a slightly higher total vertebral osteoarthritis frequency (15.5%) with very similar frequencies recorded in all segments of the spine.

Males also exhibit high frequencies of Schmorl's depressions in both the thoracic and lumbar spine (Table 51). The total frequency of Schmorl's defects in males is 29.7%, (19/64 vertebrae). No defects are noted in the 55 available female vertebrae. This difference is statistically significant ($\chi^2 = 12.73$; $P < 0.01$). Higher frequencies of Schmorl's defects are noted in older individuals. Males in the old adult age group exhibit a higher frequency (52.9%) of defects than males in the young adult age category (21.3%). The difference is not, however, statistically significant.

TABLE 49: Frequency of occurrence of osteoarthritis at major joints in the Eastern necropolis of Mursa series

	Shoulder		Elbow		Hip		Knee	
	A^1/O^2	%	A/O	%	A/O	%	A/O	%
Female								
Young adult[3]	1/3	33.3	3/3	100.0	2/5	40.0	2/4	50.0
Old adult	0/1	0.0	1/1	100.0	0/1	0.0	1/1	100.0
Total	1/4	25.0	4/4	100.0	2/6	33.3	3/5	60.0
Male								
Young adult	0/2	0.0	0/2	0.0	0/6	0.0	0/2	0.0
Old adult	1/1	100.0	1/1	100.0	1/1	100.0	1/1	100.0
Total	1/3	33.3	1/3	33.3	1/7	14.3	1/3	33.3

[1] A = number of joints affected with osteoarthritis. Osteoarthritis was scored as present if at least one joint element showed evidence of osteoarthritic change.

[2] O = number of joints observed. A joint was scored as present if at least one joint element was completely present, or if two or three elements were partially present.

[3] Young adult = individuals aged between 16 to 35 years; Old adult = individuals older than 36 years.

TABLE 50: Frequency of occurrence of vertebral osteoarthritis in the Eastern necropolis of Mursa series

	Cervical		Thoracic		Lumbar		Total	
	A[1]/O[2]	%	A/O	%	A/O	%	A/O	%
Female								
Young adult[3]	2/18	11.1	2/31	6.4	0/10	0.0	4/59	6.8
Old adult	1/9	11.1	0/9	0.0	0/5	0.0	1/23	4.3
Total	3/27	11.1	2/40	5.0	0/15	0.0	5/82	6.1
Male								
Young adult	0/18	0.0	0/32	0.0	0/15	0.0	0/65	0.0
Old adult	4/8	50.0	7/12	58.3	3/5	60.0	14/25	56.0
Total	4/26	15.4	7/44	15.9	3/20	15.0	14/90	15.5

[1] A = number of vertebrae affected with osteoarthritis or osteophytosis.
[2] O = number of vertebrae observed.
[3] Young adult = individuals aged between 16 to 35 years; Old adult = individuals older than 36 years.

TABLE 51: Frequency of occurrence of Schmorl's depressions in the Eastern necropolis of Mursa series

	Thoracic		Lumbar		Total	
	A[1]/O[2]	%	A/O	%	A/O	%
Female						
Young adult[3]	0/31	0.0	0/10	0.0	0/41	0.0
Old adult	0/9	0.0	0/5	0.0	0/14	0.0
Total	0/40	0.0	0/15	0.0	0/55	0.0
Male						
Young adult	9/32	28.1	1/15	6.7	10/47	21.3
Old adult	4/12	33.3	5/5	100.0	9/17	52.9
Total	13/44	29.5	6/20	30.0	19/64	29.7

[1] A = number of vertebrae with Schmorl's depressions.
[2] O = number of vertebrae observed.
[3] Young adult = individuals aged between 16 to 35 years; Old adult = individuals older than 36 years.

3.3. THE ZMAJEVAC SKELETAL SERIES

Zmajevac is located in the north-eastern corner of continental Croatia, close to Croatia's borders with Hungary and Yugoslavia, approximately 35 km north-east of Osijek. Rescue excavations in 1998 revealed the existence of a Late Antique cemetery. This cemetery was systematically excavated in 1999 and 2000. During these campaigns 37 individuals were recovered. The majority of the remains were recovered from single primary inhumations. Five graves, however, contained two individuals. No consistent combination of individuals is apparent in these graves. The graves consist of two subadults (grave 7), a subadult and an adult female (graves 25 and 28), an adult male and an adult female (grave 27), and two adult females (grave 1). Bone preservation and completeness of the recovered remains was excellent (Figure 12). Artifacts recovered from the site date the use of the cemetery to the 4th century AD (Šimić, 1998, Filipović, personal communication).

The age and sex distribution in the series is presented in Table 52. The series is characterized by an underrepresentation of subadults from the youngest (0-1 year) age category who comprise only 5.4% of the total sample, and an even distribution of males and females. Subadults comprise 24.3% (9/37) of the total sample. Peak mortality for females is between 46-55 years (35.7% of females died during this interval), for males between 36-45 years (42.8% of males died during this time period). This difference is reflected in mean ages at death. The average age at death for adult females is 43.1 years (SD = 13.2), for adult males 40.5 years (SD = 11.4).

Frequencies of alveolar bone disease are presented in Table 53. Alveolar bone disease is not present in subadults, and has a low (11.6%) overall frequency in adults. Females exhibit slightly higher total frequencies (12.6%) than males (10.8%). Sex differences are, however, present only in the old adult

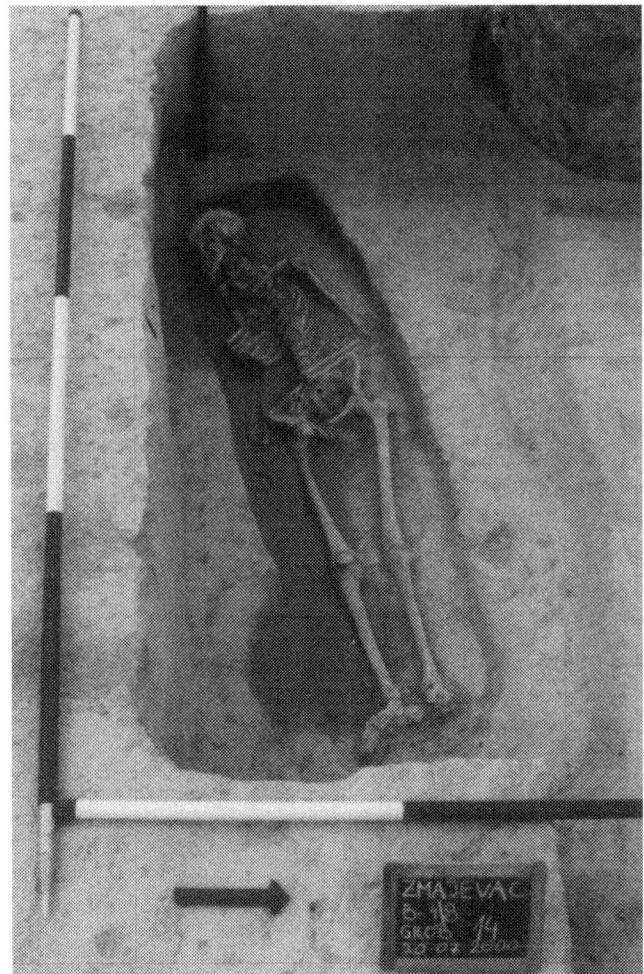

Figure 12. Adult female skeleton from Zmajevac. Excellent bone preservation facilitates identification of osteopathologies.

TABLE 52: Age and sex distribution in the Zmajevac series

Age category	Subadult N[1]	%[2]	Female N	%	Male N	%	Total N	%
Birth -1	2	22.2					2	5.4
2- 5	4	44.4					4	10.8
6-10	2	22.2					2	5.4
11-15	1	11.2					1	2.7
16-20			1	7.1	1	7.1	2	5.4
21-25			0		0		0	
26-30			2	14.4	2	14.4	4	10.8
31-35			1	7.1	1	7.1	2	5.4
36-40			1	7.1	3	21.4	4	10.8
41-45			2	14.4	3	21.4	5	13.5
46-50			2	14.3	0		2	5.4
51-55			3	21.4	3	21.5	6	16.3
56-60			1	7.1	1	7.1	2	5.4
60+			1	7.1	0		1	2.7
Total	9	100.0	14	100.0	14	100.0	37	100.0

Mean age at death[3] x = 43.05 x = 40.50
                      sd = 13.17 sd = 11.39

[1] N = number of individuals dying.
[2] % = % of individuals dying.
[3] Mean age at death is calculated using median values of each age category (for example, 23 for the age category 21-25), and 65 for the age category 60+.

TABLE 53: Frequency of alveolar bone disease in the Zmajevac series

Age category	Subadult A[1]/O[2]	%[3]	Female A/O	%	Male A/O	%
Young adult[4]			0/84	0.0	0/107	0.0
Old adult			30/154	19.5	37/234	15.8
Total	0/64	0.0	30/238	12.6	37/341	10.8

[1] A = number of tooth sockets with periodontal or periapical abscess, or antemortem tooth loss.
[2] O = number of tooth sockets observed.
[3] % = % of tooth sockets with periodontal or periapical abscess, or antemortem tooth loss.
[4] Young adult = individuals aged between 16 to 35 years; Old adult = individuals older than 36 years.

TABLE 54: Frequency of carious lesions in the Zmajevac series

Age category	Subadult A[1]/O[2]	%[3]	Female A/O	%	Male A/O	%
Young adult[4]			0/76	0.0	5/103	4.8
Old adult			15/156	9.6	28/177	15.8
Total	4/79	5.1	15/232	6.5	33/280	11.8

[1] A = number of teeth with carious lesions.
[2] O = number of teeth observed.
[3] % = % of teeth with carious lesions.
[4] Young adult = individuals aged between 16 to 35 years; Old adult = individuals older than 36 years.

age category. Adults younger than 35 years exhibit no evidence of alveolar bone disease.

Adult caries frequencies are also low - 6.5% in females, 11.8% in males, and 9.4% overall (Table 54). Subadults exhibit only 4 carious lesions (4/79 or 5.1%). The modal category for severity of lesion in females is grade 3, in males grade 2. Both sexes show a similar distribution of carious lesions. Carious lesions are most frequently located interproximally (in 8/15 or 53.3% of all carious lesions in females, and in 19/33 or 57.6% of all carious lesions in males). In males carious lesions are also recorded on the root of the tooth (in 7/33 or 21.2%), on the occlusal (5/33 or 15.1%), and on the buccal surface (2/33 or 6.1%) of the tooth. In females lesions are recorded on the occlusal surface (in 6/15 or 40%), and on the root (1/15 or 6.7%) of the tooth.

Enamel hypoplasia frequencies are summarized in Tables 55-57. Hypoplasias are most frequently recorded in maxillary central incisors - 50.0%, followed by mandibular canines - 48.0% and maxillary canines - 31.8%.

TABLE 55: Hypoplasia frequencies by individual in the Zmajevac series

Tooth	N[1]	NwLEH	%wLEH
Maxillary I1[2]	14	7	50.0
Maxillary C	22	7	31.8
Mandibular C	25	12	48.0

[1] N = number of teeth observed; NwLEH = number of teeth with one or more LEH; %wLEH = % of N with one or more LEH.
[2] I = incisor; C = canine.

As is true for most of the series, subadults are poorly represented in the analyzed sample. Only 8 teeth are available for analysis (3 central maxillary incisors, 2 maxillary and 3 mandibular canines). Two of these, one central incisor and one mandibular canine exhibit hypoplastic defects. Males exhibit slightly higher frequencies of hypoplastic defects than females, particularly in the canines, suggesting possible greater subadult stress in males. This is supported by analysis of the mean number of hypoplasias per tooth (Table 57). When the mean number of defects in each tooth with hypoplasias is averaged for males and females, males have a greater number of defects per tooth in all three teeth categories analyzed.

Cribra orbitalia frequencies (Table 58) also suggest greater subadult stress in males. Cribra orbitalia is noted in 4/12 males with intact orbits. No females exhibit this condition. Of the

TABLE 56: Hypoplasia frequencies in the Zmajevac series for subadults and adults

Tooth	Subadults		All adults		Females		Males	
	Nw/N[1]	%wLEH[2]	Nw/N	%wLEH	Nw/N	%wLEH	Nw/N	%wLEH
Maxillary I1[3]	1/3	33.3	6/11	54.5	3/5	60.0	3/6	50.0
Maxillary C	0/2	0.0	7/20	35.0	1/9	11.1	6/11	54.5
Mandibular C	1/3	33.3	11/22	50.0	4/10	40.0	7/12	58.3

[1] Nw = number of individuals with one or more LEH; N = number of individuals observed.
[2] %wLEH = % of N with one or more LEH.
[3] I = incisors; C = canines.

TABLE 57: Mean number of hypoplasias in incisors and canines in the Zmajevac series

Tooth	Subadults			All adults			Females			Males		
	Mean	N	S.D.	Mean	N	S.D.	Mean	N	S.D.	Mean	N	S.D.
MaxillaryI1[1]	0.33	3	0.58	0.64	11	0.67	0.60	5	0.55	0.67	6	0.82
Maxillary C	0.00	2	0.00	0.45	20	0.69	0.11	9	0.33	0.73	11	0.79
Mandibular C	0.33	3	0.58	0.64	22	0.73	0.40	10	0.52	0.83	12	0.83

[1] I = incisors; C = canines.

TABLE 58: Frequency of occurrence of cribra orbitalia in the Zmajevac series

Age/sex	Cribra orbitalia			Active lesions	
	O[1]	A1[2]	%	A2[3]	% of A1
0 - 0.9	0	0	0.0	0	0.0
1 - 3.9	2	0	0.0	0	0.0
4 - 9.9	2	1	0.0	1	100.0
10 - 14.9	1	0	0.0	0	0.0
All subadults	5	1	20.0	1	100.0
Adult females	6	0	0.0	0	0.0
Adult males	12	4	33.3	0	0.0
All adults	18	4	22.2	0	0.0

[1] O = number of frontal bones observed.
[2] A1 = number of frontal bones in which at least one orbit shows evidence of cribra orbitalia.
[3] A2 = number of frontal bones in which cribra orbitalia is active at time of death.

five preserved subadult frontals with intact orbits, one exhibits active, moderate, bilateral cribra orbitalia.

There is no skeletal evidence of infectious disease in the series.

Healed cranial fractures are noted in 2 adults with preserved crania. Both are recorded in males (2/11 or 18.2% of preserved male crania). Both fractures are shallow, well healed depression fractures with no evidence of subsequent infection. One is located on the left, the other on the right posterior parietal bones. One "parry" fracture on the midshaft of the

right ulna is recorded in an adult female. One adult male exhibits probable traumatic myositis ossificans on the left pubic bone in the form of a relatively large, irregular bone exostosis on the dorsal side of the bone. The exososis is 22 mm high, and 15 mm wide.

One adult male exhibits spondylolisis on the fifth lumbar vertebra.

Osteoarthritis frequencies in the series are summarized in Table 59. The overall frequencies in both sexes are low. Females exhibit highest frequencies of osteoarthritis in the knee, males in the elbow. In both sexes osteoarthritis is generally confined to adults over 35 years of age. All of the cases reported reflect mild or moderate degrees of osteoarthritis.

The overall frequency of vertebral osteoarthritis in the series is low (35/448 or 7.8%). Comparing the different regions of the spine (Table 60), greatest involvement occurs in the thoracic spine (24/240; 10.0%), followed by the cervical (6/113; 5.3%) and lumbar (5/95; 5.2%) regions. Males exhibit higher overall frequencies than females, 10.1% compared to 5.4%. The difference is not, however, statistically significant.

The frequencies of Schmorl's depressions in the series are summarized in Table 61. The overall frequency of Schmorl's depressions in the sample is 15.8% (53/335). Schmorl's depressions are more common in lumbar (17/95; 17.9%) than in thoracic (36/240; 15.0%) vertebrae. Males exhibit higher frequencies of Schmorl's defects in both segments of the spine but, once again, these differences are not statistically significant.

TABLE 59: Frequency of occurrence of osteoarthritis at major joints in the Zmajevac series

	Shoulder		Elbow		Hip		Knee	
	A[1]/O[2]	%	A/O	%	A/O	%	A/O	%
Female								
Young adult[3]	0/4	0.0	0/4	0.0	0/4	0.0	0/3	0.0
Old adult	2/9	22.2	1/10	10.0	3/10	30.0	4/10	40.0
Total	2/13	15.4	1/14	7.1	3/14	21.4	4/13	30.8
Male								
Young adult	0/4	0.0	0/4	0.0	0/4	0.0	1/4	25.0
Old adult	1/9	11.1	3/8	37.5	2/9	22.2	2/9	22.2
Total	1/13	7.7	3/12	25.0	2/13	15.4	3/13	23.1

[1] A = number of joints affected with osteoarthritis. Osteoarthritis was scored as present if at least one joint element showed evidence of osteoarthritic change.
[2] O = number of joints observed. A joint was scored as present if at least one joint element was completely present, or if two or three elements were partially present.
[3] Young adult = individuals aged between 16 to 35 years; Old adult = individuals older than 36 years.

TABLE 60: Frequency of occurrence of vertebral osteoarthritis in the Zmajevac series

	Cervical		Thoracic		Lumbar		Total	
	A[1]/O[2]	%	A/O	%	A/O	%	A/O	%
Female								
Young adult[3]	0/16	0.0	0/27	0.0	0/10	0.0	0/53	0.0
Old adult	2/37	5.4	8/95	8.4	2/35	5.7	12/167	7.2
Total	2/53	3.8	8/122	6.5	2/45	4.4	12/220	5.4
Male								
Young adult	0/20	0.0	0/36	0.0	0/15	0.0	0/71	0.0
Old adult	4/40	10.0	16/82	19.5	3/35	8.6	23/157	14.6
Total	4/60	6.7	16/118	13.5	3/50	6.0	23/228	10.1

[1] A = number of vertebrae affected with osteoarthritis or osteophytosis.
[2] O = number of vertebrae observed.
[3] Young adult = individuals aged between 16 to 35 years; Old adult = individuals older than 36 years.

TABLE 61: Frequency of occurrence of Schmorl's depressions in the Zmajevac series

	Thoracic		Lumbar		Total	
	A[1]/O[2]	%	A/O	%	A/O	%
Female						
Young adult[3]	9/27	33.3	2/10	20.0	11/37	29.7
Old adult	7/95	7.4	3/35	8.6	10/130	7.7
Total	16/122	13.1	5/45	11.1	21/167	12.6
Male						
Young adult	5/36	13.9	5/15	33.3	10/51	19.6
Old adult	15/82	18.3	7/35	20.0	22/117	18.8
Total	20/118	16.9	12/50	24.0	32/168	19.0

[1] A = number of vertebrae with Schmorl's depressions.
[2] O = number of vertebrae observed.
[3] Young adult = individuals aged between 16 to 35 years; Old adult = individuals older than 36 years.

3.4. THE LATE ANTIQUE VINKOVCI SKELETAL SERIES

Roman *Cibalae* (Vinkovci) was founded on the ruins of a large Celtic village destroyed during the Baton uprising in Pannonia (6-8 AD). The town quickly gained in importance and developed from a municipium to a colony. Two Roman emperors, Valentinian I (364-375), and his brother and co-ruler Valens (364-378) were born in Cibalae. The skeletal material which comprises this series was recovered during two campaigns carried out in 1976 and 1977. A total of 34 individuals was recovered. Most individuals (18) were recovered from single inhumations. Eight graves, however, contained the remains of two individuals. In 3 cases these were the remains of an adult male and a subadult, in 2 cases two adult females were present in the grave, while combinations consisting of an adult female and a subadult, an adult male and female, and two adult males are present as single cases. Recovered material artifacts date the use of the cemetery to the 4th century AD.

The age and sex distribution of the series is presented in Table 62. The series is characterized by an absence of subadults from the youngest (0-1 year) age category, and an even distribution of males and females. Subadults comprise 26.5% of the total sample with the highest mortality recorded in the 6-10 years age category. Peak mortality for females is between 41-45 years (25.0% of all adult females died during this interval), for males between 36-45 years (46.0% of males died during this time period). This difference is reflected in mean ages at death. The average age at death for adult females is 39.4 years (SD = 12.4), for adult males 36.5 years (SD = 8.7).

Alveolar bone disease frequencies are presented in Table 63. Alveolar bone disease is not present in subadults, and has a low (7.7%) overall frequency in adults. Females exhibit considerably higher frequencies (15.0%) than males (2.7%). This difference is statistically significant ($\chi^2 = 19.73$; P < 0.01). As both males and females in the young adult age category exhibit little or no evidence of alveolar bone disease, the observed sex differences in the frequencies of alveolar bone disease are probably related to the longer average female life-span.

Caries frequencies (Table 64) are also higher in females than in males (8.7% compared to 4.0%), although in this case the

TABLE 62: Age and sex distribution in the Late Antique Vinkovci series

Age category	Subadult N[1]	%[2]	Female N	%	Male N	%	Total N	%
Birth -1	0						0	
2- 5	3	33.3					3	8.9
6-10	4	44.5					4	11.7
11-15	2	22.2					2	5.9
16-20			0		0		0	
21-25			2	16.7	2	15.4	4	11.7
26-30			1	8.3	2	15.4	3	8.9
31-35			2	16.8	1	7.8	3	8.9
36-40			1	8.3	3	23.0	4	11.7
41-45			3	25.0	3	23.0	6	17.6
46-50			1	8.3	2	15.4	3	8.9
51-55			1	8.3	0		1	2.9
56-60			0		0		0	
60+			1	8.3	0		1	2.9
Total	9	100.0	12	100.0	13	100.0	34	100.0

Mean age at death[3]   x = 39.42   x = 36.46
                        sd = 12.44   sd = 8.75

[1] N = number of individuals dying.
[2] % = % of individuals dying.
[3] Mean age at death is calculated using median values of each age category (for example, 23 for the age category 21-25), and 65 for the age category 60+.

TABLE 63: Frequency of alveolar bone disease in the Late Antique Vinkovci series

Age category	Subadult A[1]/O[2]	%[3]	Female A/O	%	Male A/O	%
Young adult[4]			2/56	3.5	0/126	0.0
Old adult			28/144	19.4	8/168	4.8
Total	0/114	0.0	30/200	15.0	8/294	2.7

[1] A = number of tooth sockets with periodontal or periapical abscess, or antemortem tooth loss.
[2] O = number of tooth sockets observed.
[3] % = % of tooth sockets with periodontal or periapical abscess, or antemortem tooth loss.
[4] Young adult = individuals aged between 16 to 35 years; Old adult = individuals older than 36 years.

TABLE 64: Frequency of carious lesions in the Late Antique Vinkovci series

Age category	Subadult A[1]/O[2]	%[3]	Female A/O	%	Male A/O	%
Young adult[4]			0/45	0.0	0/101	0.0
Old adult			12/92	13.0	10/151	6.6
Total	0/102	0.0	12/137	8.7	10/252	4.0

[1] A = number of teeth with carious lesions.
[2] O = number of teeth observed.
[3] % = % of teeth with carious lesions.
[4] Young adult = individuals aged between 16 to 35 years; Old adult = individuals older than 36 years.

difference is not statistically significant. Once again, neither males or females show evidence of carious lesions before 36 years of age. Carious lesions are, likewise, absent in subadult dentition. In both sexes the majority of the observed caries are located interproximally (in 11/12 lesions in females, and 7/10 lesions in males). Males also exhibit root (2/10) and occlusal (1/10) caries, while females exhibit one case of root caries (1/12). The modal category for severity of lesions in both males and females is grade 3.

Enamel hypoplasia frequencies are summarized in Tables 65 and 66. Hypoplasias are most frequent in maxillary canines (43.7%), followed by mandibular canines (42.1%) and maxillary central incisors (30.3%). Subadults are poorly represented in the sample with only 8 teeth (2 maxillary central incisors, 3 maxillary and 3 mandibular canines) available for analysis. One maxillary canine exhibits a shallow hypoplastic defect. In adults, hypoplastic defects are most often noted on the mandibular canines (8/16 or 50.0%). Adult males and females exhibit similar frequencies of hypoplastic defects in all teeth categories analyzed.

TABLE 65: Hypoplasia frequencies by individual in the Late Antique Vinkovci series

Tooth	N[1]	NwLEH	%wLEH
Maxillary I1[2]	13	4	30.8
Maxillary C	16	7	43.7
Mandibular C	19	8	42.1

[1] N = number of teeth observed; NwLEH = number of teeth with one or more LEH; %wLEH = % of N with one or more LEH.
[2] I = incisor; C = canine.

Cribra orbitalia (Table 67) is recorded in 4 subadults with intact orbits (4/7). Two cases were active at time of death. In adults it's presence is observed in 2 male and one female crania (3/14). All adult cases are healed and mild in expression.

Five individuals (3 subadults one male, and one female) exhibit skeletal evidence for infectious disease in the form of periostitis on the tibia. Two of the three cases noted in subadults are generalized, severe in expression and active at time of death, while one is localized and healed. Both adult cases are mild and healed. One adult female exhibits osteomyelitis of the middle third of the diaphysis of the right tibia, subsequent to fracture.

Healed fractures are noted only in adults. The fractures are located on the skull vault, radius, clavicles and tibia. One

TABLE 66: Hypoplasia frequencies in the Late Antique Vinkovci series for subadults and adults

Tooth	Subadults		All adults		Females		Males	
	Nw/N[1]	%wLEH[2]	Nw/N	%wLEH	Nw/N	%wLEH	Nw/N	%wLEH
Maxillary I1[3]	0/2	0.0	4/11	36.4	1/4	25.0	3/7	42.8
Maxillary C	1/3	33.3	6/13	46.1	2/5	40.0	4/8	50.0
Mandibular C	0/3	0.0	8/16	50.0	4/7	57.1	4/9	44.4

[1] Nw = number of individuals with one or more LEH; N = number of individuals observed.
[2] %wLEH = % of N with one or more LEH.
[3] I = incisors; C = canines.

TABLE 67: Frequency of occurrence of cribra orbitalia in the Late Antique Vinkovci series

Age/sex	Cribra orbitalia			Active lesions	
	O[1]	A1[2]	%	A2[3]	% of A1
0 - 0.9	0	0	0.0	0	0.0
1 - 3.9	0	0	0.0	0	0.0
4 - 9.9	6	3	50.0	2	66.7
10 - 14.9	1	1	100.0	0	0.0
All subadults	7	4	57.1	2	50.0
Adult females	7	1	14.3	0	0.0
Adult males	7	2	28.6	0	0.0
All adults	14	3	21.4	0	0.0

[1] O = number of frontal bones observed.
[2] A1 = number of frontal bones in which at least one orbit shows evidence of cribra orbitalia.
[3] A2 = number of frontal bones in which cribra orbitalia is active at time of death.

TABLE 68: Frequency of occurrence of vertebral osteoarthritis in the Late Antique Vinkovci series

	Cervical		Thoracic		Lumbar		Total	
	A[1]/O[2]	%	A/O	%	A/O	%	A/O	%
Female								
Young adult[3]	0/7	0.0	0/25	0.0	0/9	0.0	0/41	0.0
Old adult	0/15	0.0	6/37	16.2	6/14	42.8	12/66	18.2
Total	0/22	0.0	6/62	9.7	6/23	26.1	12/107	11.2
Male								
Young adult	0/18	0.0	0/45	0.0	0/23	0.0	0/86	0.0
Old adult	0/24	10.0	10/50	20.0	3/24	12.5	13/98	13.3
Total	0/42	0.0	10/95	10.5	3/47	6.4	13/184	7.1

[1] A = number of vertebrae affected with osteoarthritis or osteophytosis.
[2] O = number of vertebrae observed.
[3] Young adult = individuals aged between 16 to 35 years; Old adult = individuals older than 36 years.

the skull and there is no evidence of infection. Fractures of the radius are present in two individuals, an adult female who exhibits a well healed fracture of the medial right radius with considerable angulation and trauma related osteoarthritic changes on the distal joint surface (1/8 females with preserved radii), and in one male who exhibits bilateral, well healed spiral fractures of the distal radii (1/10 males with preserved radii). One adult male exhibits a well healed fracture of the middle third of the right clavicle (1/8 males with preserved clavicles), and a healed depression fracture of the proximal lateral joint surface of the left tibia (1/7 males with preserved tibias). A fracture of the right tibia (complicated by subsequent osteomyelitis) is also noted in an adult female (1/5 females with preserved tibiae).

Osteoarthritis frequencies in major joints are low in the series, and with the exception of one case of mild osteoarthritis in the knee of a young adult male, restricted to individuals older than 36 years. Females exhibit one case of mild osteoarthritis in the shoulder, and a moderately severe case of osteoarthritis in the hip, while males exhibit one case of osteoarthritis in the shoulder, and one in the knee.

The total female vertebral osteoarthritis frequency is 11.2% (Table 68), with greatest involvement in the lumbar region of the spine. Males exhibit a slightly lower total vertebral osteoarthritis frequency (7.1%) with greatest involvement in the thoracic segment of the spine. In both sexes vertebral osteoarthritis is restricted to individuals older than 36 years.

Females also exhibit higher frequencies of Schmorl's depressions in both the thoracic and lumbar spine (Table 69). The total frequency of Schmorl's defects in females is 16.5%, (14/85 vertebrae). No defects are noted in the young adult female age category. Males exhibit a lower overall frequency of Schmorl's defects (13.4%), but show a less pronounced age-dependence (young adults have higher total frequencies and higher frequencies of Schmorl's defects in lumbar vertebrae than males from the old adult age category).

healed depression fracture, with smooth margins and a slightly porous floor, is present on the left parietal of an adult female (1/7 preserved female crania). The fracture is in the shape of the letter "L" with the long arm measuring 50 mm and the short 35 mm. The fracture did not penetrate the inner table of

TABLE 69: Frequency of occurrence of Schmorl's depressions in the Late Antique Vinkovci series

	Thoracic A[1]/O[2]	%	Lumbar A/O	%	Total A/O	%
Female						
Young adult[3]	0/25	0.0	0/9	0.0	0/34	0.0
Old adult	9/37	24.3	5/14	35.7	14/51	27.4
Total	9/62	14.5	5/23	21.7	14/85	16.5
Male						
Young adult	4/45	8.9	6/23	26.1	10/68	14.7
Old adult	6/50	12.0	3/24	12.5	9/74	12.2
Total	10/95	10.5	9/47	19.1	19/142	13.4

[1] A = number of vertebrae with Schmorl's depressions.
[2] O = number of vertebrae observed.
[3] Young adult = individuals aged between 16 to 35 years; Old adult = individuals older than 36 years.

3.5. CHARACTERISTICS OF THE COMPOSITE ANTIQUE SERIES

The composite antique series is the most homogenous composite series both in terms of the territory it covers (it is confined to Eastern Slavonia), and in temporal span (it is limited to the 4th century AD). It is comprised of four skeletal series similar in size, with the range of recovered individuals from 26 in Štrbinci to 37 in Zmajevac. Three series are related

TABLE 70: Age and sex distribution in the Antique composite series

Age category	Subadult N[1]	%[2]	Female N	%	Male N	%	Total N	%
Birth -1	5	14.7					5	4.0
2- 5	11	32.3					11	8.8
6-10	9	26.5					9	7.2
11-15	9	26.5					9	7.2
16-20			2	4.3	4	8.9	6	4.8
21-25			5	10.9	5	11.1	10	8.0
26-30			7	15.2	6	13.4	13	10.4
31-35			7	15.2	4	8.9	11	8.8
36-40			3	6.5	7	15.5	10	8.0
41-45			8	17.5	8	17.8	16	12.8
46-50			4	8.7	3	6.7	7	5.6
51-55			6	13.0	4	8.9	10	8.0
56-60			1	2.2	2	4.4	3	2.4
60+			3	6.5	2	4.4	5	4.0
Total	34	100.0	46	100.0	45	100.0	125	100.0

Mean age at death[3]		x = 39.10		x = 37.75	
		sd = 12.40		sd = 12.68	

[1] N = number of individuals dying.
[2] % = % of individuals dying.
[3] Mean age at death is calculated using median values of each age category (for example, 23 for the age category 21-25), and 65 for the age category 60+.

to urban centers (*Mursa, Certissia* and *Cibalae*), while the Zmajevac series may reflect life conditions in a frontier military outpost.

Croatian skeletal series from the Antique period have, so far, received little attention. Biological data has been published for a small sub-sample of the Štrbinci series (Šlaus, 1998a), and for a small series from Split on the Dalmatian coast (Šlaus, 1999). This is unfortunate as this is an important period of time characterized by numerous political, religious and social changes, related to the political and economical crises which led to the fall of the Western Roman Empire. One reason for our current lack of knowledge is the absence of investigated Late Antique cemeteries in continental Croatia. Ongoing investigations of several cemeteries in Eastern Slavonia, and Baranja will hopefully rectify this in the future.

The age and sex distribution of the series is presented in Table 70. Subadults comprise 27.2% of the total sample but are clearly underrepresented in the youngest (birth-1 year) age category (only 5 individuals or 4.0% of the total Antique composite series). Subadult mortality in the sample is highest from 2-5 years (32.3% of the subadult subsample).

Males and females are evenly represented in the adult sample (45 and 46 individuals respectively). The average age at death of adults over 15 years is 39.1 years for females, and 37.7 years for males. This small difference (1.35 years) in average life-spans is reflected in similar mortality profiles. Both sexes exhibit high mortality between 21-35 years (41.3% of all adult female deaths, and 33.4% of all adult male deaths) with an additional peak between 41-45 years (17.5% of female and 17.8% of all male deaths). Few individuals (10 females or 21.7% of all adult female deaths, and 8 males or 17.7% of all adult male deaths) lived to be older than 50 years.

The frequencies of alveolar bone disease in the Antique composite series are summarized in Table 71. Alveolar bone disease is present in only 1 of the 301 (0.3%) subadult tooth sockets available for inspection. In adults the total frequency is 8.6% (165/1916) with an uneven distribution between males and females. While frequencies in the young adult age category are similarly low (1.1% for females, and 0.8% for males), females older than 36 years exhibit considerably higher frequencies than males from the same age group (18.0% compared to 11.0%). This difference is statistically significant (χ^2 =7.52, P< .01). Total female frequency (11.3%) is also higher than total male frequency (6.3%). This difference is, also, statistically significant (χ^2=12.05, P< .01). As frequencies of alveolar bone disease are similar in the young adult age category, but significantly different in the old adult age category, one could argue that they reflect

TABLE 71: Frequency of alveolar bone disease in the Antique composite series

Age category	Subadult A[1]/O[2]	%[3]	Female A/O	%	Male A/O	%
Young adult[4]			4/347	1.1	4/481	0.8
Old adult			95/527	18.0	62/561	11.0
Total	1/301	0.3	99/874	11.3	66/1042	6.3

[1] A = number of tooth sockets with periodontal or periapical abscess, or antemortem tooth loss.
[2] O = number of tooth sockets observed.
[3] % = % of tooth sockets with periodontal or periapical abscess, or antemortem tooth loss.
[4] Young adult = individuals aged between 16 to 35 years; Old adult = individuals older than 36 years.

differences in average life spans. The average adult female life span is, however, only slightly longer (1.35 years) than the adult male life span. Other factors may have therefore contributed to the observed higher frequency of alveolar bone disease in females. Higher frequencies of dental disease in females have been recorded in numerous archaeological populations (for example Larsen, 1983; Lukacs, 1992; Lukacs and Pal 1993). This difference is often explained by one of three factors: 1) earlier eruption of teeth in girls and consequently, longer exposure of girl's teeth to the cariogenic oral environment, 2) easier access to food supplies by women during food preparation, and 3) the effects of hormonal fluctuations and pregnancy. Based on the available data it is hard to say to what degree, if any, these factors contributed to the observed higher frequencies of alveolar bone disease in females from the Antique composite series. There is no ethnographic or historical documentation of dietary practices and food preparation for these populations. Total adult caries frequencies (Table 72) are similar (9.6% in males, and 9.2% in females) with males in the young adult age category exhibiting significantly higher frequencies of caries than females (5.3% compared to 2.0%, χ^2=4.12, P< .05). Further systematic analyses of dental disease in other Antique populations from continental Croatia are, therefore, necessary to evaluate if the observed difference in male/female frequencies of alveolar bone disease are the result of random variation in a small sample, or the result of specific, as yet unidentified, factors.

The overall frequency of carious lesions in the Antique composite series is 8.2%. Subadults contribute little with only

TABLE 72: Frequency of carious lesions in the Antique composite series

Age category	Subadult A[1]/O[2]	%[3]	Female A/O	%	Male A/O	%
Young adult[4]			6/306	2.0	23/434	5.3
Old adult			59/398	14.8	67/500	13.4
Total	5/306	1.6	65/704	9.2	90/934	9.6

[1] A = number of teeth with carious lesions.
[2] O = number of teeth observed.
[3] % = % of teeth with carious lesions.
[4] Young adult = individuals aged between 16 to 35 years; Old adult = individuals older than 36 years.

5 teeth (5/306 or 1.6%) exhibiting carious lesions. Adult male and female total frequencies are similar (9.6% and 9.2% respectively), as are frequencies in the old adult age group (13.4% and 14.8% respectively). As already stated, males in the young adult age category exhibit significantly higher frequencies of carious lesions than females.

Both sexes display the same modal category, grade 2, for severity of carious lesion. The distribution of carious lesions is also similar. Carious lesions are most frequently located interproximally (in 55/90 or 61.1% of all carious lesions in males, and in 45/65 or 69.2% of all carious lesions in females). In males this is followed by root (15/90 or 16.7%), occlusal (13/90 or 14.4%) and buccal caries (7/90 or 7.8%). In females by occlusal (12/65 or 18.5%), buccal (5/65 or 7.7%) and root (3/65 or 4.6%) caries. The only noticeable sex difference in the distribution of caries is the relatively high frequency of root caries in males. These caries are, however, present only in individuals from the old adult age category and are not responsible for the significantly higher frequency of caries in young adult males.

TABLE 73: Hypoplasia frequencies by individual in the Antique composite series

Tooth	N[1]	NwLEH	%wLEH
Maxillary I1[2]	50	18	36.0
Maxillary C	68	28	41.2
Mandibular C	75	33	44.0

[1] N = number of teeth observed; NwLEH = number of teeth with one or more LEH; %wLEH = % of N with one or more LEH.
[2] I = incisor; C = canine.

Enamel hypoplasia frequencies are summarized in Tables 73-76. Hypoplasias are most frequent in mandibular canines - 44.0%, followed by maxillary canines - 41.2% and maxillary central incisors - 36.0%. Out of the 193 analyzed teeth, 79 (40.9%) exhibit evidence of hypoplasia.

Although slightly better than in the Prehistoric composite series, subadults are still poorly represented in the analyzed sample. Of the 31 subadult teeth available for analysis (10 central maxillary incisors, 10 maxillary and 11 mandibular canines), 14 (45.2%) exhibit hypoplastic defects (Table 74). In this series, hypoplasia in subadults is most frequently recorded in maxillary canines.

Adults exhibit a lower total frequency of hypoplasias (65/162 or 40.1%) than subadults. A breakdown of the adult sample by sex (Table 74) shows that, compared to females, adult males exhibit slightly higher frequencies of hypoplastic defects in all tooth categories analyzed. Controlling for age (Table 75), males consistently exhibit higher frequencies of hypoplastic defects than females in both the young adult, and old adult age categories for all teeth analyzed except for mandibular canines where females in the old adult age category exhibit a slightly higher frequency than males. A breakdown of the adult sample by age also shows that young adults experienced more episodes of hypoplasia inducing

TABLE 74: Hypoplasia frequencies in the Antique composite series for subadults and adults

Tooth	Subadults		All adults		Females		Males	
	Nw/N[1]	%wLEH[2]	Nw/N	%wLEH	Nw/N	%wLEH	Nw/N	%wLEH
Maxillary I1[3]	4/10	40.0	14/40	35.0	4/15	26.7	10/25	40.0
Maxillary C	6/10	60.0	22/58	37.9	6/26	23.1	16/32	50.0
Mandibular C	4/11	36.4	29/64	45.3	13/30	43.3	16/34	47.1

[1] Nw = number of individuals with one or more LEH; N = number of individuals observed.
[2] %wLEH = % of N with one or more LEH.
[3] I = incisors; C = canines.

TABLE 75: Hypoplasia frequencies in adult dentition in the Antique composite series

Sex/age	Maxillary I1[1]		Maxillary C		Mandibular C	
	Nw/N[2]	%wLEH[3]	Nw/N	%wLEH	Nw/N	%wLEH
Female						
Young adult[4]	3/7	42.9	4/13	30.8	7/12	58.3
Old adult	1/8	12.5	2/13	15.4	6/18	33.3
Male						
Young adult	7/13	53.8	9/15	60.0	10/15	66.7
Old adult	3/12	25.0	7/17	41.2	6/19	31.6

[1] I = incisors; C = canines.
[2] Nw = number of individuals with one or more LEH; N = number of individuals observed.
[3] %wLEH = % of N with one or more LEH.
[4] Young adult = individuals aged between 16 to 35 years; Old adult = individuals older than 36 years.

Cribra orbitalia is observed in 17 of the 82 crania (20.7%) with intact orbits. The overall subadult frequency is 33.3% with the majority of lesions (4/6) active at time of death. In adults the lesion has a frequency of 17.2% with all of the lesions exhibiting some degree of healing.

Sex differences in healing lesion frequencies also indicate greater subadult stress in males. Male lesion frequencies (27.8%) are considerably higher than female (3.6%) frequencies. This difference is marginally not significant (χ^2=3.4, P< .07).

Skeletal evidence for infectious disease is present in subadults and adults. As

TABLE 76: Mean number of hypoplasias in incisors and canines in the Antique composite series

Tooth	Subadults			All adults			Females			Males		
	Mean	N	S.D.	Mean	N	S.D.	Mean	N	S.D.	Mean	N	S.D.
Maxillary I1[1]	0.60	10	0.84	0.35	40	0.48	0.27	15	0.46	0.40	25	0.50
Maxillary C	0.90	10	0.87	0.38	58	0.49	0.23	26	0.43	0.50	32	0.51
Mandibular C	0.64	11	0.92	0.47	64	0.54	0.43	30	0.51	0.47	34	0.55

[1] I = incisors; C = canines.

stress in all three tooth categories than adults who lived to be older than 36 years.

The mean number of hypoplasias per tooth (Table 76) shows that adults have consistently lower mean numbers of defects than subadults. This suggests that multiple occurrence of stress incidents is an important factor in the mortality of children. Analysis of the mean number of defects per tooth also supports the hypothesis of greater subadult stress in males. When the number of defects in each tooth with hypoplasias is averaged for the different groups in the sample, males consistently exhibit a greater number of defects per tooth, in all tooth categories analyzed, than females.

Cribra orbitalia frequencies are summarized in Table 77. In the Antique composite series the expression of this condition ranges from slight pitting to moderate sievelike lesions with diplotic expansion.

TABLE 77: Frequency of occurrence of cribra orbitalia in the Antique composite series

Age/sex	Cribra orbitalia			Active lesions	
	O[1]	A1[2]	%	A2[3]	% of A1
0 - 0.9	2	0	0.0	0	0.0
1 - 3.9	4	1	25.0	1	100.0
4 - 9.9	8	4	50.0	3	75.0
10 - 14.9	4	1	25.0	0	0.0
All subadults	18	6	33.3	4	66.7
Adult females	28	1	3.6	0	0.0
Adult males	36	10	27.8	0	0.0
All adults	64	11	17.2	0	0.0

[1] O = number of frontal bones observed.
[2] A1 = number of frontal bones in which at least one orbit shows evidence of cribra orbitalia.
[3] A2 = number of frontal bones in which cribra orbitalia is active at time of death.

with the Prehistoric composite series, because of the different preservation of the recovered remains, periostitis frequencies are calculated not "by individual", but by bone.

TABLE 78: Frequency of occurrence of active periosteal lesions in the Antique composite series

Sex	Periosteal lesions		
	A1[1]	A2[2]	% of A1
Subadults	25	16	64.0
Adult females	7	0	0.0
Adult males	2	1	50.0
All adults	9	1	11.1
Total	34	17	50.0

[1] A1 = number of bones with periostitis.
[2] A2 = number of bones with periostitis active at time of death.

In comparison to adults, subadults show less resistance to infectious disease. Endocranial periostitis is present on 2 (one parietal and one occipital) of the 77 recovered subadult cranial vault bones (2.6%). Periostitis on the tibia is present in 15 of the 39 recovered subadult tibiae (38.5%), and on 5 of the 119 recovered adult tibiae (4.2%). Furthermore, while most of the subadult lesions show no evidence of healing, only one of the adult lesions was active at time of death (Table 78). One case of osteomyelitis, subsequent to fracture, is noted on the middle third of the diaphysis of the tibia in an adult female.

Skeletal evidence of healed fractures is present in both subadults and adults. The types of fractures identified include depressed lesions on the cranial vault, long bone fractures, rib fractures and vertebral compression fractures. Fractures of the cranium are present in one subadult (1/19 or 5.3% of preserved subadult cranial vaults), 4 males (4/34 or 11.8% of preserved male cranial vaults) and one female (1/33 or 3.0%). All of the fractures are healed depression fractures with smooth margins and slightly porous floors. None penetrated the inner table of the skull and none exhibit evidence of subsequent infection. The predominance of cranial fractures in adult males is indicative for their participation in violent activities. The distribution of other types of fractures in the series supports this hypothesis. Most of the long bone fractures (both recorded fractures of the tibia and one

of the two recorded fractures of the radius) are noted in males, as is the only clavicle and vertebral fracture. Rib fractures are evenly distributed in the series (in 1 subadult, 2 females and 2 males), while defensive "parry" fractures on the midshaft of the ulna are noted only in females (in one female from Mursa and one from Zmajevac).

Enthesophytes are recorded on one male innominate, one male tibia, and on 4 female and 4 male calcanei (at the insertion site of the Achilles tendon). There is no skeletal evidence for dislocation in the series. Spondylolysis is present in the fifth lumbar vertebra of 2 males (in 2/30 or 6.7% of males with complete lumbar spines, or in 2/50 or 4.0% of adults with preserved lumbar spines).

Osteoarthritis frequencies in the series are summarized in Table 79. Of the four major joints in the skeleton, osteoarthritis is, in both sexes, most frequently recorded in the knee. Osteoarthritis is more common in females than in males, and more common in the old adult than the young adult age group.

TABLE 79: Frequency of occurrence of osteoarthritis at major joints in the Antique composite series

	Shoulder		Elbow		Hip		Knee	
	A[1]/O[2]	%	A/O	%	A/O	%	A/O	%
Female								
Young adult[3]	1/12	8.3	3/13	23.1	2/18	11.1	2/12	16.7
Old adult	4/18	22.2	2/19	10.5	4/20	20.0	6/18	33.3
Total	5/30	16.7	5/32	15.6	6/38	15.8	8/30	26.7
Male								
Young adult	1/14	7.1	0/15	0.0	0/19	0.0	3/13	23.1
Old adult	3/19	15.8	5/20	25.0	3/20	15.0	3/19	15.8
Total	4/33	12.1	5/35	14.3	3/39	7.7	6/32	18.7

[1] A = number of joints affected with osteoarthritis. Osteoarthritis was scored as present if at least one joint element showed evidence of osteoarthritic change.
[2] O = number of joints observed. A joint was scored as present if at least one joint element was completely present, or if two or three elements were partially present.
[3] Young adult = individuals aged between 16 to 35 years; Old adult = individuals older than 36 years.

TABLE 80: Frequency of occurrence of vertebral osteoarthritis in the Antique composite series

	Cervical		Thoracic		Lumbar		Total	
	A[1]/O[2]	%	A/O	%	A/O	%	A/O	%
Female								
Young adult[3]	2/41	4.9	2/101	2.0	0/34	0.0	4/176	2.3
Old adult	3/78	3.8	18/173	10.4	8/69	11.6	29/320	9.1
Total	5/119	4.2	20/274	7.3	8/103	7.8	33/496	6.6
Male								
Young adult	0/84	0.0	0/160	0.0	0/73	0.0	0/317	0.0
Old adult	12/87	13.8	38/168	22.6	10/74	13.5	60/329	18.2
Total	12/171	7.0	38/328	11.6	10/147	6.8	60/646	9.3

[1] A = number of vertebrae affected with osteoarthritis or osteophytosis.
[2] O = number of vertebrae observed.
[3] Young adult = individuals aged between 16 to 35 years; Old adult = individuals older than 36 years.

The overall frequency of vertebral osteoarthritis in the series is low (93/1142 or 8.1%). Comparing the different regions of the spine (Table 80), greatest involvement occurs in the thoracic region (58/602 or 9.6%), followed by the lumbar (18/250 or 7.2%) and cervical (17/290 or 5.9%) regions. No sex differences are present in the young adult age category, but males older than 36 years exhibit significantly higher total frequencies of vertebral osteoarthritis than females (18.2% compared to 9.1%, $\chi^2 = 8.1$; P < .01). This, statistically significant, difference appears to be primarily related to higher frequencies of vertebral osteoarthritis in the thoracic spine where males older than 36 years exhibit significantly higher frequencies than females (22.6% compared to 10.4%, $\chi^2 = 5.9$; P < .02).

The frequencies of Schmorl's depressions in the series are summarized in Table 81. The overall frequency of Schmorl's depressions in the sample is 14.1% (120/852). Frequencies of Schmorl's depressions in the thoracic and lumbar spine are similar (12.6% and 17.6% respectively). Both sexes exhibit higher frequencies in the old adult age category. Male frequencies are consistently higher than female but none of the differences are statistically significant.

TABLE 81: Frequency of occurrence of Schmorl's depressions in the Antique composite series

	Thoracic		Lumbar		Total	
	A^1/O^2	%	A/O	%	A/O	%
Female						
Young adult[3]	9/101	8.9	2/34	5.9	11/135	8.1
Old adult	21/173	12.1	13/69	18.8	34/242	14.0
Total	30/274	10.9	15/103	14.6	45/377	11.9
Male						
Young adult	18/160	11.2	14/73	19.2	32/233	13.7
Old adult	28/168	16.7	15/74	20.3	43/242	17.8
Total	46/328	14.0	29/147	19.7	75/475	15.8

[1] A = number of vertebrae with Schmorl's depressions.

[2] O = number of vertebrae observed.

[3] Young adult = individuals aged between 16 to 35 years; Old adult = individuals older than 36 years.

Data from the Antique composite series suggest different levels of subadult stress between males and females. These differences are not reflected in the mortality profiles of adult males and females. Both sexes show similar periods of greatest mortality, and females, on average, live only 1.35 years longer than males. However, males consistently exhibit higher frequencies of hypoplastic defects in all tooth categories analyzed, as well as a higher mean number of hypoplasias per tooth than females. Males also exhibit a marginally not significant higher frequencies of cribra orbitalia than females. Together, the cribra orbitalia and enamel hypoplasia data strongly suggest that males in the Antique composite series experienced greater subadult stress than females. Sex differences in the series are not limited only to subadult stress, but are also present in the frequencies of healed trauma. Males exhibit higher frequencies of cranial and long bone trauma

than females (with the exception of midshaft ulna fractures which are limited to females) suggesting higher levels of interpersonal violence in adult males.

4. BIOARCHAEOLOGY OF THE EARLY MEDIEVAL PERIOD

The Early medieval period in continental Croatia can be divided into three parts: 1) the post-Hunnic period, 2) the Avar period, and 3) the post-Avar period. It is a period of marked political instability and warfare.

The post-Hunnic period begins with the death of Atilla in 453 and the emergence of the Eastern Goths, Langobards and Gepids. Most of continental Croatia, except for it's most eastern parts which were held by the Gepids, became part of the Gothic kingdom (Šišić, 1925). After the death of Theodoric in 526 and the destruction of the Gothic kingdom by the Byzantine emperor Justinian in 554, Pannonia was annexed to the Eastern Roman Empire. In return for their help in the wars against the Ostrogoths, the Langobards were given permission by Justinian to occupy north-western Slavonia where they came into contact with the Gepids. This resulted in war between the new neighbors which was inconclusive until the Langobards formed a pact with the Avars, a horse-riding nomadic people first noted by medieval writers in 557 when they sent their envoys to Justinian. Together, the Langobards and Avars destroyed the Gepid kingdom in 567. Soon after their victory, however, the Langobards were forced to leave for Italy under pressure from the Avars.

The Avar period begins in 569 with the Avar invasion of the empty areas in Pannonia (Šišić, 1925; Klaić, 1971). The Avars were a conglomerate of different ethnic groups including Central Asian populations, Bulgars, Kutrigurs, the remains of the conquered Germanic tribes, and Slavs (Liptak, 1983). Various opinions have been voiced regarding the nature of the alliance between the Slavic tribes and the Avars. These opinions range from a belief in an amicable relationship between the two peoples, in which the Avars and Slavs are viewed as equal partners, to a belief in which the Avars were the warrior elite and therefore absolute masters in the state (Brandt, 1980; Klaić, 1990). The period of Avar dominance is generally divided by archaeologists into two periods, the Early Avar period from 569 to around 630, and the Late Avar period from about 650 to 803. The early Avar period is characterized by aggressive and expansionist politics, warfare, and the exaction of tribute from the Byzantine Empire to the amount of 27 tons of gold for the period from 575 to 626 (Kovačević, 1963). This period culminated with the unsuccessful attempt by the Avars and Slavs to capture Constantinopolis in 626. The crushing military defeat under the walls of Constantinopolis had a huge effect on the Avar state and was followed by a Slav uprising. The uprising resulted in the formation of a powerful Slavic tribal federation, known as Samo's Alliance which collapsed after the death of

Samo in 658. Avar power weakened but was revived in about 650 by a new wave of migrations from Central Asia which consolidated the Avar state. The Late Avar period is, however, characterized by defensive politics, a complete lack of tribute as witnessed by an absence of Byzantine coins in the Carpathian basin from around 670, and a greater reliance on agriculture. At the end of the 8th century, the Avars came into conflict with the Franks by helping their enemy the Bavarian duke Trasil. The Franks retaliated, and in 803 the Frankish emperor Charlemagne destroyed the Avar state in Pannonia.

After the destruction of the Avar state, a Slavic duchy called Slovinja, with it's center in Sisak, was formed. Militarily, politically and culturally this state was dependent on the Frankish Empire and was put under the vassal command of the Furlanian margrave. Frankish rule soon, however, became oppressive resulting in an uprising led by the Pannonian duke Ljudevit (Klaić, 1971). The uprising was unsuccessful and was followed by renewed Frankish rule over continental Croatia and their subsequent conflicts during the first half of the 9th century with Bulgarians in eastern Slavonia.

During the 9th and 10th centuries continental Croatia was continually raided by the Hungarians, another horse-riding, Central Asian population which settled permanently in modern Hungary after the battle of Augsburg in 955. During the first half of the 10th century the Croat ruler Tomislav (910-928) took Slovinje away from the Hungarians and secured a border with the Hungarians on the banks of the Drava river. The Croat state, however, soon suffered a period of weakness during which the Hungarians retook parts of eastern Slavonia and Srijem.

The early Medieval period is represented by two skeletal series and one isolated find. The skeletal series were recovered from Vinkovci (a Gepid population) and from Privlaka (a Late Avar period population). The isolated find is a skull recovered from

Jopić cave in the Kordun region and is included in the sample because it is a rare example of cranial deformation, a practice which has previously been documented in other Hunnic, Gepid and Avar series, as well as a rare example of peri-mortem trauma. The geographical location of the sites is presented in Figure 13.

4.1. THE VINKOVCI GEPID SKELETAL SERIES

Gepid cemeteries are rare in Croatia. The primary reason for this is that the main centers of Gepid power were located to the east of continental Croatia, in neighboring Yugoslavia where their presence is first recorded in the beginning of the 5th century. After the death of Atilla they gained prominence and established a kingdom which culminated with their occupation of *Sirmium* which become their administrative center. The Vinkovci Gepid series contains the remains of 34 individuals recovered in 1976 and 1977 during rescue excavations at the PIK Vinkovci site. Use of the cemetery is dated to the first half of the 6th century (Dizdar, personal communication). Bone preservation in the series is poor to moderate as is the completeness of the recovered skeletons.

The age and sex distribution of the series is presented in Table 82. The series is characterized by an underrepresentation of subadults from the youngest (0-1 year, and 2-5 years) age categories, and a relatively even distribution of males and females. Despite their clear underrepresentation subadults comprise 29.4% (10/34) of the total sample. Peak mortality for females is between 31-40 years, 45.4% of females died during this interval. Males display a more evenly distributed mortality distribution with the highest mortality between 31-35 years (23.0% of the male sample). Males, however, appear to be at greater risk during young adulthood. Almost twice as many died before achieving 31 years than females (46.2% compared to 27.3%). This difference is reflected in average ages at death which are 36.6 years (SD = 9.77), for adult females, and 33.0 years (SD = 12.1) for adult males.

The frequencies of alveolar bone disease are summarized in Table 83. Alveolar bone disease is not present in subadults and has a relatively low overall frequency in adults (28/344 or 8.1%). Females exhibit considerably higher frequencies (15.2%) than males (4.4%). This difference is statistically significant ($\chi^2 = 8.7$, P < 0.01). The difference

Figure 13. The geographical locations of the Early medieval sites:
1. Vinkovci, 2. Jopićeva špilja, 3. Privlaka

TABLE 82: Age and sex distribution in the Vinkovci Gepid series

Age category	Subadult N[1]	%[2]	Female N	%	Male N	%	Total N	%
Birth -1	1	10.0					1	2.9
2- 5	0						0	
6-10	5	50.0					5	14.7
11-15	4	40.0					4	11.8
16-20			0		2	15.4	2	5.9
21-25			1	9.1	2	15.4	3	8.8
26-30			2	18.2	2	15.4	4	11.8
31-35			3	27.2	3	23.0	6	17.7
36-40			2	18.2	1	7.7	3	8.8
41-45			1	9.1	0		1	2.9
46-50			0		1	7.7	1	2.9
51-55			2	18.2	2	15.4	4	11.8
56-60			0		0		0	
60+			0		0		0	
Total	10	100.0	11	100.0	13	100.0	34	100.0

Mean age at death[3]   x = 36.63   x = 33.00

                          sd = 9.77   sd = 12.07

[1] N = number of individuals dying.

[2] % = % of individuals dying.

[3] Mean age at death is calculated using median values of each age category (for example, 23 for the age category 21-25), and 65 for the age category 60+.

TABLE 83: Frequency of alveolar bone disease in the Vinkovci Gepid series

Age category	Subadult A[1]/O[2]	%[3]	Female A/O	%	Male A/O	%
Young adult[4]			0/54	0.0	1/150	0.7
Old adult			18/64	28.1	9/76	11.8
Total	0/138	0.0	18/118	15.2	10/226	4.4

[1] A = number of tooth sockets with periodontal or periapical abscess, or antemortem tooth loss.

[2] O = number of tooth sockets observed.

[3] % = % of tooth sockets with periodontal or periapical abscess, or antemortem tooth loss.

[4] Young adult = individuals aged between 16 to 35 years; Old adult = individuals older than 36 years.

TABLE 84: Frequency of carious lesions in the Vinkovci Gepid series

Age category	Subadult A[1]/O[2]	%[3]	Female A/O	%	Male A/O	%
Young adult[4]			0/42	0.0	1/129	0.8
Old adult			1/25	4.0	6/52	11.5
Total	3/120	2.5	1/67	1.5	7/181	3.9

[1] A = number of teeth with carious lesions.

[2] O = number of teeth observed.

[3] % = % of teeth with carious lesions.

[4] Young adult = individuals aged between 16 to 35 years; Old adult = individuals older than 36 years.

appears to be the result of differences in the old age category although the difference between the frequency of alveolar bone disease in old adult females and old adult males is not statistically significant. ($\chi^2 = 3.8$, P < 0.08).

Caries frequencies are summarized in Table 84. Both subadults and adults exhibit low frequencies, with typically, frequencies highest in the old adult age category. Only one carious lesion is recorded in the female sample. In males the modal category for severity of lesion is grade 2. In adults carious lesions are most frequently located interproximally (in 5/8 of all carious lesions) followed by occlusal and lingual lesions. In subadults, two carious lesions are located bucally, and one is located interproximally.

Enamel hypoplasia frequencies are summarized in Tables 85-86. Hypoplasias are most frequent in the mandibular canines - 55.6%, followed by maxillary canines - 40.0% and maxillary central incisors - 9.1%.

TABLE 85: Hypoplasia frequencies by individual in the Vinkovci Gepid series

Tooth	N[1]	NwLEH	%wLEH
Maxillary I1[2]	11	1	19.1
Maxillary C	15	6	40.0
Mandibular C	18	10	55.6

[1] N = number of teeth observed; NwLEH = number of teeth with one or more LEH; %wLEH = % of N with one or more LEH.

[2] I = incisor; C = canine.

Subadults are poorly represented in the sample. Only 18 teeth were available for analysis (5 central maxillary incisors, 6 maxillary and 7 mandibular canines). The highest frequency of hypoplastic defects is recorded in mandibular canines (Table 86). Adults are also poorly represented in the series with only 6 maxillary incisors, 9 maxillary and 11 mandibular canines available for analysis. Adult frequencies are slightly higher than subadult which may reflect small sample size. As in subadults, the highest frequency of hypoplasias is recorded in mandibular canines (63.6%). A breakdown of the adult sample by sex shows that adult males and females exhibit similar frequencies of hypoplastic teeth.

Cribra orbitalia frequencies are summarized in Table 87. Eight subadult frontal bones with intact orbits were available for analysis, five of which exhibit cribra orbitalia. Only one case was, however, active at time of death, and of the remaining 4 cases, all are slight in severity. Two males (2/11 males with

TABLE 86: Hypoplasia frequencies in the Vinkovci Gepid series for subadults and adults

Tooth	Subadults		All adults		Females		Males	
	Nw/N[1]	%wLEH[2]	Nw/N	%wLEH	Nw/N	%wLEH	Nw/N	%wLEH
Maxillary I1[3]	1/5	20.0	0/6	0.0	0/0	0.0	0/6	0.0
Maxillary C	2/6	33.3	4/9	44.4	2/3	66.7	2/6	33.3
Mandibular C	3/7	42.9	7/11	63.6	1/3	33.3	6/8	75.0

[1] Nw = number of individuals with one or more LEH; N = number of individuals observed.
[2] %wLEH = % of N with one or more LEH.
[3] I = incisors; C = canines.

TABLE 87: Frequency of occurrence of cribra orbitalia in the Vinkovci Gepid series

Age/sex	Cribra orbitalia			Active lesions	
	O[1]	A1[2]	%	A2[3]	% of A1
0 - 0.9	1	0	0.0	0	0.0
1 - 3.9	0	0	0.0	0	0.0
4 - 9.9	3	2	66.7	1	50.0
10 - 14.9	4	3	75.0	0	0.0
All subadults	8	5	62.5	1	20.0
Adult females	4	0	0.0	0	0.0
Adult males	11	2	18.2	0	0.0
All adults	15	2	13.3	0	0.0

[1] O = number of frontal bones observed.
[2] A1 = number of frontal bones in which at least one orbit shows evidence of cribra orbitalia.
[3] A2 = number of frontal bones in which cribra orbitalia is active at time of death.

preserved orbits) also show healing cribra orbitalia lesions. Cribra orbitalia is not recorded in females.

Only one case of periostitis is noted in the series. A subadult aged between 11.5-12.5 years exhibits active, moderate endocranial periostitis on the frontal bone. No cases of periostitis on the medial surfaces of the tibia are noted on any of the 14 preserved subadult and 24 preserved adult tibiae.

Three individuals, two males (2/11 recovered male crania) and one subadult (1/8 recovered subadult crania), exhibit healed depression fractures on the cranial vault. Two fractures are located on the frontal bone (in the one subadult and in one male), while one is located on the posterior left parietal. None of the fractures penetrated the inner table of the skull and none show evidence of infection.

Enthesophytes are common in the series and are recorded on the patellae and calcanei. Enthesophytes are recorded on 3/7 preserved male

calcanei, on 2/6 male patellae , and on 6/9 recovered female patellae.

Benign cortical defects are noted in 3 males. One exhibits deep defects at the insertion sites of the pectoralis major and latissimus dorsi muscles on the right humerus. Two exhibit bilateral deep rhomboid fossae on the medial clavicles (both more pronounced on the left side).

Osteoarthritis frequencies in major joints are low in the series, and restricted to individuals older than 36 years. Females exhibit one case of moderate osteoarthritis in the shoulder (1/5 recovered shoulder joints), and two moderate cases of osteoarthritis in the knee (2/8 recovered knee joints). Males exhibit one case of mild osteoarthritis in the shoulder (1/7 recovered shoulder joints).

The total female vertebral osteoarthritis frequency is 12.1% (Table 88), with involvement only in the thoracic region of the spine. Males exhibit a considerably lower total vertebral osteoarthritis frequency (1.8%) with greatest involvement in the lumbar segment of the spine. This difference is statistically significant ($\chi^2 = 5.3$, P < 0.03) as is the difference in thoracic spine involvement between females and males ($\chi^2 = 9.1$, P < 0.01).

Females also exhibit higher frequencies of Schmorl's depressions in both the thoracic and lumbar spine (Table 89).

TABLE 88: Frequency of occurrence of vertebral osteoarthritis in the Vinkovci Gepid series

	Cervical		Thoracic		Lumbar		Total	
	A[1]/O[2]	%	A/O	%	A/O	%	A/O	%
Female								
Young adult[3]	0/3	0.0	1/9	11.1	0/0	0.0	1/12	8.3
Old adult	0/16	0.0	6/19	31.6	0/11	0.0	6/46	13.0
Total	0/19	0.0	7/28	25.0	0/11	0.0	7/58	12.1
Male								
Young adult	0/24	0.0	0/33	0.0	0/15	0.0	0/72	0.0
Old adult	0/9	0.0	0/21	0.0	2/10	20.0	2/40	5.0
Total	0/33	0.0	0/54	0.0	2/25	8.0	2/112	1.8

[1] A = number of vertebrae affected with osteoarthritis or osteophytosis.
[2] O = number of vertebrae observed.
[3] Young adult = individuals aged between 16 to 35 years; Old adult = individuals older than 36 years.

TABLE 89: Frequency of occurrence of Schmorl's depressions in the Vinkovci Gepid series

	Thoracic		Lumbar		Total	
	A[1]/O[2]	%	A/O	%	A/O	%
Female						
Young adult[3]	2/9	22.2	0/0	0.0	2/9	22.2
Old adult	7/19	36.8	3/11	27.3	10/30	33.3
Total	9/28	32.1	3/11	27.3	12/39	30.8
Male						
Young adult	6/33	18.2	0/15	0.0	6/48	12.5
Old adult	4/21	19.0	0/10	0.0	4/31	12.9
Total	10/54	18.5	0/25	0.0	10/79	12.6

[1] A = number of vertebrae with Schmorl's depressions.

[2] O = number of vertebrae observed.

[3] Young adult = individuals aged between 16 to 35 years; Old adult = individuals older than 36 years.

The total frequency of Schmorl's defects in females is 30.8%, (12/39 vertebrae), compared to 12.6% (10/79) in males. The difference is not, however, statistically significant.

4.2. THE SKULL FROM JOPIĆ CAVE

This is an isolated find recovered in 1988 from Jopić cave in the Kordun region. The site consists of the disturbed remains of a prehistoric necropolis with numerous animal remains, chief among them the remains of dogs, boars and stags. One isolated well preserved, artificially deformed human skull was also recovered (Figure 14). The skull is dated to the Late Avar period (Malez et al. 1988). It is included in this analysis because it is a rare example of an artificially deformed skull, as well as a rare case of peri-mortem trauma.

The skull is almost certainly female based on the following morphological traits. The superior margins of the orbits are very sharp, the zygomatics are small as are the mastoid processes. The skull is very smooth and gracile with no pronounced muscle ridges on the occipital bone. Age at death is estimated at between 25-35 years based on palatine suture closure (Mann and Jantz, 1988), alveolar bone resorption and tooth occlusal surface wear.

The skull shows fronto-occipital artificial cranial deformation, possibly caused by binding. The maximum length (glabella-opisthocranion) of the skull is 161 mm. Maximum breadth (euryon-euryon) is 119 mm, and it's height (basion-bregma) is 139 mm. The highest point of the skull is above bregma and is 152 mm distant from basion.

Similar types of artificial cranial deformation have been recorded in other Early medieval European series from Burgundy and Thuringia, through Hungary and the Carpathian basin, and well into the territory of modern Russia (Liptak, 1983).

The skull exhibits a well healed, oval depression fracture with a maximum diameter of 12 mm on the posterior part of the right parietal bone, approximately 14 mm anterior of Lambda. The margins of the fracture are smooth and the floor is slightly porous. There is no evidence of infection.

Clear evidence of peri-mortem trauma is present on the left temporal bone (Figure 15). This fracture is consistent with blunt force trauma that penetrated the endocranium. Concentric radiating fractures encircle the impact area as well as a small linear fracture line which radiates away from the impact area (Figure 16). The fracture is clearly peri-mortem because of the in-bending of the adhering bone fragments, the lack of discoloration on the margins of the fracture lines, and the concentric curvature of the surrounding fracture lines. There is slight beveling on the endocranial surface of the margin of the superior fracture line.

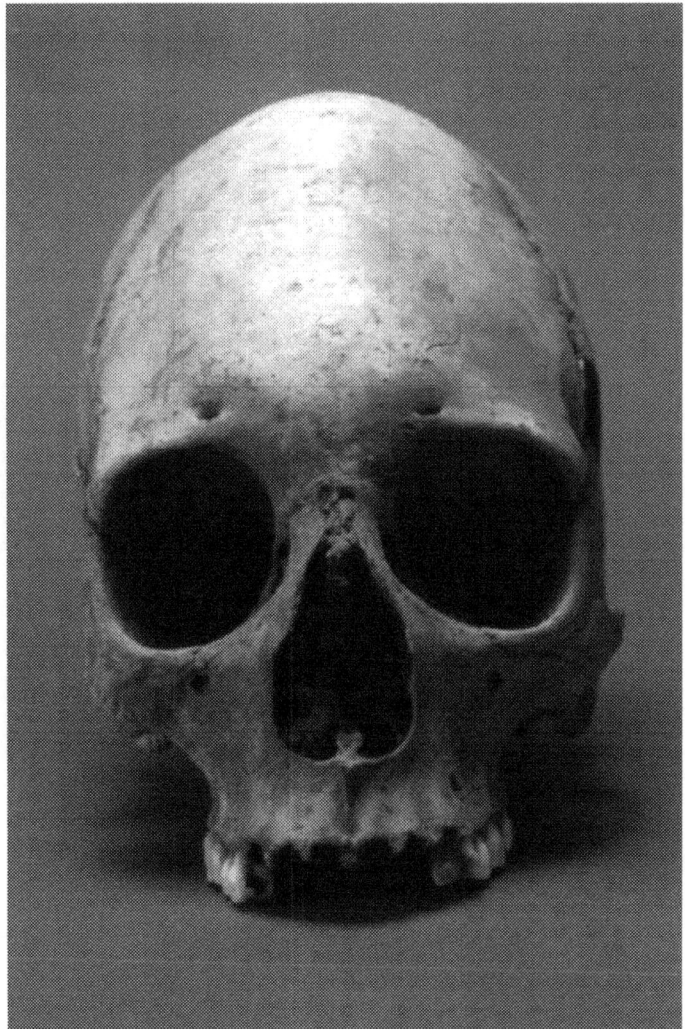

Figure 14. Fronto-occipital artificial skull deformation in the adult female from Jopić cave.

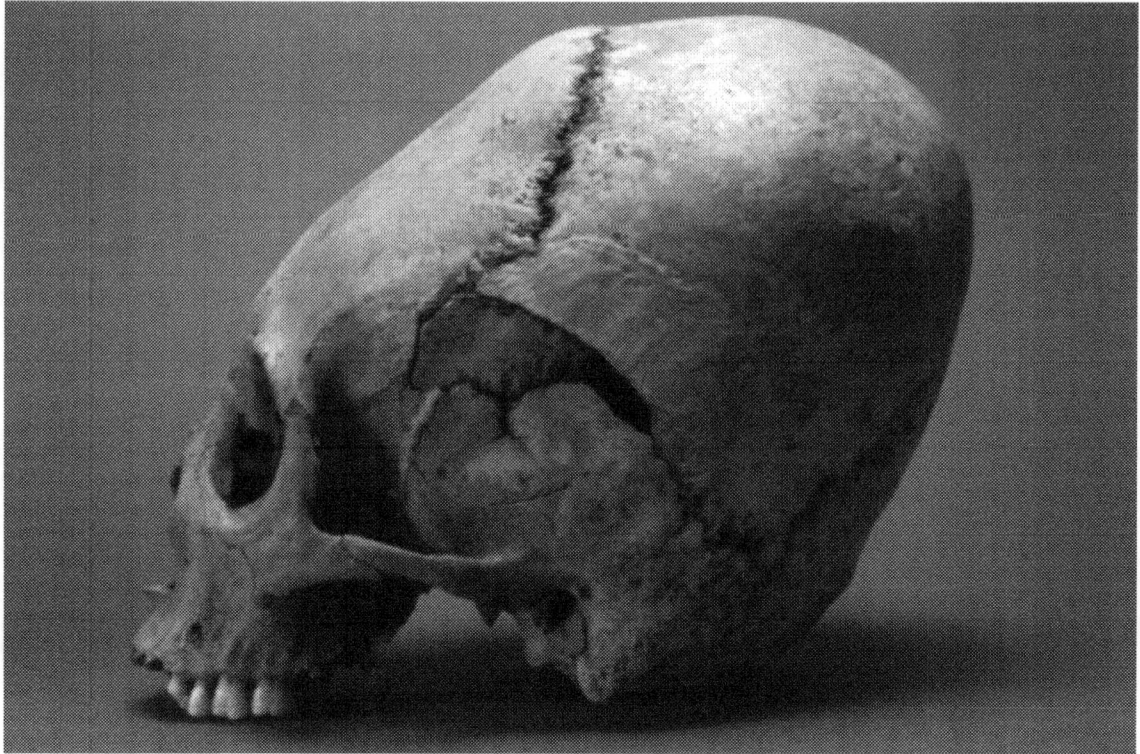

Figure 15. Peri-mortem trauma on the left temporal bone of the same individual.

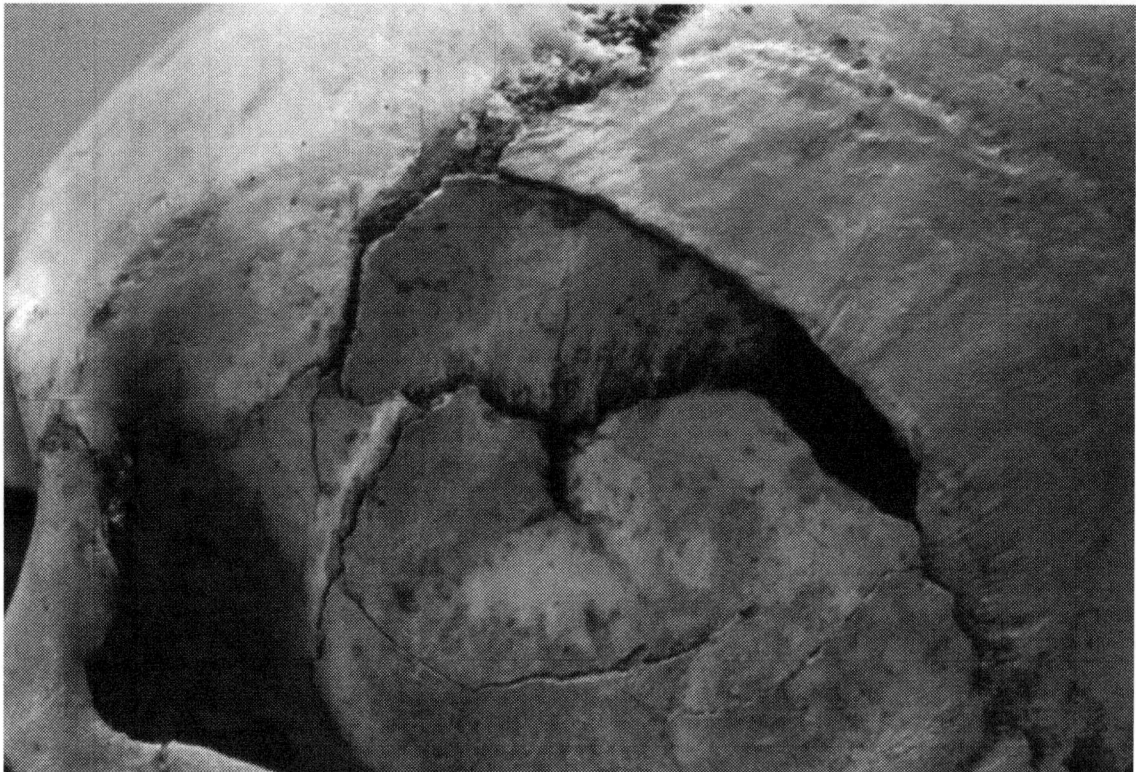

Figure 16. Detailed view of the impact area. Note concentric curvature of surrounding fracture lines, in-bending of the adhering bone fragments, and lack of discoloration on margins of fracture lines.

4.3. THE PRIVLAKA SKELETAL SERIES

The Privlaka skeletal series is the largest individual skeletal series reported on in this book. The material was recovered from the "Gole Njive" complex on the outskirts of Privlaka, approximately 11 km south-east of Vinkovci. Construction activities carried out in 1972 revealed the existence of a large Early medieval cemetery. The site was systematically excavated from 1973 to 1980. During these campaigns the presence of 230 graves aligned in, more or less, parallel rows was recorded. Artifacts recovered from the site date the use of the cemetery to between 700 to 800, or to the Late Avar period (Šmalcelj, 1973, 1976).

TABLE 90: Age and sex distribution in the Privlaka series

Age category	Subadult N[1]	%[2]	Female N	%	Male N	%	Total N	%
Birth -1	3	8.2					3	1.6
2- 5	11	29.7					11	6.1
6-10	14	37.8					14	7.7
11-15	9	24.3					9	5.0
16-20			5	6.8	3	4.2	8	4.4
21-25			17	23.3	6	8.5	23	12.7
26-30			14	19.2	14	19.7	28	15.6
31-35			13	17.8	15	21.2	28	15.6
36-40			10	13.7	12	16.9	22	12.1
41-45			5	6.8	11	15.5	16	8.8
46-50			3	4.1	4	5.6	7	3.9
51-55			1	1.4	2	2.8	3	1.6
56-60			1	1.4	2	2.8	3	1.6
60+			4	5.5	2	2.8	6	3.3
Total	37	100.0	73	100.0	71	100.0	181	100.0

Mean age at death[3] $x = 33.04$ $x = 35.94$
                       $sd = 11.62$ $sd = 10.28$

[1] N = number of individuals dying.
[2] % = % of individuals dying.
[3] Mean age at death is calculated using median values of each age category (for example, 23 for the age category 21-25), and 65 for the age category 60+.

The age and sex distribution of the series is presented in Table 90. Subadults comprise 20.4% of the total sample and are, as is frequently the case, clearly underrepresented in the youngest (birth-1 year) age category (only 3 individuals or 1.6% of the total series). Subadult mortality in the series is highest from 6-10 years (37.8% of the subadult subsample).

Males and females are evenly represented in the adult sample (71 and 73 individuals respectively). The average age at death of adults over 15 years is 33.0 years for females, and 35.9 years for males. This relatively small difference (2.9 years) in average life-spans is reflected in similar mortality profiles. The highest mortality rates for females are recorded from 21

to 30 years (42.5% of the female sample), while males exhibit highest mortality between the ages of 26-35 years (40.9%). In both sexes only 6 individuals (8.2% of all adult female deaths, and 8.4% of all adult male deaths) live to be older than 50 years.

Alveolar bone disease frequencies are summarized in Table 91. None of the 639 recovered subadult tooth sockets exhibits evidence of alveolar bone disease. In adults the total frequency is 14.0% (393/2811) with an even total distribution between males and females (13.4% in females compared to 14.6% in males). However, while total frequencies and frequencies in the old adult age group are similar, females in the young adult age category exhibit more than twice as much alveolar bone disease as males (7.8% compared to 3.1%). This difference is statistically significant ($\chi^2=13.2$, P< .01).

The same pattern is present in the distribution of caries. Caries frequencies (Table 92) are very low in subadults (0.9%), similar between males and females in the old adult age category and in total values, and considerably higher in young adult females than young adult males (10.2%

TABLE 92: Frequency of carious lesions in the Privlaka series

Age category	Subadult A[1]/O[2] %[3]	Female A/O	%	Male A/O	%
Young adult[4]		80/787	10.2	31/518	6.0
Old adult		48/322	14.9	59/351	16.8
Total	5/516 0.9	128/1109	11.5	90/869	10.4

[1] A = number of teeth with carious lesions.
[2] O = number of teeth observed.
[3] % = % of teeth with carious lesions.
[4] Young adult = individuals aged between 16 to 35 years; Old adult = individuals older than 36 years.

TABLE 91: Frequency of alveolar bone disease in the Privlaka series

Age category	Subadult A[1]/O[2] %[3]	Female A/O	%	Male A/O	%
Young adult[4]		76/970	7.8	20/646	3.1
Old adult		128/547	23.4	169/648	26.1
Total	0/639 0.0	204/1517	13.4	189/1294	14.6

[1] A = number of tooth sockets with periodontal or periapical abscess, or antemortem tooth loss.
[2] O = number of tooth sockets observed.
[3] % = % of tooth sockets with periodontal or periapical abscess, or antemortem tooth loss.
[4] Young adult = individuals aged between 16 to 35 years; Old adult = individuals older than 36 years.

compared to 6.0%). This difference is also statistically significant ($\chi^2=5.5$, P< .02).

Both sexes display the same modal category, grade 2, for severity of carious lesion. The distribution of carious lesions is also similar. Carious lesions are most frequently located interproximally (in 61/128 or 47.6% of all carious lesions in females, and in 35/90 or 38.9% of all carious lesions in males). In females this is followed by root (43/128 or 33.6%), occlusal (16/128 or 12.5%) and buccal caries (8/128 or 6.2%), and in males by root (32/90 or 35.5%), occlusal (17/90 or 18.9%), buccal (5/90 or 5.5%), and lingual (1/90 or 1.1%) caries.

Enamel hypoplasia frequencies are summarized in Tables 93-96. Hypoplasias are most frequent in the maxillary central

TABLE 93: Hypoplasia frequencies by individual in the Privlaka series

Tooth	N[1]	NwLEH	%wLEH
Maxillary I1[2]	58	30	51.7
Maxillary C	79	39	49.4
Mandibular C	105	52	49.5

[1] N = number of teeth observed; NwLEH = number of teeth with one or more LEH; %wLEH = % of N with one or more LEH.
[2] I = incisor; C = canine.

incisors - 51.7%, followed by mandibular canines - 49.5% and maxillary canines - 49.4%. Of the 242 analyzed teeth, 121 (50.0%) exhibit evidence of hypoplasia.

Although slightly better than in other skeletal series, subadults are still poorly represented. Of the 34 subadult teeth available for analysis (11 central maxillary incisors, 10 maxillary and 13 mandibular canines), 26 (76.5%) exhibit hypoplastic defects (Table 94). In this series, hypoplasia in subadults is most frequently recorded in maxillary canines.

A breakdown of the adult sample by sex shows that adult males and females exhibit very similar frequencies of hypoplastic defects. Of the 115 female teeth available for analysis 53 (46.1%) exhibit hypoplastic defects. In males, 42/93 (45.2%) of the teeth available for analysis exhibit hypoplastic defects.

The mean number of hypoplasias per tooth (Table 95) also shows similar values for males and females. Subadults consistently exhibit a higher number of defects per tooth then adults.

Controlling for age in the adult sample (Table 96), shows a consistently higher frequency of defects in individuals who died as young adults.

Cribra orbitalia frequencies are summarized in Table 97. In the Privlaka series the expression of this condition ranges from slight pitting to moderate sievelike lesions with diplotic expansion.

Cribra orbitalia is observed in 42 of the 150 crania (28.0%) with intact orbits. The overall subadult frequency is 51.7% with the majority of lesions (11/15 or 73.3%) active at time of death. In adults the lesion has a frequency of 22.3% with

TABLE 96: Hypoplasia frequencies in adult dentition in the Privlaka series

Sex/age	Maxillary I1[1] Nw/N[2]	%wLEH[3]	Maxillary C Nw/N	%wLEH	Mandibular C Nw/N	%wLEH
Female						
Young adult[4]	12/18	66.7	12/27	44.4	17/35	48.6
Old adult	2/6	33.3	2/11	18.2	8/18	44.4
Male						
Young adult	6/17	35.3	12/20	60.0	10/20	50.0
Old adult	2/6	33.3	5/11	45.4	7/19	36.8

[1] I = incisors; C = canines.
[2] Nw = number of individuals with one or more LEH; N = number of individuals observed.
[3] %wLEH = % of N with one or more LEH.
[4] Young adult = individuals aged between 16 to 35 years; Old adult = individuals older than 36 years.

TABLE 94: Hypoplasia frequencies in the Privlaka series for subadults and adults

Tooth	Subadults Nw/N[1]	%wLEH[2]	All adults Nw/N	%wLEH	Females Nw/N	%wLEH	Males Nw/N	%wLEH
Maxillary I1[3]	8/11	72.7	22/47	46.8	14/24	58.3	8/23	34.8
Maxillary C	8/10	80.0	31/69	44.9	14/38	36.8	17/31	54.8
Mandibular C	10/13	76.9	42/92	45.6	25/53	47.2	17/39	43.6

[1] Nw = number of individuals with one or more LEH; N = number of individuals observed.
[2] %wLEH = % of N with one or more LEH.
[3] I = incisors; C = canines.

TABLE 95: Mean number of hypoplasias in incisors and canines in the Privlaka series

Tooth	Subadults Mean	N	S.D.	All adults Mean	N	S.D.	Females Mean	N	S.D.	Males Mean	N	S.D.
Maxillary I1[1]	1.00	11	0.78	0.51	47	0.58	0.58	24	0.50	0.43	23	0.66
Maxillary C	1.20	10	0.79	0.55	69	0.68	0.45	38	0.64	0.68	31	0.70
Mandibular C	1.08	13	0.76	0.61	92	0.74	0.62	53	0.74	0.59	39	0.75

[1] I = incisors; C = canines .

TABLE 97: Frequency of occurrence of cribra orbitalia in the Privlaka series

Age/sex	Cribra orbitalia			Active lesions	
	O[1]	A1[2]	%	A2[3]	% of A1
0 - 0.9	3	1	33.3	1	100.0
1 - 3.9	4	1	25.0	1	100.0
4 - 9.9	15	9	60.0	8	88.9
10 - 14.9	7	4	57.1	1	25.0
All subadults	29	15	51.7	11	73.3
Adult females	62	12	19.3	0	0.0
Adult males	59	15	25.4	0	0.0
All adults	121	27	22.3	0	0.0

[1] O = number of frontal bones observed.

[2] A1 = number of frontal bones in which at least one orbit shows evidence of cribra orbitalia.

[3] A2 = number of frontal bones in which cribra orbitalia is active at time of death.

all of the lesions exhibiting some degree of healing. No significant sex differences in healing lesion frequencies are noted indicating similar levels of subadult stress in males and females. The difference between the frequency of cribra orbitalia in subadults (51.7%) and adults (22.3%) is, however, statistically significant ($\chi^2 = 4.1$, P< .05).

Skeletal evidence for infectious disease is present in subadults and adults. In subadults, active, moderately severe endocranial periostitis on the occipital bone is present in one individual. Two individuals exhibit periostitis on the mandible, one healed and localized on the left ramus, and one active along the body. Periostitis on the tibiae is present in 9 of 37 recovered subadults (24.3%), or on 13/70 recovered subadult tibiae (18.6%). Most of these lesions (8/13 or 61.5%) were active at time of death. Two subadults exhibit periostitis on the fibula, both active at time of death.

In adults, skeletal evidence for infectious disease is seen on the endocranial surface of the frontal and left parietal bone (both from a female aged between 17.5-19.5 years, and both healed at time of death), and on the mandible of a female aged between 21-25 years. In the postcranial skeleton periostitis is recorded on the humerus, femur, tibia and fibula. Periostitis on the tibial shaft is present in 4/73 (5.5%) females, or on 7/157 (4.4%) recovered female tibiae, and in 8/71 (11.3%) males, or on 13/143 (9.1%) recovered male tibiae. Periostits is also present on the fibula, in 2/73 (2.7%) females, and in 3/71 (4.2%) males, on the femur, in 1/73 (1.4%) females, and 2/71 (2.8%) males, and on the humerus, in 1/71 (1.4%) males. Compared to subadults, adults exhibit more resistance

to infectious disease, 18/20 (90.0%) periosteal lesions on the tibiae were healed at time of death, as were 8/9 (88.9%) periosteal lesions on the fibulae.

There is one case of osteomyelitis subsequent to fracture in the series, recorded in an adult female, located on the distal third of the diaphysis of the right femur.

Skeletal evidence of healed fractures is present only in adults. The types of fractures identified include depressed lesions on the cranial vault, long bone fractures, and fractures of the clavicle. Cranial fractures are recorded in one female (1/61 females with recovered cranial vaults or 1.6%). This individual, aged between 40-45 years, has two small, well healed depression fractures on the posterior part of the right parietal bone, approximately 12 mm superior of Lambda. The fractures have smooth margins and floors, and show no evidence of infection. Postcranial fractures are noted on the clavicle, in 2/56 (3.6%) females with preserved clavicles, and 3/61 (4.9%) males, humerus, in 1/71 (1.4%) females with preserved humerii, and 3/68 (4.4%) males, radius, in 2/65 (3.1%) females with preserved radii, and 1/64 (1.6%) males, ulna, in 1/63 (1.6%) females with preserved ulnae, and 2/67 (3.0%) males, femur, in 2/72 (2.8%) females with preserved femora, tibia, in 2/67 (3.0%) males with preserved tibiae, and fibula in 2/60 (3.3) males with preserved fibulae.

There is one case of dislocation in the series. This is a long standing dislocation in a 60+ years old female. The dislocated joint is the right elbow which exhibits severe

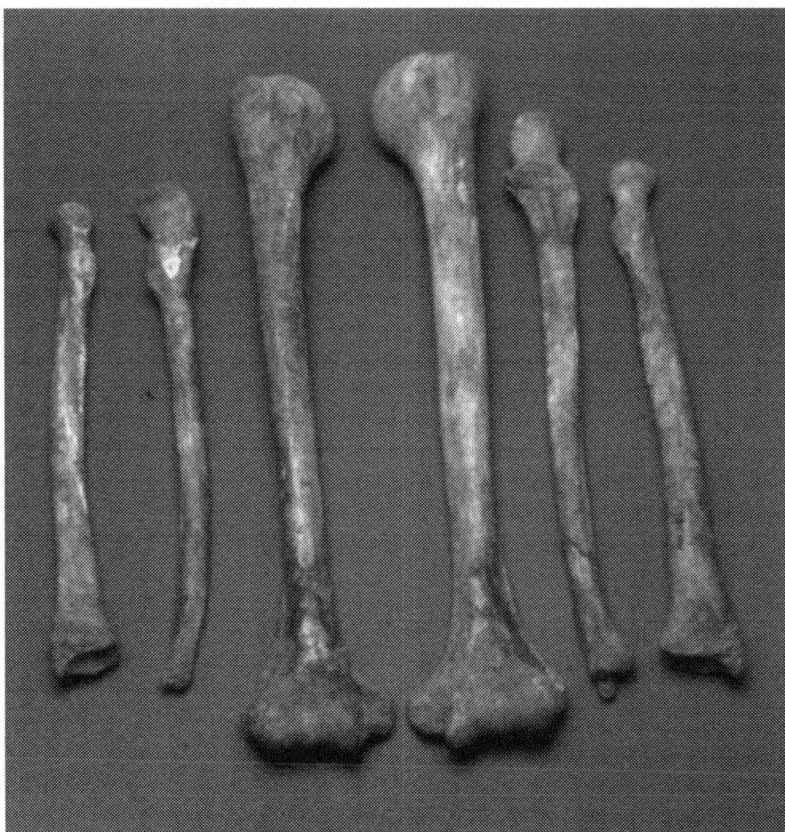

Figure 17. Probable case of postparalytic deformity in the right arm of an adult male from Privlaka.

Figure 18. Comparison of distal radial surfaces in the same individual.
The right radius exhibits considerable atrophy.

porosity, osteophyte development and the formation of a new humero-radial joint, approximately 33 mm. superior of the original one. The new joint is severely pitted. The head of the right radius is not present. The proximal right ulna shows severe porosis, bone destruction and osteophyte development.

There is one probable case of postparalytic deformity in the series. The case is recorded in a 25-30 years old male and is located in the right arm. The right humerus, radius and ulna are considerably lighter, and more gracile than the ones on the left side (Figure 17). The difference is more pronounced in the radius and ulna than in the humerus. The difference in maximum lengths between the right and left humerus is 5 mm (294 mm compared to 299 mm), in epicondylar breadth 4 mm (59 mm compared to 63 mm), and in maximum vertical diameter of the head 3 mm (43 mm compared to 46 mm). The difference in maximum lengths of the radius is more pronounced and equals 22 mm (228 mm compared to 206 mm). The right distal radial joint surface is also considerably smaller than the left (Figure 18). The distal right ulna is missing so comparison of maximum lengths are not possible, but this bone is also clearly much smaller and gracile than the left ulna. This is best seen by comparing the transverse diameters which are 17 mm on the left side, and 11 mm on the right (the right ulna practically has no interosseus crest).

TABLE 98: Frequency of occurrence of osteoarthritis at major joints in the Privlaka series

	Shoulder		Elbow		Hip		Knee	
	A[1]/O[2]	%	A/O	%	A/O	%	A/O	%
Female								
Young adult[3]	3/32	9.3	12/44	27.3	1/43	2.3	2/41	4.9
Old adult	6/14	42.9	10/23	43.5	5/22	22.7	12/20	60.0
Total	9/46	19.6	22/67	32.8	6/65	9.2	14/61	22.9
Male								
Young adult	1/25	4.0	11/35	31.4	1/33	3.0	12/34	35.3
Old adult	4/16	25.0	19/29	65.5	3/27	11.1	11/25	44.0
Total	5/41	12.2	30/64	46.9	4/60	6.7	23/59	38.9

[1] A = number of joints affected with osteoarthritis. Osteoarthritis was scored as present if at least one joint element showed evidence of osteoarthritic change.

[2] O = number of joints observed. A joint was scored as present if at least one joint element was completely present, or if two or three elements were partially present.

[3] Young adult = individuals aged between 16 to 35 years; Old adult = individuals older than 36 years.

Enthesophytes are recorded mostly in males and are present in one individual on the right humerus, in two individuals on the left radii, in one individual on the right ulna, in two individuals on the right and left femurs, in four individuals on the right fibulae, and in one individual bilaterally on the calcanei. In females enthesophytes are recorded in 6 individuals, in each case on the calcaneus.

Spondylolysis is present in the fifth lumbar vertebra of 3 males (in 3/43 or 7.0% of males with complete lumbar spines), and in 1 female (1/40, or 2.5% of females with intact lumbar spines).

Osteoarthritis frequencies in the series are summarized in Table 98. Of the four

TABLE 99: Frequency of occurrence of vertebral osteoarthritis in the Privlaka series

	Cervical		Thoracic		Lumbar		Total	
	A[1]/O[2]	%	A/O	%	A/O	%	A/O	%
Female								
Young adult[3]	4/85	4.7	0/43	0.0	0/103	0.0	4/231	1.7
Old adult	12/34	35.3	14/30	46.7	23/43	53.5	49/107	45.8
Total	16/119	13.4	14/73	19.2	23/146	15.7	53/338	15.7
Male								
Young adult	3/45	0.0	6/31	19.3	5/107	4.7	14/183	7.6
Old adult	7/28	25.0	15/31	48.4	30/66	45.4	52/125	41.6
Total	10/73	13.7	21/62	33.9	35/173	20.2	66/308	21.4

[1] A = number of vertebrae affected with osteoarthritis or osteophytosis.
[2] O = number of vertebrae observed.
[3] Young adult = individuals aged between 16 to 35 years; Old adult = individuals older than 36 years.

TABLE 100: Frequency of occurrence of Schmorl's depressions in the Privlaka series

	Thoracic		Lumbar		Total	
	A[1]/O[2]	%	A/O	%	A/O	%
Female						
Young adult[3]	5/43	11.6	12/103	11.6	17/146	11.6
Old adult	1/30	3.3	2/43	4.6	3/73	4.1
Total	6/73	8.2	14/146	9.6	20/219	9.1
Male						
Young adult	7/31	22.6	19/107	17.7	26/138	18.8
Old adult	13/31	41.9	21/66	31.8	34/97	35.0
Total	20/62	32.2	40/173	23.1	60/235	25.5

[1] A = number of vertebrae with Schmorl's depressions.
[2] O = number of vertebrae observed.
[3] Young adult = individuals aged between 16 to 35 years; Old adult = individuals older than 36 years.

major joints in the skeleton, osteoarthritis is, in both sexes, most frequently recorded in the elbow. In both sexes this is followed by the knee, shoulder and hip. Osteoarthritis frequencies are similar between males and females and more common in the old adult than the young adult age group.

The overall frequency of vertebral osteoarthritis in the series is 18.4% (119/646). Comparing the different regions of the spine (Table 99), greatest involvement occurs in the thoracic region (35/135 or 25.9%), followed by the lumbar (58/319 or 18.2%) and cervical (26/192 or 13.5%) regions. No sex differences are present in the total and old adult age categories, but young males exhibit significantly higher total frequencies of vertebral osteoarthritis than females (7.6% compared to 1.7%, $\chi^2 = 6.54$; P < .02). This, statistically significant, difference appears to be primarily related to higher frequencies of vertebral osteoarthritis in the thoracic spine where young males exhibit significantly higher frequencies than females (19.3% compared to none, $\chi^2 = 5.38$; P < .03).

The frequencies of Schmorl's depressions in the series are summarized in Table 100. The overall frequency of Schmorl's depressions in the sample is 17.6% (80/454). Frequencies of Schmorl's depressions in the thoracic and lumbar spine are similar (19.2% in the thoracic and 16.9% in the lumbar spine). Total male frequencies are significantly higher than female frequencies (25.5% compared to 9.1%, $\chi^2 = 13.93$; P < .01). This difference appears to be the result of differences in the old age category where males exhibit significantly higher frequencies of Schmorl's defects than females (35.0% compared to 4.1%, $\chi^2 = 14.40$; P < .01).

4.4. CHARACTERISTICS OF THE COMPOSITE EARLY MEDIEVAL SERIES

Similar to the Antique composite series this is a relatively homogenous series. In terms of the territory that it covers it is, with the exception of the isolated skull from Jopić cave, restricted to an area circumscribed by an 11 km radius around Vinkovci. The temporal span covers the period from the 6th to the end of the 8th century. It is comprised of two series, one large and one small, and an isolated find.

Historical sources indicate that this was a period of marked political instability characterized by migrations, warfare and uprisings. Both of the analyzed series come from short-lived and militarily destroyed kingdoms. The Gepid kingdom lasted from 454 to 567 when it was destroyed by the Langobards and Avars, while the Avar kingdom lasted only slightly longer, from 569 to 803 when it was destroyed by the Franks.

The age and sex distribution of the series is presented in Table 101. Subadults comprise 21.7% of the total sample and are clearly underrepresented in the youngest (birth-1 year) age category (only 4 individuals or 1.8% of the total Early medieval composite series). Subadult mortality in the sample is highest from 6-10 years (40.4% of the subadult subsample or 8.8% of the complete sample).

Males and females are evenly represented (84 and 85 individuals respectively). The average age at death of adults over 15 years is 33.5 years for females, and 35.5 years for males. This small difference (2.0 years) in average life-spans is reflected in similar mortality profiles. The highest mortality rates for females are recorded from 21-30 years (34 individuals or 40.0%), for males from 26-35 years (34 individuals or 37.0%). Few individuals (8 females or 9.4% of all adult female deaths, and 8 males or 9.5% of all adult male deaths) lived to be older than 50 years.

TABLE 101: Age and sex distribution in the Early medieval composite series

Age category	Subadult N[1]	%[2]	Female N	%	Male N	%	Total N	%
Birth -1	4	8.5					4	1.8
2- 5	11	23.4					11	5.1
6-10	19	40.4					19	8.8
11-15	13	27.7					13	6.0
16-20			5	5.9	5	5.9	10	4.6
21-25			18	21.2	8	9.5	26	12.0
26-30			16	18.8	16	19.1	32	14.8
31-35			17	20.0	18	21.5	35	16.3
36-40			12	14.1	13	15.5	25	11.6
41-45			6	7.1	11	13.1	17	7.9
46-50			3	3.5	5	5.9	8	3.7
51-55			3	3.5	4	4.7	7	3.2
56-60			1	1.2	2	2.4	3	1.4
60+			4	4.7	2	2.4	6	2.8
Total	47	100.0	85	100.0	84	100.0	216	100.0

Mean age at death[3]   x = 33.50   x = 35.49
                        sd = 11.34   sd = 10.56

[1] N = number of individuals dying.

[2] % = % of individuals dying.

[3] Mean age at death is calculated using median values of each age category (for example, 23 for the age category 21-25), and 65 for the age category 60+.

TABLE 102: Frequency of alveolar bone disease in the Early medieval composite series

Age category	Subadult A[1]/O[2]	%[3]	Female A/O	%	Male A/O	%
Young adult[4]			76/1024	7.4	21/796	2.6
Old adult			146/611	23.9	178/724	24.6
Total	0/777	0.0	222/1635	13.6	199/1520	13.1

[1] A = number of tooth sockets with periodontal or periapical abscess, or antemortem tooth loss.

[2] O = number of tooth sockets observed.

[3] % = % of tooth sockets with periodontal or periapical abscess, or antemortem tooth loss.

[4] Young adult = individuals aged between 16 to 35 years; Old adult = individuals older than 36 years.

TABLE 103: Frequency of carious lesions in the Early medieval composite series

Age category	Subadult A[1]/O[2]	%[3]	Female A/O	%	Male A/O	%
Young adult[4]			80/829	9.6	32/647	4.9
Old adult			49/347	14.1	65/403	16.1
Total	8/636	1.3	129/1176	11.0	97/1050	9.2

[1] A = number of teeth with carious lesions.

[2] O = number of teeth observed.

[3] % = % of teeth with carious lesions.

[4] Young adult = individuals aged between 16 to 35 years; Old adult = individuals older than 36 years.

The frequencies of alveolar bone disease and carious lesions are summarized in Tables 102 and 103. Alveolar bone disease is not present in any of the 777 subadult tooth sockets available for inspection. The total adult frequency is 13.3% (421/3155) with similar total frequencies for males and females (13.1% and 13.6% respectively). Frequencies in the old adult age category are also similar, but young females exhibit significantly more alveolar bone disease than young males (7.4% compared to 2.6%, $\chi^2=17.47$, P< .01).

The overall frequency of carious lesions in the Early medieval composite series is 8.2%, exactly the same as the frequency recorded for the Antique composite series. Subadults contribute little with only 8 teeth (8/636 or 1.3%) exhibiting carious lesions. Adult male and female total frequencies are similar (9.2% and 11.0% respectively), as are frequencies in the old adult age group (16.1% and 14.1% respectively). Following the pattern recorded in alveolar bone disease, young females exhibit significantly higher frequencies of carious lesions than males (9.6% compared to 4.9%, $\chi^2=9.29$, P< .01). As previously discussed, higher frequencies of dental disease in females have been recorded in numerous populations. As the statistically significant differences are contained to the young adult age category, it seems likely that they were caused by one of the three previously discussed factors. Unfortunately, as in the Antique series, there is no ethnographic or historical data on dietary practices and food preparation for these populations. Thus, further systematic analyses of dental disease in other Early medieval populations from continental Croatia are necessary to evaluate if the observed differences in male/female frequencies of dental disease are the result of random variation in a small sample, or the result of specific, as yet unidentified, factors.

Both sexes display the same modal category, grade 2, for severity of carious lesion. The distribution of carious lesions is also similar. Carious lesions are most frequently located

TABLE 104: Hypoplasia frequencies by individual in the Early medieval composite series

Tooth	N[1]	NwLEH	%wLEH
Maxillary I1[2]	69	31	44.9
Maxillary C	94	45	47.9
Mandibular C	123	62	50.4

[1] N = number of teeth observed; NwLEH = number of teeth with one or more LEH; %wLEH = % of N with one or more LEH.

[2] I = incisor; C = canine.

TABLE 105: Hypoplasia frequencies in the Early medieval composite series for subadults and adults

Tooth	Subadults		All adults		Females		Males	
	Nw/N[1]	%wLEH[2]	Nw/N	%wLEH	Nw/N	%wLEH	Nw/N	%wLEH
Maxillary I1[3]	9/16	56.2	22/53	41.5	14/24	58.3	8/29	27.6
Maxillary C	10/16	62.5	35/78	44.9	16/41	39.0	19/37	51.3
Mandibular C	13/20	65.0	49/103	47.6	26/56	46.4	23/47	48.9

[1] Nw = number of individuals with one or more LEH; N = number of individuals observed.
[2] %wLEH = % of N with one or more LEH.
[3] I = incisors; C = canines.

TABLE 106: Mean number of hypoplasias in incisors and canines in the Early medieval composite series

Tooth	Subadults			All adults			Females			Males		
	Mean	N	S.D.	Mean	N	S.D.	Mean	N	S.D.	Mean	N	S.D.
Maxillary I1[1]	0.81	16	0.83	0.45	53	0.57	0.58	24	0.50	0.34	29	0.61
Maxillary C	0.87	16	0.81	0.55	78	0.68	0.46	41	0.64	0.67	37	0.72
Mandibular C	0.95	20	0.89	0.65	103	0.76	0.61	56	0.69	0.70	47	0.80

[1] I = incisors; C = canines.

interproximally (in 39/97 or 40.2% of all carious lesions in males, and in 62/129 or 48.1% of all carious lesions in females). In both sexes this is followed by root (32/97 or 33.0% in males, 43/129 or 33.3% in females), occlusal (19/97 or 19.6% in males, 16/129 or 12.4% in females) and buccal caries (5/97 or 5.1% in males, 8/129 or 6.2 % in females). Males also exhibit 2 (2/97 or 2.1%) lingual caries. Subadults exhibit 8 carious lesions, 4 located on the root, 3 on the buccal surface of the tooth, and only one interproximally.

Enamel hypoplasia frequencies are summarized in Tables 104-107. Of the 286 teeth available for analysis, 138 (48.2%) exhibit hypoplastic defects. Hypoplasias are most frequent in the mandibular canines - 50.4%, followed by maxillary canines - 47.9% and maxillary central incisors - 44.9%.

Subadults are better represented than in the Prehistoric and Antique composite series. Of the 52 subadult teeth available for analysis (16 central maxillary incisors, 16 maxillary and 20 mandibular canines), 32 (61.5%) exhibit hypoplastic defects (Table 105). In this series, hypoplasia in subadults is most frequently recorded in mandibular canines, followed by maxillary canines and maxillary central incisors.

A breakdown of the adult sample by sex shows that males and females exhibit similar frequencies of hypoplastic defects. Hypoplastic defects are

recorded in 50/113 (44.2%) of male teeth available for study, and in 56/121 (46.3%) female teeth. Subadults, once again, consistently exhibit higher frequencies of hypoplasia inducing stress than adults. The same pattern is evident when the mean number of hypoplasias is compared (Table 106). Subadults consistently, in all three tooth categories analyzed, exhibit a higher number of defects in the teeth affected than individuals who lived into adulthood. Males and females exhibit similar values. Controlling for age (Table 107), young adults exhibit higher frequencies of hypoplastic defects than old adults with the exception of female mandibular canines and male maxillary central incisors.

Cribra orbitalia frequencies are summarized in Table 108. In the Early medieval composite series the expression of this condition ranges from slight pitting to moderate sievelike lesions with some diplotic expansion.

TABLE 107: Hypoplasia frequencies in adult dentition in the Early medieval composite series

Sex/age	Maxillary I1[1]		Maxillary C		Mandibular C	
	Nw/N[2]	%wLEH[3]	Nw/N	%wLEH	Nw/N	%wLEH
Female						
Young adult[4]	12/18	66.7	13/29	44.8	16/37	43.2
Old adult	2/6	33.3	3/12	25.0	10/19	52.6
Male						
Young adult	5/21	23.8	14/24	58.3	15/26	57.7
Old adult	3/8	37.5	5/13	38.5	8/21	38.1

[1] I = incisors; C = canines.
[2] Nw = number of individuals with one or more LEH; N = number of individuals observed.
[3] %wLEH = % of N with one or more LEH.
[4] Young adult = individuals aged between 16 to 35 years; Old adult = individuals older than 36 years.

TABLE 108: Frequency of occurrence of cribra orbitalia in the Early medieval composite series

| Age/sex | Cribra orbitalia | | | Active lesions | |
	O[1]	A1[2]	%	A2[3]	% of A1
0 - 0.9	4	1	25.0	1	100.0
1 - 3.9	4	1	25.0	1	100.0
4 - 9.9	18	11	61.1	9	81.8
10 - 14.9	11	7	63.6	1	14.3
All subadults	37	20	54.0	12	60.0
Adult females	66	12	18.2	0	0.0
Adult males	70	17	24.3	0	0.0
All adults	136	29	21.3	0	0.0

[1] O = number of frontal bones observed.

[2] A1 = number of frontal bones in which at least one orbit shows evidence of cribra orbitalia.

[3] A2 = number of frontal bones in which cribra orbitalia is active at time of death.

Cribra orbitalia is observed in 49 of the 173 crania (28.3%) with intact orbits. The overall subadult frequency is 54.0% with most of the lesions (12/20) active at time of death. In subadults the lesion first appears at approximately 6 months of age and increases in frequency to a maximum of 63.6% between ages 10 and 14.9. In adults the lesion has a frequency of 21.3% with all of the lesions exhibiting some degree of healing. No significant sex differences are present in cribra orbitalia frequencies in adults.

Skeletal evidence for infectious disease is present in subadults and adults. Periostitis frequencies are presented by bone because of differential preservation of the recovered remains, and the need to compare them with the Prehistoric and Antique composite series.

Subadults exhibit active endocranial periostitis on one frontal (1/38 recovered subadult frontal bones or 2.6%) and one occipital bone (1/35 or 2.9%). Periostitis on the mandible is present in 2/41 (4.9%) recovered mandibles. In the postcranial skeleton periostitis is recorded in 13/70 (18.6%) available subadult tibiae, and on 2/54 (3.7%) fibulae. Adults exhibit endocranial periostitis on the frontal (1/137 or 0.7%), and parietal bone (1/279 or 0.3%). One case (1/134 or 0.7%) is noted in the mandible. In the postcranial skeleton periostitis

TABLE 109: Frequency of occurrence of active periosteal lesions in the Early medieval composite series

| Sex | Periosteal lesions | | |
	A1[1]	A2[2]	% of A1
Subadults	19	13	68.4
Adult females	14	2	14.3
Adult males	22	2	9.1
All adults	36	4	11.1
Total	55	17	30.9

[1] A1 = number of bones with periostitis.

[2] A2 = number of bones with periostitis active at time of death.

is recorded in the humerus (1/302 or 0.3%), femur (3/304 or 0.9%), tibia (20/300 or 6.7%), and fibula (9/253 or 3.5%).

As is evident from these numbers subadults, similar to the pattern observed in the Prehistoric and Antique composite series, show less resistance to infectious disease than adults. This is further corroborated when the numbers of active and healed cases of periostitis are compared (Table 109). Most subadult lesions (68.4%) show no evidence of healing, while the same is true for only 11.1% of adult cases.

One case of osteomyelitis, subsequent to fracture, is noted in the femur (1/304 or 0.3%) of an adult female.

Skeletal evidence of healed fractures is almost exclusive to adults. Only one fracture, a healed depression fracture on the frontal bone (1/38 preserved subadult cranial vaults or 2.6%) is recorded in subadults. In adults, fractures are recorded in the cranium and postcranium. Cranial fractures are noted in 2 females (2/69 or 2.9% of females with recovered cranial vaults), and 2 males (2/72 or 2.8%). One was fatal (the blunt force trauma to the female recovered from Jopić cave), while three are well healed depression fractures that did not penetrate the inner table of the skull. Postcranial fractures are recorded on the clavicle, in 2/59 or 3.4% females with recovered clavicles, and 3/66 or 4.5% males with recovered clavicles, humerus, in 1/77 or 1.3% females, and 3/73 or 4.1% males, radius, in 2/71 or 2.8% females, and 1/69 or 1.4% males, ulna, in 1/69 or 1.4% females, and 2/71 or 2.8% males, femur, in 2/80 or 2.5% females, tibia, in 2/71 or 2.8% males, and fibula, in 2/64 or 3.1% males.

It is interesting to note that for some reason the political instability of the period does not translate into high frequencies of skeletal trauma. The frequencies, for instance, of cranial trauma in the series are considerably lower than those recorded in the Prehistoric and Antique composite series. Postcranial fractures are also low, below 5% for both sexes in all bones analyzed. There is no evidence of "beaten-up" individuals - individuals with several fractures, and the frequencies of "parry" fractures to the ulna are below 3% for both sexes. The reasons for this apparent lack of skeletal trauma are unclear, and open to different interpretations. Both of the series analyzed come from small settlement cemeteries. If the political destruction of the Avar and Gepid kingdoms was sudden, the result of battles fought on, at present, unknown locations, it is possible that the victims were not buried in their village cemeteries but were buried on the battlefield, or disposed of in some other manner. The lack of skeletal trauma in the cemetery series may reflect a relatively peaceful incorporation of the survivors into the new state, Avar in the case of the surviving Gepids, and Frankish in the case of the surviving Avars. Further systematic analysis of trauma patterns in Early medieval series from continental Croatia are necessary to determine if the observed low frequencies of trauma in the Gepid and Avar series analyzed in this book are the result of small sample size, or a realistic reflection of the incidence of trauma in Early medieval populations from Croatia.

Enthesophytes are recorded on the patellae, calcaneii, and long bones. Enthesophytes on the patellae are present in 2 males and 4 females. Enthesophytes at the insertion site of the Achilles

TABLE 110: Frequency of occurrence of osteoarthritis at major joints in the Early medieval composite series

	Shoulder		Elbow		Hip		Knee	
	A^1/O^2	%	A/O	%	A/O	%	A/O	%
Female								
Young adult[3]	3/33	9.1	12/45	26.7	1/46	2.2	2/44	4.5
Old adult	7/18	38.9	10/28	35.7	5/27	18.5	14/25	56.0
Total	10/51	19.6	22/73	30.1	6/73	8.2	16/69	23.1
Male								
Young adult	1/30	3.3	11/41	26.8	1/38	2.6	12/39	30.8
Old adult	5/18	27.8	19/30	63.3	3/28	10.7	11/26	42.3
Total	6/48	12.5	30/71	42.2	4/66	6.1	23/65	35.4

[1] A = number of joints affected with osteoarthritis. Osteoarthritis was scored as present if at least one joint element showed evidence of osteoarthritic change.

[2] O = number of joints observed. A joint was scored as present if at least one joint element was completely present, or if two or three elements were partially present.

[3] Young adult = individuals aged between 16 to 35 years; Old adult = individuals older than 36 years.

tendon on the calcaneus are noted in 6 females and 3 males. Males also exhibit enthesophytes on the following long bones: humerus, one individual; radius, two individuals; ulna, one individual; femur, 2 individuals; and fibula, 4 individuals.

One, long standing dislocation of the elbow is noted in the series.

Spondylolysis is present in the fifth lumbar vertebra of one female (1/43 females with intact lumbar spines or 2.3%), and 3 males (3/47 males with intact lumbar spines or 6.4%).

Osteoarthritis frequencies in the series are summarized in Table 110. Of the four major joints in the skeleton, osteoarthritis is, in both sexes, most frequently recorded in the elbow. In both sexes this is followed by the knee, shoulder, and hip. No significant sex differences are present in the frequencies of osteoarthritis except in the frequencies of osteoarthritis in the knee in young adults where young males

exhibit significantly higher frequencies than young females (30.8% compared to 4.5%, $\chi^2 = 5.7$; P < .02). Osteoarthritis is more common in the old adult than the young adult age group.

The overall frequency of vertebral osteoarthritis in the series is 15.7% (128/816) which is higher than the frequencies recorded in the Prehistoric and Antique composite series. Comparing the different regions of the spine (Table 111), greatest involvement occurs in the thoracic region 19.3% (42/217), followed by the lumbar 16.9% (60/355) and cervical 10.6% (26/244) regions. No sex differences are noted.

The frequencies of Schmorl's depressions in the series are

TABLE 112: Frequency of occurrence of Schmorl's depressions in the Early medieval composite series

	Thoracic		Lumbar		Total	
	A^1/O^2	%	A/O	%	A/O	%
Female						
Young adult[3]	7/52	13.5	12/103	11.6	19/155	12.3
Old adult	8/49	16.3	5/54	9.3	13/103	12.6
Total	15/101	14.8	17/157	10.8	32/258	12.4
Male						
Young adult	13/64	20.3	19/122	15.6	32/186	17.2
Old adult	17/52	32.7	21/76	27.6	38/128	29.7
Total	30/116	25.9	40/198	20.2	70/314	22.3

[1] A = number of vertebrae with Schmorl's depressions.

[2] O = number of vertebrae observed.

[3] Young adult = individuals aged between 16 to 35 years; Old adult = individuals older than 36 years.

TABLE 111: Frequency of occurrence of vertebral osteoarthritis in the Early medieval composite series

	Cervical		Thoracic		Lumbar		Total	
	A^1/O^2	%	A/O	%	A/O	%	A/O	%
Female								
Young adult[3]	4/88	4.5	1/52	1.9	0/103	0.0	5/243	2.1
Old adult	12/50	24.0	20/49	40.8	23/54	42.6	55/153	35.9
Total	16/138	11.6	21/101	20.8	23/157	14.6	60/396	15.1
Male								
Young adult	3/69	4.3	6/64	9.4	5/122	4.1	14/255	5.5
Old adult	7/37	18.9	15/52	28.8	32/76	42.1	54/165	32.7
Total	10/106	9.4	21/116	18.1	37/198	18.7	68/420	16.2

[1] A = number of vertebrae affected with osteoarthritis or osteophytosis.

[2] O = number of vertebrae observed.

[3] Young adult = individuals aged between 16 to 35 years; Old adult = individuals older than 36 years.

summarized in Table 112. The overall frequency of Schmorl's depressions in the sample is 17.8% (102/572). Frequencies of Schmorl's depressions are slightly higher in the thoracic spine (20.7% or 45/217) than in the lumbar (16.0% or 57/355). Both sexes exhibit higher total frequencies in the old adult age category but this is much more pronounced in males. Total male frequencies are significantly higher than female (22.3% compared to 12.4%, $\chi^2 = 6.11$; P < .02). This difference is primarily due to differences present in the old adult age category where males exhibit significantly higher frequencies of Schmorl's defects than females (29.7% compared to 12.6%, $\chi^2 = 5.53$; P < .02).

5. BIOARCHAEOLOGY OF THE LATE MEDIEVAL PERIOD

The political status of continental Croatia in the 10th and 11th centuries is, because of conflicting historical interpretations, at present unclear. In all likelihood this was a period of anarchy during which sovereignty changed between Hungary and Croatia (Klaić, 1971).

After the death of the Croatian king Zvonimir in uncertain circumstances in 1091, the Hungarian king Ladislav I annexed continental Croatia and build a system of "*županijas*" based on an old Slavic system. Royal *županijas* were established as organizational units which incorporated royal holdings. Alongside these, smaller tribal *župas*, counties of free people obliged to serve in the military, functioned (Klaić, 1990). Ladislav's heir Koloman defeated the Croatian king Petar Svačić and crowned himself as king of Hungary, Croatia and Dalmatia in 1102. Under Hungarian rule, in the 12th and 13th centuries, continental Croatia achieved an almost independent position with the Hercegs and Bans as leaders (Klaić, 1990). Economic changes characterize this period, primarily the emergence of secular elites, and the rise in importance of monastic orders, chief among them the Templars and the Hospitallers (Dobronić, 1984). Towns were built and given special privileges until the short, but devastating, Mongol invasion in 1242 highlighted the weaknesses of open settlements. This experience prompted king Bela IV to construct a defensive system based on walled towns. Walled towns were built from the end of the 13th century, either as centers of local noble power, or as free royal towns subject directly to the king. Areas under the city walls were frequently occupied by foreigners, called *hospites*, mostly of Flemish, Wallon or Rhenish origin. Some towns which acquired the status of a free royal town during this period are Varaždin (in 1209), Vukovar (1231), Virovitica (1234), Petrinja (1240), Zagreb (1242), and Koprivnica (1356) (Macan, 1992).

With the development of free royal towns, and a widespread transition from barter to a monetary system, a new phase of feudalism began which lasted from the 12/13th to the 16th century. The separation of crafts and trade from agriculture lead to the development of a new type of settlement called "*varos*". These trading centers did not develop inside walled towns, but around, and below them, as suburbia.

The Late medieval period is represented by six skeletal series. The series were recovered from sites in Đakovo (phase I of the medieval Đakovo cemetery), Vinkovci, Lobor, Ščitarjevo, Đelekovec and Stenjevac. The geographical locations of the sites are presented in Figure 19. As can be seen, the analyzed sites basically cover all of continental Croatia. Four of the analyzed series (Vinkovci, Lobor, Ščitarjevo and Đelekovec) are relatively small and contain between 10 to 20 individuals. The remaining two (Đakovo phase I, and Stenjevac) are larger and contain 31 and 84 individuals respectively.

5.1. THE ĐAKOVO PHASE I SKELETAL SERIES

The Đakovo phase I skeletal series was recovered from the medieval Đakovo cemetery. Đakovo is first mentioned in historical sources as an estate given in a deed by prince Koloman to the bishop of Bosnia in 1239. The see of the bishop gradually developed into a market, and later a town. The medieval cemetery is located in the center of modern Đakovo, in the area behind the present "Church of all Saints". Excavations carried out from 1995 to 1997 revealed the presence of 486 graves arranged in, more or less, regular rows. All of the deceased were buried in simple, trapezoidal or rectangular burial pits with no evidence of grave architecture.

Archaeological evidence indicates two phases of burial in the cemetery. These phases are recognizable by different stratigraphical relationships, as well as by specific material remains (Filipec, 1996, 1997). The first phase begins in the middle of the 11th century, and lasts up to 1242 when it was interrupted by the Mongol invasion. The second phase begins in the aftermath of the Mongol invasion and lasts until 1536 when Đakovo was captured by the Turks. Craniometric analyses of recovered skulls from the cemetery confirm the presence of two distinct populations in the recovered remains (Šlaus and Filipec, 1998). Bone preservation and completeness of the skeletons is poor to average. Because of this, and because of the need to be certain regarding the

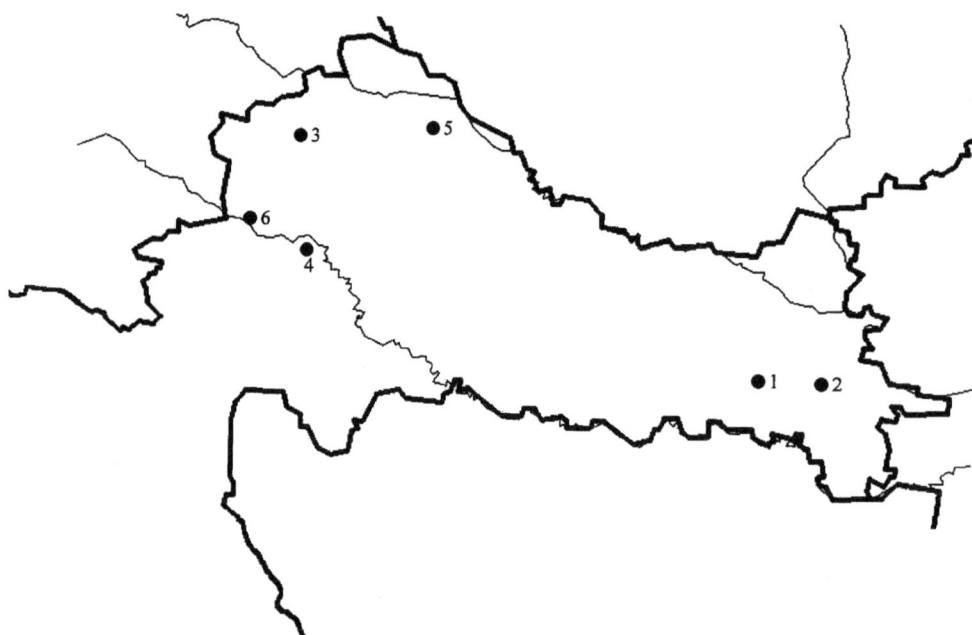

Figure 19. The geographical locations of the Late medieval sites: 1. Đakovo, 2. Vinkovci, 3. Lobor, 4. Ščitarjevo, 5. Đelekovec, 6. Stenjevac

TABLE 113: Age and sex distribution in the Đakovo, burial phase I, series

Age category	Subadult N[1]	%[2]	Female N	%	Male N	%	Total N	%
Birth -1	0						0	
2- 5	1	33.3					1	3.2
6-10	1	33.3					1	3.2
11-15	1	33.4					1	3.2
16-20			1	7.7	0		1	3.2
21-25			3	23.1	6	40.0	9	29.1
26-30			4	30.7	1	6.7	5	16.1
31-35			1	7.7	5	33.3	6	19.4
36-40			1	7.7	0		1	3.2
41-45			0		2	13.3	2	6.5
46-50			1	7.7	0		1	3.2
51-55			0		0		0	
56-60			1	7.7	0		1	3.2
60+			1	7.7	1	6.7	2	6.5
Total	3	100.0	13	100.0	15	100.0	31	100.0

Mean age at death[3]   x = 33.92   x = 32.13
                        sd = 14.47   sd = 11.45

[1] N = number of individuals dying.

[2] % = % of individuals dying.

[3] Mean age at death is calculated using median values of each age category (for example, 23 for the age category 21-25), and 65 for the age category 60+.

chronological phase of a burial, the sample for analysis was greatly reduced.

The age and sex distribution in the series is presented in Table 113. Subadults are poorly represented in the series. They are completely absent in the youngest (0-1 year) age category, and represented by only three individuals in all of the other remaining subadult age categories. Subadults comprise 9.7% of the total sample.

Peak mortality for both males and females is between 21-30 years (53.8% of all adult females, and 46.7% of all males died during this interval). The similar mortality distribution is reflected in similar mean ages at death. The average age at

TABLE 114: Frequency of alveolar bone disease in the Đakovo, burial phase I, series

Age category	Subadult A[1]/O[2]	%[3]	Female A/O	%	Male A/O	%
Young adult[4]			0/130	0.0	7/226	3.1
Old adult			28/64	43.7	0/19	0.0
Total	0/15	0.0	28/194	14.4	7/245	2.9

[1] A = number of tooth sockets with periodontal or periapical abscess, or antemortem tooth loss.

[2] O = number of tooth sockets observed.

[3] % = % of tooth sockets with periodontal or periapical abscess, or antemortem tooth loss.

[4] Young adult = individuals aged between 16 to 35 years; Old adult = individuals older than 36 years.

death for adult females is 33.9 years (SD = 14.5), for adult males 32.1 years (SD = 11.4).

The frequencies of alveolar bone disease are presented in Table 114. Alveolar bone disease is not present in subadults, and has a low (8.0% or 35/439) overall frequency in adults. Females exhibit considerably higher total frequencies (14.4%) than males (2.9%). This difference is statistically significant (χ^2 = 15.29; P < 0.01). The difference is not caused by differences in the young adult age category, in which both sexes exhibit very little or no evidence of alveolar bone disease, but by differences in the old adult age category in which females have considerably higher frequencies of alveolar bone disease than males (43.7% compared to none, χ^2 = 6.20; P < 0.02).

Total caries frequencies (Table 115) are, however, similar in males and females (7.0% and 5.0% respectively), and are not significantly different in either the young adult, or old age categories. No lesions are recorded in subadult dentition. In adult females the majority of the observed lesions are located interproximally (in 3/8 lesions), in males occlusally (in 8/16 lesions). Females also exhibit buccal (3/8) and occlusal (2/8) caries, while males exhibit interproximal (7/16) and buccal (1/16) lesions. The modal category for severity of lesions is grade 2 in both sexes.

TABLE 115: Frequency of carious lesions in the Đakovo, burial phase I, series

Age category	Subadult A[1]/O[2]	%[3]	Female A/O	%	Male A/O	%
Young adult[4]			5/133	3.8	15/202	7.4
Old adult			3/26	11.5	1/28	3.6
Total	0/15	0.0	8/159	5.0	16/230	7.0

[1] A = number of teeth with carious lesions.

[2] O = number of teeth observed.

[3] % = % of teeth with carious lesions.

[4] Young adult = individuals aged between 16 to 35 years; Old adult = individuals older than 36 years.

TABLE 116: Hypoplasia frequencies by individual in the Đakovo, burial phase I, series

Tooth	N[1]	NwLEH	%wLEH
Maxillary I1[2]	14	7	50.0
Maxillary C	14	7	50.0
Mandibular C	18	8	44.4

[1] N = number of teeth observed; NwLEH = number of teeth with one or more LEH; %wLEH = % of N with one or more LEH.

[2] I = incisor; C = canine.

Enamel hypoplasia frequencies are presented in Table 116. Hypoplasias are more frequent in maxillary incisors and canines (50.0%) than in mandibular canines. No subadult teeth were available for analysis. In adults, hypoplastic defects are recorded in 2/6 female and 5/8 male maxillary incisors, in 3/6 female and 4/8 male maxillary canines, and in 1/7 female and 7/11 male mandibular canines.

Cribra orbitalia is recorded in both of the subadults recovered with intact orbits. Both cases were active at time of death. In adults it's presence is observed in 2 female (2/9) and 3 male crania (3/10). All adult cases were healed and mild in expression.

Skeletal evidence for infectious disease is recorded in subadults and adults. One subadult exhibits bilateral, severe, active periostitis on the complete medial surfaces of the tibiae. In the adult sample five individuals, 4 males (4/9 males with intact tibias), and one female (1/8) exhibit skeletal evidence for infectious disease in the form of periostitis on the tibia. In all cases, except for one male, the lesion is unilateral, and localized to the middle or distal third of the medial side of the diaphysis of the tibia. The one male mentioned has bilateral, healed, mild periostitis along the complete medial surfaces of the tibias. No cases of osteomyelitis are noted in the sample.

Healed fractures are noted only in adults. Cranial fractures are recorded in 3 individuals, 2 males (2/12 males with complete crania), and one female (1/10). In males, the fractures are located on the right parietal bone, in the female, on the occipital bone. All fractures are well healed, oval, depression fractures, with slightly porous floors and rounded margins. They did not penetrate the inner table of the skull and there is no evidence of infection. In the postcranium, two "parry" fractures on the midshafts of the left ulna are present in two males (2/8 males with recovered ulnas). In both cases the fractures are well healed, with no evidence of angulation or infection.

Osteoarthritis frequencies in major joints are low in the series and restricted to individuals older than 36 years. One female exhibits mild osteoarthritis in the elbow, while one exhibits a moderate case of osteoarthritis in the knee. Osteoarthritis is not recorded in males.

The total female vertebral osteoarthritis frequency is 17.2% (5/29), with greatest involvement in the cervical region of the spine. Males exhibit no vertebral osteoarthritis. The old adult age category in males is, however, poorly represented, only 25 vertebrae were available for analysis.

Males exhibit higher total frequencies of Schmorl's depressions (Table 117) than females (53.5% compared to none). This difference is statistically significant ($\chi^2 = 5.69$; P < 0.02).

5.2. THE LATE MEDIEVAL VINKOVCI SKELETAL SERIES

This is a small skeletal series recovered from various sites in Vinkovci (Duga Ulica, Prolaz A. Ullman, and Croatia osiguranje) during rescue excavations carried out in 1988, 1991 and 1993. A total of 6 graves was eventually excavated, 5 of which contain multiple inhumations. These graves are Grave 1-which contains the remains of 2 females and a child, Grave 2-which contains one male, one female and one child, Grave 4-which contains a female and child, Grave 5-which contains one male, one female and one child, and Grave 6-which contains one male, two females and two subadults. The graves are dated to the Late medieval period (Dizdar, personal communication).

The age and sex distribution of the series is presented in Table 118. Subadults comprise 41.2% of the total sample (7/17). Males and females are unevenly represented with 7 females and 3 males comprising the adult sample. Peak mortality for adults appears to be between 31-35 years. The average age at death for adult females is 37.3 years (SD = 11.0), for adult males 29.7 years (SD = 5.8).

The frequencies of alveolar bone disease are presented in Table 119. Alveolar bone disease is not present in subadults, and has a low (5.1%) overall frequency in adults. Females exhibit slightly higher frequencies (6.9%) than males (3.2%) but this difference is not statistically significant.

Adult caries frequencies are also low - 12.3% in females, 7.8% in males, and 10.5% overall (Table 120). Subadults exhibit no carious lesions. The modal category for severity of lesion in both males and females is grade 2. Both sexes show a similar distribution of carious lesions. Lesions are most frequently located interproximally (in 4/9 of all carious lesions in females, and in 1/4 of all carious lesions in males). In males carious lesions are also recorded on the root of the tooth (1/4), the occlusal (1/4), and buccal (1/4) surface, while in females lesions are recorded on the occlusal (3/9), root (1/9), and buccal (1/9) surface of the tooth.

TABLE 117: Frequency of occurrence of Schmorl's depressions in the Đakovo, burial phase I, series

	Thoracic		Lumbar		Total	
	A^1/O^2	%	A/O	%	A/O	%
Female						
Young adult[3]	0/8	0.0	0/7	0.0	0/15	0.0
Old adult	0/0	0.0	0/0	0.0	0/0	0.0
Total	0/8	0.0	0/7	0.0	0/15	0.0
Male						
Young adult	0/8	0.0	2/10	20.0	2/18	11.1
Old adult	13/15	86.7	8/10	80.0	21/25	84.0
Total	13/23	56.2	10/20	50.0	23/43	53.5

[1] A = number of vertebrae with Schmorl's depressions.
[2] O = number of vertebrae observed.
[3] Young adult = individuals aged between 16 to 35 years; Old adult = individuals older than 36 years.

TABLE 118: Age and sex distribution in the Late medieval Vinkovci series

Age category	Subadult N[1]	%[2]	Female N	%	Male N	%	Total N	%
Birth -1	1	14.2					1	5.9
2- 5	2	28.6					2	11.7
6-10	2	28.6					2	11.7
11-15	2	28.6					2	11.7
16-20			0		0		0	
21-25			1	14.3	1	33.3	2	11.7
26-30			1	14.3	0		1	5.9
31-35			2	28.5	2	66.7	4	23.7
36-40			0		0		0	
41-45			1	14.3	0		1	5.9
46-50			1	14.3	0		1	5.9
51-55			1	14.3	0		1	5.9
56-60			0		0		0	
60+			0		0		0	
Total	7	100.0	7	100.0	3	100.0	17	100.0

Mean age at death[3]   x = 37.29   x = 29.67
                       sd = 10.96   sd = 5.77

[1] N = number of individuals dying.
[2] % = % of individuals dying.
[3] Mean age at death is calculated using median values of each age category (for example, 23 for the age category 21-25), and 65 for the age category 60+.

generalized periostitis on the endocranial surfaces of the frontal and right parietal bone. Two subadults exhibit bilateral, moderately severe, active periostitis on the medial shafts of the tibiae, and one exhibits severe, bilateral, active periostitis on the diaphyses of the tibiae and fibulae. The female exhibits active, moderately severe, periostitis along the complete diaphyses of the right tibia and fibula.

Skeletal evidence for trauma is present in one male. This individual, aged between 31-35 years, exhibits two well healed fractures, one on the distal right ulna, and one on the distal right radius. There is slight angulation, and some associated osteoarthritis on the distal joint surfaces.

Osteoarthritis is not recorded in any of the recovered adult major joints.

Vertebral osteoarthritis is noted in only one male lumbar vertebra (1/13 recovered male vertebra).

One Schmorl's lesion is recorded in the lumbar vertebra of an adult female.

TABLE 119: Frequency of alveolar bone disease in the Late medieval Vinkovci series

Age category	Subadult A[1]/O[2]	%[3]	Female A/O	%	Male A/O	%
Young adult[4]			0/47	0.0	3/94	3.2
Old adult			7/54	13.0	0/0	0.0
Total	0/16	0.0	7/101	6.9	3/94	3.2

[1] A = number of tooth sockets with periodontal or periapical abscess, or antemortem tooth loss.
[2] O = number of tooth sockets observed.
[3] % = % of tooth sockets with periodontal or periapical abscess, or antemortem tooth loss.
[4] Young adult = individuals aged between 16 to 35 years; Old adult = individuals older than 36 years.

TABLE 120: Frequency of carious lesions in the Late medieval Vinkovci series

Age category	Subadult A[1]/O[2]	%[3]	Female A/O	%	Male A/O	%
Young adult[4]			4/41	9.8	4/51	7.8
Old adult			5/32	15.6	0/0	0.0
Total	0/7	0.0	9/73	12.3	4/51	7.8

[1] A = number of teeth with carious lesions.
[2] O = number of teeth observed.
[3] % = % of teeth with carious lesions.
[4] Young adult = individuals aged between 16 to 35 years; Old adult = individuals older than 36 years.

Enamel hypoplasia is not recorded in this series. However, only 4 adult maxillary, and 7 adult mandibular canines were available for analysis.

Healed cribra orbitalia is observed in one of the 3 female frontals with preserved orbits, and in one of the 3 male frontals. One subadult frontal with intact orbits was also recovered but shows no evidence of the lesion.

Skeletal evidence for infectious disease is present in 4 subadults, and one female. In subadults periostitis is recorded on the cranium and postcranium. One subadult, aged between birth and 1 year, exhibits severe, active

5.3. THE LOBOR SKELETAL SERIES

This is a small skeletal series recovered from the Lobor site in north-western Croatia. Rescue excavations carried out in 1998 revealed the presence of a small Late medieval cemetery. Based on burial ritual and finds from the graves, mostly bronze or iron S-links, cast metal rings, and silver coins, use of the cemetery is dated to the 11th century (Filipec, 1999).

The age and sex distribution in the series is presented in Table 121. The series contains 4 subadults, 4 females and 3 males. The mean age at death for females is 47.2 years (SD = 17.7), for males 34.7 years (SD = 10.4).

TABLE 121: Age and sex distribution in the Lobor series

Age category	Subadult N[1]	%[2]	Female N	%	Male N	%	Total N	%
Birth -1	1	25.0					1	9.1
2- 5	1	25.0					1	9.1
6-10	0						0	
11-15	2	50.0					2	18.1
16-20			0		0		0	
21-25			1	25.0	1	33.3	2	18.2
26-30			0		0		0	
31-35			0		0		0	
36-40			0		1	33.3	1	9.1
41-45			0		1	33.4	1	9.1
46-50			1	25.0	0		1	9.1
51-55			1	25.0	0		1	9.1
56-60			0		0		0	
60+			1	25.0	0		1	9.1
Total	4	100.0	4	100.0	3	100.0	11	100.0

Mean age at death[3]   x = 47.25   x = 34.67
                        sd = 17.67   sd = 10.40

[1] N = number of individuals dying.
[2] % = % of individuals dying.
[3] Mean age at death is calculated using median values of each age category (for example, 23 for the age category 21-25), and 65 for the age category 60+.

TABLE 122: Frequency of alveolar bone disease in the Lobor series

Age category	Subadult A[1]/O[2]	%[3]	Female A/O	%	Male A/O	%
Young adult[4]			0/30	0.0	0/32	0.0
Old adult			14/32	43.7	3/60	5.0
Total	1/51	1.9	14/62	22.6	3/92	3.3

[1] A = number of tooth sockets with periodontal or periapical abscess, or antemortem tooth loss.
[2] O = number of tooth sockets observed.
[3] % = % of tooth sockets with periodontal or periapical abscess, or antemortem tooth loss.
[4] Young adult = individuals aged between 16 to 35 years; Old adult = individuals older than 36 years.

TABLE 123: Frequency of carious lesions in the Lobor series

Age category	Subadult A[1]/O[2]	%[3]	Female A/O	%	Male A/O	%
Young adult[4]			0/28	0.0	1/31	3.2
Old adult			4/17	23.5	4/59	6.8
Total	0/30	0.0	4/45	8.9	5/90	5.5

[1] A = number of teeth with carious lesions.
[2] O = number of teeth observed.
[3] % = % of teeth with carious lesions.
[4] Young adult = individuals aged between 16 to 35 years; Old adult = individuals older than 36 years.

The frequencies of alveolar bone disease are presented in Table 122. Alveolar bone disease is noted in one subadult tooth socket (1.9%). The overall frequency in adults is low (11.0% or 17/154). Females exhibit considerably higher total frequencies (22.6%) than males (3.3%). The difference is statistically significant ($\chi^2 = 9.35$; P < 0.01). As both sexes exhibit no alveolar bone disease in the young adult age category, but females in the old adult age category have significantly more alveolar bone disease than males (43.7% compared to 5.0%, $\chi^2 = 11.43$; P < 0.01), the difference in total frequencies may reflect the longer average female life-span in the series.

Total adult caries frequencies are also low - 8.9% in females, 5.5% in males, and 6.7% overall (Table 123). No lesions are noted in subadults. The modal category for severity of lesion in both sexes is grade 2. Of the 4 lesions recorded in females, 2 are located on the root, one is located interproximally, and one is located on the occlusal surface of the tooth. In males, 4 of the 5 recorded lesions are located interproximally, while one is located on the lingual surface of the tooth.

Enamel hypoplasia is recorded in 2 of the 4 recovered maxillary canines (in one female and one male), and in 2 of the 5 recovered mandibular canines (one subadult and one male).

One of the 2 recovered subadult frontals with intact orbits exhibits moderate, active cribra orbitalia. In adults, healed cribra orbitalia is observed in one of the 3 female frontals with preserved orbits.

Skeletal evidence for infectious disease is present in 2 of the 4 recovered subadults. One subadult, aged between 1-2 years, exhibits bilateral, moderately severe, healed periostitis on the medial shafts of the tibiae. The other subadult, aged between 12,5-13,5 years exhibits bilateral moderately severe, active periostitis on the medial shafts of the tibiae, as well as moderate, active periostitis on the right fibula.

There is one case of skeletal trauma in the series. An adult male, aged between 40-45 years, has an oval, shallow depression fracture on the right parietal bone. The lesion is 28 mm long and 11 mm wide with a slightly porous floor and well rounded margins. The fracture did not penetrate the inner table of the skull and there is no evidence of infection.

The same individual also has a well preserved tumor on the anterior side of the neck of the right femur (Figure 20). The surface of the tumor is irregular with a rounded, lumpy, cauliflower-like appearance. It's measurements are

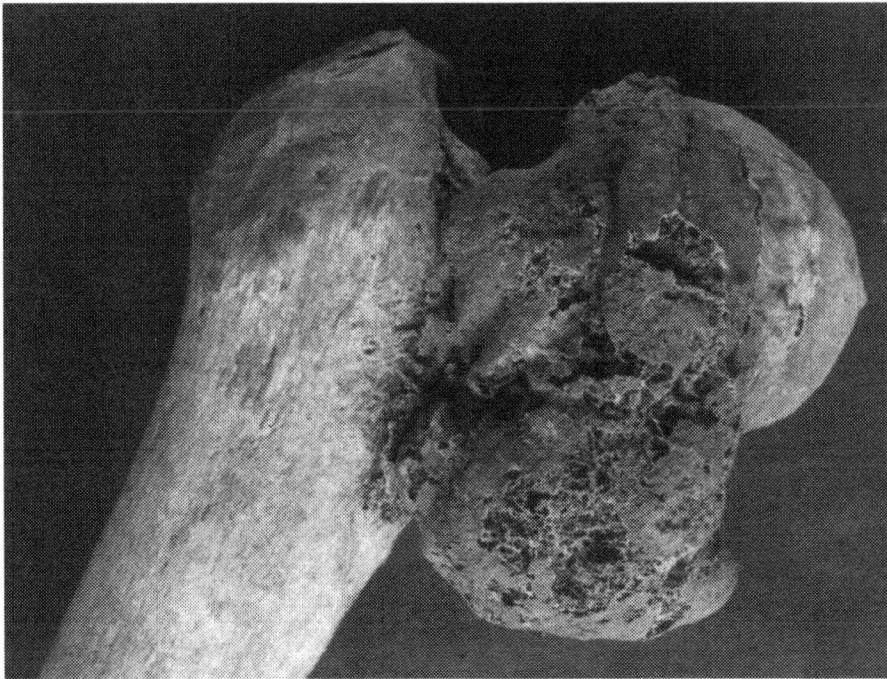

Figure 20. Tumor located on the anterior surface of the femoral neck
in an adult male from Lobor.

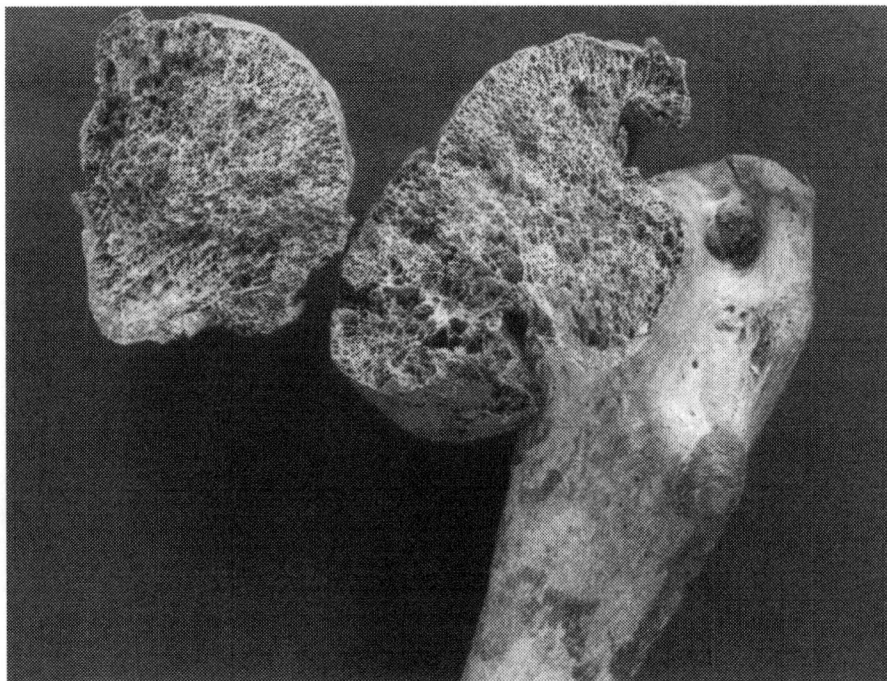

Figure 21. Cross-section of the tumor. Note dense trabecular structure
without a clear margin between the tumor and normal bone.

56 mm in the transverse direction, 89 mm in the perpendicular direction, 39 mm in the sagittal direction, and 160 mm in circumference. There is a clearly visible difference in color between normal bone tissue and the tumor. A cross-section of the tumor (Figure 21) shows a dense trabecular structure without a clear margin between the tumor and normal bone. A thin layer of compact bone covers the tumor. The head of the femur, and the right acetabulum show slight secondary degenerative change (Figure 22). Analysis of the tumor by computerized

tomography allows additional insight into the structure of the tumor. (Figure 23). The base of the tumor on the medial portion of the femoral neck is clearly seen, as is the structure of normal surrounding bone. The tumor has an internal structure of cancellous bone interspersed with compact bone. Morphologically, the observed changes are characteristic for solitary osteochondroma. Osteochondroma, one of the most common benign bone tumors recorded in skeletal series, begins as a rounded outgrowth on the periosteal surface caused by faulty

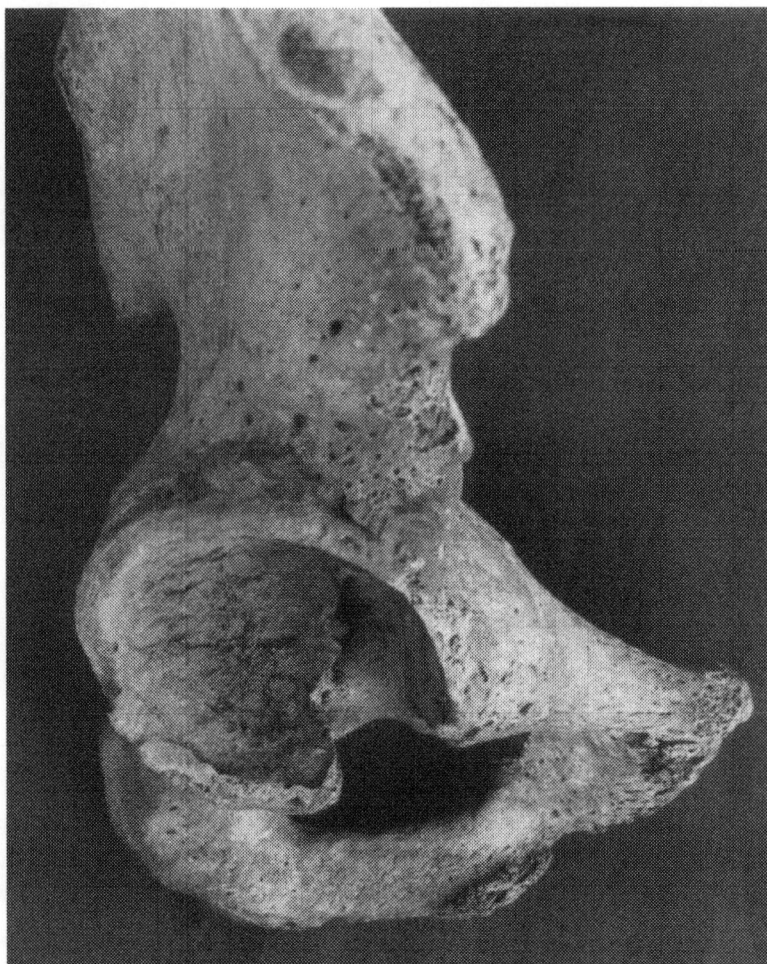

Figure 22. Right innominate of same individual. Note slight secondary degenerative change on acetabulum.

differentiation of the inner layer of the periosteum into cartilage. The final shape is determined by mechanical stresses in the affected area (Ortner and Putschar, 1981).

Osteoarthritis on the major joints is recorded in 2 female shoulders, one female elbow, and one female knee.

The total vertebral osteoarthritis frequency for females is 22.8% (Table 124). Greatest involvement is in the lumbar region of the spine. Males exhibit a lower total vertebral osteoarthritis frequency (12.7%) with, also, greatest involvement in the lumbar segment of the spine. The difference in male and females vertebral osteoarthritis frequencies is not statistically significant.

Males exhibit higher total frequencies of Schmorl's depressions in both the thoracic and lumbar spine (Table 125). The total frequency of Schmorl's defects in females is 11.9%, (7/59 vertebrae), compared to 27.4% (14/51) in males. The difference is not, however, statistically significant.

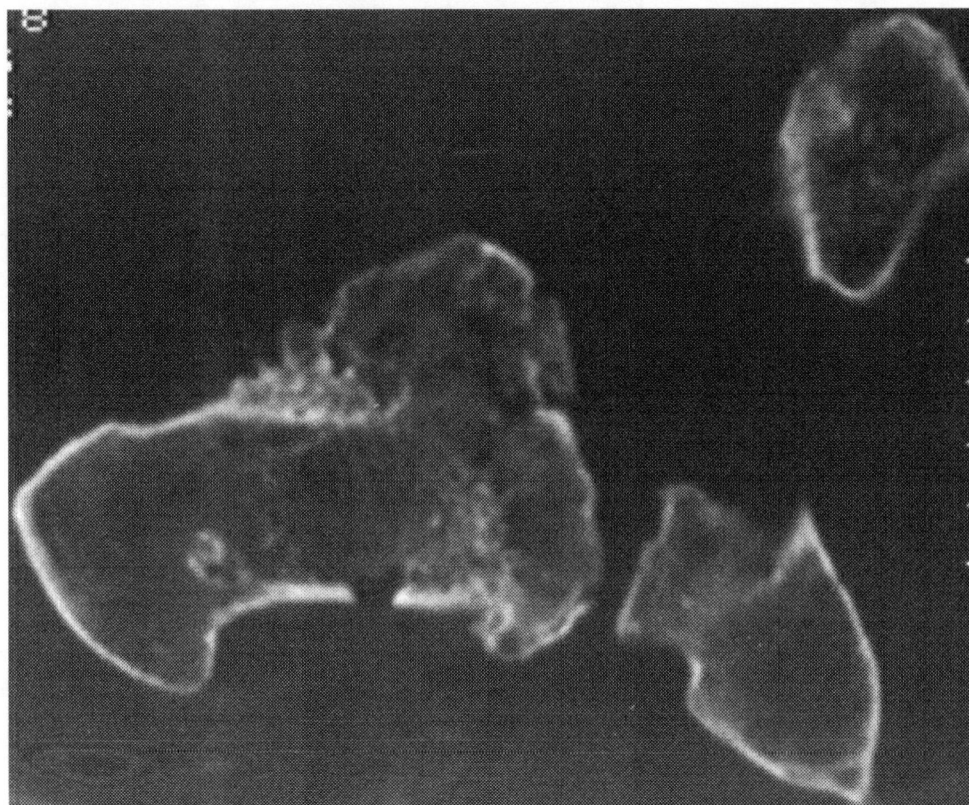

Figure 23. CAT-scan of the tumor showing internal structure and base of the tumor.

TABLE 124: Frequency of occurrence of vertebral osteoarthritis in the Lobor series

	Cervical A^1/O^2	%	Thoracic A/O	%	Lumbar A/O	%	Total A/O	%
Female								
Young adult[3]	0/7	0.0	0/12	0.0	0/5	0.0	0/24	0.0
Old adult	0/13	0.0	5/27	18.5	13/15	86.7	18/55	32.7
Total	0/20	0.0	5/39	12.8	13/20	65.0	18/79	22.8
Male								
Young adult	0/7	0.0	0/12	0.0	0/5	0.0	0/24	0.0
Old adult	1/13	7.7	5/24	20.8	3/10	30.0	9/47	19.1
Total	1/20	5.0	5/36	13.9	3/15	20.0	9/71	12.7

[1] A = number of vertebrae affected with osteoarthritis or osteophytosis.
[2] O = number of vertebrae observed.
[3] Young adult = individuals aged between 16 to 35 years; Old adult = individuals older than 36 years.

TABLE 125: Frequency of occurrence of Schmorl's depressions in the Lobor series

	Thoracic A^1/O^2	%	Lumbar A/O	%	Total A/O	%
Female						
Young adult[3]	0/12	0.0	0/5	0.0	0/17	0.0
Old adult	4/27	14.8	3/15	20.0	7/42	16.7
Total	4/39	10.2	3/20	15.0	7/59	11.9
Male						
Young adult	3/12	25.0	0/5	0.0	3/17	17.6
Old adult	6/24	25.0	5/10	50.0	11/34	32.3
Total	9/36	25.0	5/15	33.3	14/51	27.4

[1] A = number of vertebrae with Schmorl's depressions.
[2] O = number of vertebrae observed.
[3] Young adult = individuals aged between 16 to 35 years; Old adult = individuals older than 36 years.

5.4. THE ŠČITARJEVO SKELETAL SERIES

This is another small series recovered from Ščitarjevo, approximately 12 km south-east of Zagreb. In archaeological literature Ščitarjevo is primarily known as *Andautonia*, an important Roman urban center. Systematic excavation of the site from 1994 to 1999 revealed the presence of 12 Late Medieval graves located in the ruins of antique architecture (Pintarić, 2000). Based on associated material remains the graves are dated from the 11th to 13th century.

The age and sex distribution of the series is presented in Table 126. The series contains only subadults (10/13) and females (3/13). Well preserved subadult remains dominate. The average age at death for adult females is 44.7 years (SD = 10.4).

The frequencies of alveolar bone disease are presented in Table 127. Alveolar bone disease is present in 2 subadult teeth sockets (1.4%). In adult females the frequency is higher (39.3%) with, typically, frequencies much higher in the old adult age category.

Adult caries frequencies are, however, similar in the young adult and old adult categories (19.3% and 21.4% respectively), with a moderately high frequency (20.0%) overall (Table 128). Subadults exhibit only 2 lesions, both located interproximally. The modal category for severity of lesion in females is grade 2. All of the 9 recorded carious lesions in adults are located inter-proximally.

Enamel hypoplasia is present in 2/5 subadult maxillary central incisors, 1/4 subadult maxillary canines, and 1/4 subadult mandibular canines. In females, enamel hypoplasia is recorded in 1/1 recovered maxillary central incisors. All of the recorded defects are pronounced and very deep.

Cribra orbitalia frequencies are presented in Table 129. No lesions are observed in females. The total frequency in subadults is high (70.0%), with the highest frequencies recorded between 1-9.9 years.

There is considerable skeletal evidence for infectious disease in the series. In subadults, 6/10 individuals exhibit at least one case of periostitis. Periostitis is recorded on the endocranial surfaces of the parietals and frontal bone (in 2 subadults), on the tibia (in 3 subadults), on the fibula (in 2 subadults), on the humerus (in one subadult), and on the femur (in one subadult). One female exhibits bilateral periostitis on the fibulae.

Skeletal evidence for trauma is seen in subadults and adults. One subadult exhibits a well healed fracture of the sternal end of the 4. left rib. In the adult sample, one female exhibits a well healed fracture of the right distal radius with no angulation.

Mild osteoarthritis is present in the right hip of one female.

The total frequency of vertebral osteoarthritis is relatively high (33.8% or 23/68), probably reflecting the slightly higher average age of death of females in the series. Vertebral osteoarthritis is noted in 2/19 cervical vertebrae, 12/36 thoracic, and 9/13 lumbar vertebrae.

Schmorl's depressions are noted in 5/48 (10.4%) recovered adult thoracic and lumbar vertebra.

TABLE 126: Age and sex distribution in the Sčitarjevo series

Age category	Subadult N[1]	%[2]	Female N	%	Male N	%	Total N	%
Birth -1	3	30.0					3	23.1
2- 5	1	10.0					1	7.7
6-10	2	20.0					2	15.4
11-15	4	40.0					4	30.7
16-20			0		0		0	
21-25			0		0		0	
26-30			0		0		0	
31-35			1	33.3	0		1	7.7
36-40			0		0		0	
41-45			0		0		0	
46-50			1	33.3	0		1	7.7
51-55			1	33.3	0		1	7.7
56-60			0		0		0	
60+			0		0		0	
Total	10	100.0	3	100.0	0		13	100.0

Mean age at death[3]   x = 44.67
                          sd = 10.40

[1] N = number of individuals dying.

[2] % = % of individuals dying.

[3] Mean age at death is calculated using median values of each age category (for example, 23 for the age category 21-25), and 65 for the age category 60+.

TABLE 127: Frequency of alveolar bone disease in the Sčitarjevo series

Age category	Subadult A[1]/O[2]	%[3]	Female A/O	%	Male A/O	%
Young adult[4]			0/32	0.0	0/0	0.0
Old adult			33/52	63.5	0/0	0.0
Total	2/139	1.4	33/84	39.3	0/0	0.0

[1] A = number of tooth sockets with periodontal or periapical abscess, or antemortem tooth loss.

[2] O = number of tooth sockets observed.

[3] % = % of tooth sockets with periodontal or periapical abscess, or antemortem tooth loss.

[4] Young adult = individuals aged between 16 to 35 years; Old adult = individuals older than 36 years.

TABLE 128: Frequency of carious lesions in the Sčitarjevo series

Age category	Subadult A[1]/O[2]	%[3]	Female A/O	%	Male A/O	%
Young adult[4]			6/31	19.3	0/0	0.0
Old adult			3/14	21.4	0/0	0.0
Total	2/107	1.9	9/45	20.0	0/0	0.0

[1] A = number of teeth with carious lesions.

[2] O = number of teeth observed.

[3] % = % of teeth with carious lesions.

[4] Young adult = individuals aged between 16 to 35 years; Old adult = individuals older than 36 years.

TABLE 129: Frequency of occurrence of cribra orbitalia in the Sčitarjevo series

Age/sex	Cribra orbitalia O[1]	A1[2]	%	Active lesions A2[3]	% of A1
0 - 0.9	3	2	66.7	1	50.0
1 - 3.9	1	1	100.0	1	100.0
4 - 9.9	2	2	100.0	1	50.0
10 - 14.9	4	2	50.0	0	0.0
All subadults	10	7	70.0	3	42.9
Adult females	3	0	0.0	0	0.0
Adult males	0	0	0.0	0	0.0
All adults	3	0	0.0	0	0.0

[1] O = number of frontal bones observed.

[2] A1 = number of frontal bones in which at least one orbit shows evidence of cribra orbitalia.

[3] A2 = number of frontal bones in which cribra orbitalia is active at time of death.

5.5. THE ĐELEKOVEC SKELETAL SERIES

The Late medieval cemetery in Đelekovec near Koprivnica in north-western Croatia was discovered in 1975. The site was systematically excavated from 1975 to 1979. A total of 137 graves from two burial phases was uncovered. The first phase is dated to the late Bijelo Brdo culture, the second to

TABLE 130: Age and sex distribution in the Đelekovec series

Age category	Subadult N[1]	%[2]	Female N	%	Male N	%	Total N	%
Birth -1	0						0	
2- 5	0						0	
6-10	1	50.0					1	5.3
11-15	1	50.0					1	5.3
16-20			0		0		0	
21-25			1	14.3	1	10.0	2	10.5
26-30			0		0		0	
31-35			3	42.8	3	30.0	6	31.6
36-40			2	28.6	2	20.0	4	21.0
41-45			1	14.3	1	10.0	2	10.5
46-50			0		1	10.0	1	5.3
51-55			0		2	20.0	2	10.5
56-60			0		0		0	
60+			0		0		0	
Total	2	100.0	7	100.0	10	100.0	19	100.0

Mean age at death[3]   x = 34.42   x = 39.50
                        sd = 6.26   sd = 9.73

[1] N = number of individuals dying.
[2] % = % of individuals dying.
[3] Mean age at death is calculated using median values of each age category (for example, 23 for the age category 21-25), and 65 for the age category 60+.

years shorter than males. The average age at death for adult females is 34.4 years (SD = 6.3), for adult males 39.5 years (SD = 9.7).

Dental disease frequencies are summarized in Tables 131 and 132. Alveolar bone disease is present in one subadult tooth socket (1/20 or 5.0%). In adults, total alveolar bone disease frequencies are higher in females (15.6%) than in males (9.3%) with a relatively low frequency (12.3%) overall. The sex difference is not significant and is related to differences in the old adult age category where old females exhibit considerably higher frequencies of alveolar bone disease (32.9%) than old males (13.6%). This difference is statistically significant (χ^2 = 5.5, P < 0.02).

Caries frequencies (Table 132) are, again, low in subadults (11.1%), and adults (11.7%), with males exhibiting slightly higher total frequencies than females (15.7% compared to 6.7%). This difference is marginally not significant (χ^2 = 3.48, P < 0.07). The modal category for severity of lesion

the period from the 14th-16th century (Šmalcelj, 1986). Most of the graves from the first burial phase were destroyed by later building activities and inhumations from the second burial phase. The material reported on in this analysis is dated to the Late medieval period, more specifically to the period from the 11th to the 13th century (Kolar, 1976). As in Đakovo, the Mongol invasion in 1242 marks the end of the first burial phase.

The series is represented by 19 individuals. Although Đelekovec is a typical Late medieval cemetery with single primary inhumations, the assemblage for analysis includes only skulls.

The age and sex distribution of the series is presented in Table 130. Subadults are poorly represented in the series. They are completely absent in the youngest (0-1, and 2-5 years) age categories, and represented by only two individuals in the remaining subadult age categories. Subadults comprise only 10.5% of the total sample.

Peak mortality for both males and females is between 31-35 years (42.8% of all adult females, and 30.0% of all males died during this interval). Females, however, appear to be at greater stress in the younger age categories. Only 14.3% of females live longer than 41 years, compared to 40.0% of males. This difference in mortality distributions is reflected in different mean ages at death. Females, on average, live 5.1

TABLE 131: Frequency of alveolar bone disease in the Đelekovec series

Age category	Subadult A[1]/O[2]	%[3]	Female A/O	%	Male A/O	%
Young adult[4]			3/107	2.8	4/94	4.2
Old adult			26/79	32.9	15/110	13.6
Total	1/20	5.0	29/186	15.6	19/204	9.3

[1] A = number of tooth sockets with periodontal or periapical abscess, or antemortem tooth loss.
[2] O = number of tooth sockets observed.
[3] % = % of tooth sockets with periodontal or periapical abscess, or antemortem tooth loss.
[4] Young adult = individuals aged between 16 to 35 years; Old adult = individuals older than 36 years.

TABLE 132: Frequency of carious lesions in the Đelekovec series

Age category	Subadult A[1]/O[2]	%[3]	Female A/O	%	Male A/O	%
Young adult[4]			2/89	2.2	5/82	6.1
Old adult			6/31	19.3	19/71	26.8
Total	2/18	11.1	8/120	6.7	24/153	15.7

[1] A = number of teeth with carious lesions.
[2] O = number of teeth observed.
[3] % = % of teeth with carious lesions.
[4] Young adult = individuals aged between 16 to 35 years; Old adult = individuals older than 36 years.

in subadults and adults is grade 2. The two carious lesions recorded in subadults are located interproximally. In females carious lesions are located interproximally in 6/8 cases, and on the root of the tooth in 2/8 cases. In males, 20/24 lesions are located interproximally, 2/24 are located occlusally, and 2/24 are located on the root of the tooth.

Enamel hypoplasia is recorded in 3/5 central maxillary incisors, 5/9 maxillary canines and 8/12 mandibular canines. Subadults are poorly represented with only 3 teeth, an incisor and a maxillary and mandibular canine available for analysis. The incisor and mandibular canine have deep hypoplastic defects. In adults, males and females exhibit similarly high frequencies. In females hypoplastic defects are noted on 1/2 incisors, 2/3 maxillary, and 2/6 mandibular canines. In males, defects are recorded on 1/2 incisors, 3/5 maxillary, and 5/5 mandibular canines.

Active, moderately severe cribra orbitalia is present in both subadults with preserved orbits. In the adult sample, healing cribra orbitalia lesions are noted in 2/6 female and 4/10 male frontals.

TABLE 133: Age and sex distribution in the Stenjevac series

Age category	Subadult N[1]	%[2]	Female N	%	Male N	%	Total N	%
Birth -1	2	7.4					2	2.4
2- 5	8	29.6					8	9.5
6-10	10	37.1					10	11.9
11-15	7	25.9					7	8.3
16-20			2	7.1	2	6.9	4	4.8
21-25			5	17.9	4	13.8	9	10.7
26-30			5	17.9	2	6.9	7	8.3
31-35			8	28.6	6	20.8	14	16.7
36-40			2	7.1	5	17.3	7	8.3
41-45			2	7.1	7	24.1	9	10.7
46-50			0		1	3.4	1	1.2
51-55			3	10.7	0		3	3.6
56-60			0		1	3.4	1	1.2
60+			1	3.6	1	3.4	2	2.4
Total	27	100.0	28	100.0	29	100.0	84	100.0

Mean age at death[3]   x = 33.61   x = 36.00
                      sd = 11.45   sd = 10.92

[1] N = number of individuals dying.
[2] % = % of individuals dying.
[3] Mean age at death is calculated using median values of each age category (for example, 23 for the age category 21-25), and 65 for the age category 60+.

Skeletal evidence for infectious disease is noted in one subadult. This individual, aged between 7-9 years, exhibits slight, healed endocranial periostitis on the occipital bone.

Cranial trauma is present in one male and one female. Both fractures are healed depression fractures with smooth floors and rounded margins on the occipital bone. Neither penetrated the inner table of the skull and neither shows evidence of infection.

As this series contains only skulls, data for physical stress could not be gathered.

5.6. THE STENJEVAC SKELETAL SERIES

The Stenjevac series is the largest collection from the Late medieval period. The site, located on the western outskirts of Zagreb, had previously been recognized as an important Antique site. At one point it was even considered as the possible location of *Andautonia* until the site was conclusively located in Ščitarjevo. Excavations carried out in 1982 revealed the presence of a large Late medieval cemetery located in the orchard of the Parish church of the "Assumption of the Virgin" (Gregl, 1982). Systematic excavations carried out from 1983 to 1993 revealed the presence of 161 graves aligned in, more or less, parallel rows. Artifacts recovered from the site date the use of the cemetery to between the 10th to 12th century (Simoni, 1988).

TABLE 134: Frequency of alveolar bone disease in the Stenjevac series

Age category	Subadult A[1]/O[2]	%[3]	Female A/O	%	Male A/O	%
Young adult[4]			34/270	12.6	11/152	7.2
Old adult			28/111	25.2	56/239	23.4
Total	1/358	0.3	62/381	16.3	67/391	17.1

[1] A = number of tooth sockets with periodontal or periapical abscess, or antemortem tooth loss.
[2] O = number of tooth sockets observed.
[3] % = % of tooth sockets with periodontal or periapical abscess, or antemortem tooth loss.
[4] Young adult = individuals aged between 16 to 35 years; Old adult = individuals older than 36 years.

TABLE 135: Frequency of carious lesions in the Stenjevac series

Age category	Subadult A[1]/O[2]	%[3]	Female A/O	%	Male A/O	%
Young adult[4]			12/199	6.0	19/126	15.1
Old adult			13/70	18.6	24/121	19.8
Total	10/261	3.8	25/269	9.3	43/247	17.4

[1] A = number of teeth with carious lesions.
[2] O = number of teeth observed.
[3] % = % of teeth with carious lesions.
[4] Young adult = individuals aged between 16 to 35 years; Old adult = individuals older than 36 years.

TABLE 136: Hypoplasia frequencies by individual in the Stenjevac series

Tooth	N[1]	NwLEH	%wLEH
Maxillary I1[2]	24	16	66.7
Maxillary C	21	11	52.4
Mandibular C	32	19	59.4

[1] N = number of teeth observed; NwLEH = number of teeth with one or more LEH; %wLEH = % of N with one or more LEH.

[2] I = incisor; C = canine.

The age and sex distribution of the series is presented in Table 133. The total sample for analysis consists of 84 well preserved skeletons. Subadults comprise 32.1% of the total sample but are, once again, clearly underrepresented in the youngest (birth-1 year) age category (only 2 individuals or 2.4% of the total series). Subadult mortality in the series is highest from 6-10 years (37.1% of the subadult sample).

Males and females are evenly represented in the adult sample (29 and 28 individuals respectively). The average age at death of adults over 15 years is 33.6 years for females, and 36.0 years for males. This relatively small difference (2.4 years) in average life-spans is reflected in similar mortality profiles. The highest mortality rates for both sexes are recorded from 31 to 35 years (28.6% of the female sample, and 20.8% of the male).

Frequencies of alveolar bone disease are summarized in Table 134. Alveolar bone disease is present in only one subadult tooth socket (0.3%). In adults the overall frequency is 16.7% (129/772) with an even total distribution between males and females (17.1% in males, compared to 16.3% in females). Similarities in the frequencies of alveolar bone disease are present in both the young adult and old adult age categories.

This is not true, however, for the distribution of carious lesions in the series (Table 135). Males exhibit a considerably higher total frequency than females (17.4% compared to 9.3%). This difference is statistically significant ($\chi^2 = 5.1$, P< .03). The difference appears to be related to differences in the young adult age category where males exhibit a significantly higher frequency of carious lesions than females (15.1% compared to 6.0%, $\chi^2 = 5.0$, P< .03). Caries frequencies are, once again, very low in subadults (3.8%).

The modal category for severity of lesion is grade 2 for females, and grade 1 for males. The distribution of carious lesions in females is similar to the distribution recorded in numerous other series. Lesions are most frequently located interproximally (in 10/25 or 40.0% of all carious lesions in females), followed by occlusal (9/25 or 36%), root (5/25 or 20.0%), and buccal (1/25 or 4.0%) lesions. In males carious lesions are most frequently recorded on the root of the tooth (18/43 or 41.9%), followed by occlusal (13/43 or 30.2%), interproximal (10/43 or 23.2%), and buccal (2/43 or 4.6%) lesions. In subadults, 7/10 recorded lesions are located interproximally, 2/10 are located on the root of the tooth, and one is located on the buccal surface.

Enamel hypoplasia frequencies are high in the series, 46/77 (59.7%) of the analyzed teeth exhibit hypoplastic defects. Hypoplasias are most frequent in the maxillary central incisors - 66.7%, followed by mandibular canines - 59.4% and maxillary canines - 52.4% (Table 136). Of the 242 analyzed teeth, 121 (50.0%) exhibit evidence of hypoplasia.

Subadults are poorly represented in the series. The frequencies of hypoplastic defects are, however, very high in the assemblage (Table 137). Of the 17 subadult teeth available for analysis, 15 (88%) exhibit hypoplastic defects. The highest

TABLE 137: Hypoplasia frequencies in the Stenjevac series for subadults and adults

Tooth	Subadults NwN[1]	Subadults %wLEH[2]	All adults Nw/N	All adults %wLEH	Females Nw/N	Females %wLEH	Males Nw/N	Males %wLEH
Maxillary I1[3]	6/7	85.7	10/17	58.8	4/8	50.0	6/9	66.7
Maxillary C	3/3	100.0	8/18	44.4	2/8	25.0	6/10	60.0
Mandibular C	6/7	85.7	13/25	52.0	5/12	41.7	8/13	61.5

[1] Nw = number of individuals with one or more LEH; N = number of individuals observed.

[2] %wLEH = % of N with one or more LEH.

[3] I = incisors; C = canines.

TABLE 138: Mean number of hypoplasias in incisors and canines in the Stenjevac series

Tooth	Subadults Mean	Subadults N	Subadults S.D.	All adults Mean	All adults N	All adults S.D.	Females Mean	Females N	Females S.D.	Males Mean	Males N	Males S.D.
Maxillary I1[1]	1.29	7	0.75	1.00	17	0.93	0.87	8	0.99	1.11	9	0.93
Maxillary C	1.33	3	0.57	0.61	18	0.78	0.37	8	0.74	0.80	10	0.79
Mandibular C	1.29	7	0.76	0.84	25	0.94	0.50	12	0.67	1.15	13	0.95

[1] I = incisors; C = canines.

65

TABLE 139: Frequency of occurrence of cribra orbitalia in
the Stenjevac series

Age/sex	Cribra orbitalia			Active lesions	
	O[1]	A1[2]	%	A2[3]	% of A1
0 - 0.9	2	1	50.0	1	100.0
1 - 3.9	6	3	50.0	2	66.7
4 - 9.9	11	9	81.8	7	77.8
10 - 14.9	1	1	100.0	0	0.0
All subadults	20	14	70.0	10	71.4
Adult females	12	4	33.3	0	0.0
Adult males	14	4	28.6	0	0.0
All adults	26	8	30.8	0	0.0

[1] O = number of frontal bones observed.

[2] A1 = number of frontal bones in which at least one orbit shows evidence of cribra orbitalia.

[3] A2 = number of frontal bones in which cribra orbitalia is active at time of death.

frequency is recorded in maxillary canines where all three recovered teeth exhibit deep hypoplastic defects. Hypoplasia frequencies are also high in adults. Slightly more than half (31/60 or 51.7%) of the analyzed teeth exhibit hypoplastic lines. The highest frequency in adults is recorded in maxillary central incisors (58.8%).

A breakdown of the adult sample by sex shows that adult males exhibit higher frequencies than females in all three tooth categories analyzed. The total frequency of hypoplastic defects in male teeth (20/32 or 62.5%) is almost twice as high as that recorded in females (11/28 or 39.3%). The difference is not, however, statistically significant.

Males also exhibit a higher mean number of hypoplasias per tooth (Table 138) than females. Two teeth categories in males (maxillary central incisors, and mandibular canines) exhibit a mean number of defects per tooth higher than 1.00. Such high values are not recorded in any of the female teeth categories. Even higher values are recorded in subadult teeth. In all three tooth categories analyzed the mean number of defects per tooth in subadults is greater than 1.00.

Cribra orbitalia frequencies are summarized in Table 139. In the Stenjevac series the expression of this condition ranges from slight pitting to severe sievelike lesions with considerable diplotic expansion (Figure 24).

Cribra orbitalia is observed in 22 of the 46 crania (47.8%) with intact orbits. The overall subadult frequency is 70.0% with the majority of lesions (10/14 or 71.4%) active at time of death. In adults the lesion has a frequency of 30.8% with all of the lesions exhibiting some degree of healing. No significant sex differences in healing lesion frequencies are noted.

Skeletal evidence for infectious disease is present in subadults and adults. Periostitis frequencies are high in subadults. More than half (15/27 or 55.5%) of the subadults in the sample exhibit at least one case of periostitis. Periostitis is recorded on the endocranial surfaces of the parietals and frontal bone in 2 individuals (2/23 subadults with preserved craniums), on the clavicle in one individual (1/11 subadults with preserved clavicles), humerus in one individual (1/19), radius in one individual (1/12), femur in one individual (1/19), tibia in 14 individuals (14/17), and fibula in 3 individuals (3/11).

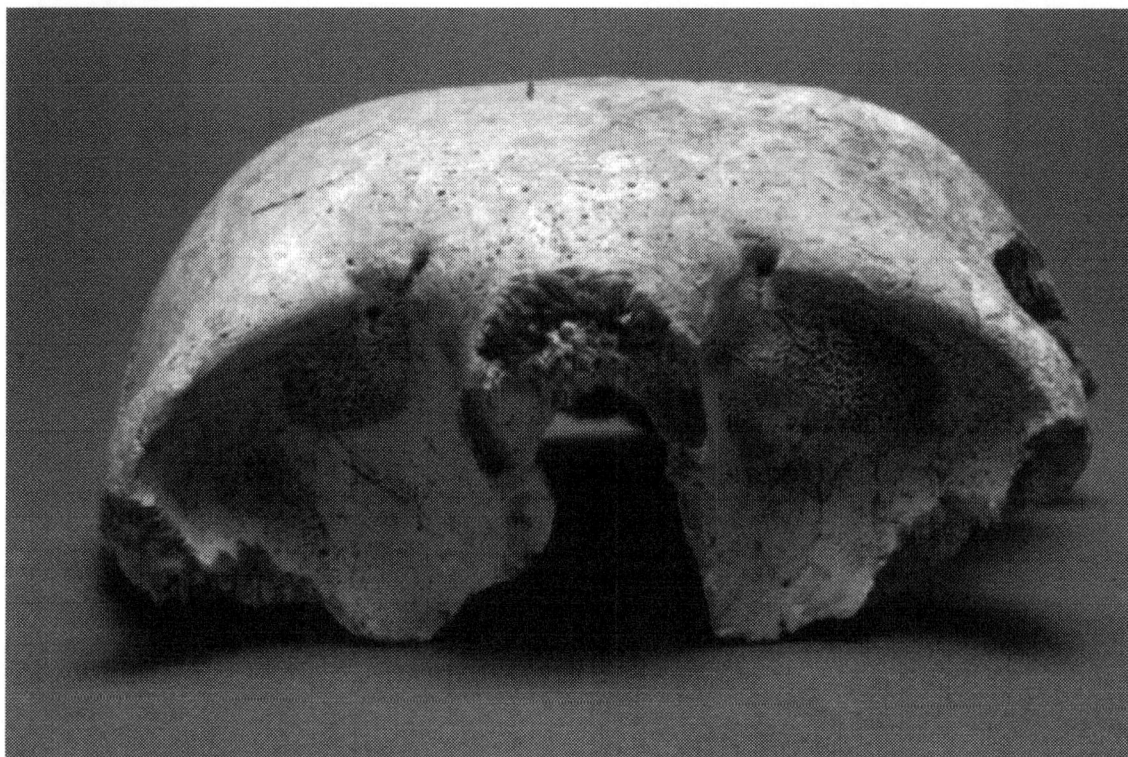

Figure 24. Severe, active cribra orbitalia in a subadult from Stenjevac.

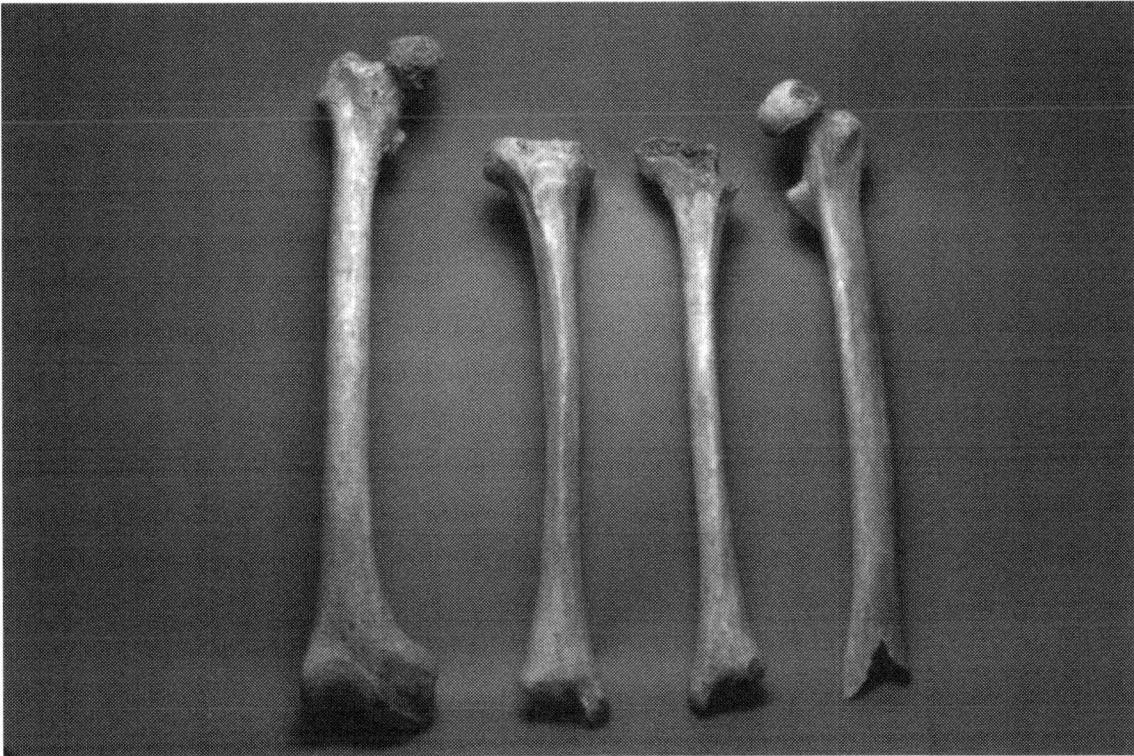

Figure 25. Probable case of postparalytic deformity in the left leg of an adult female from Stenjevac.

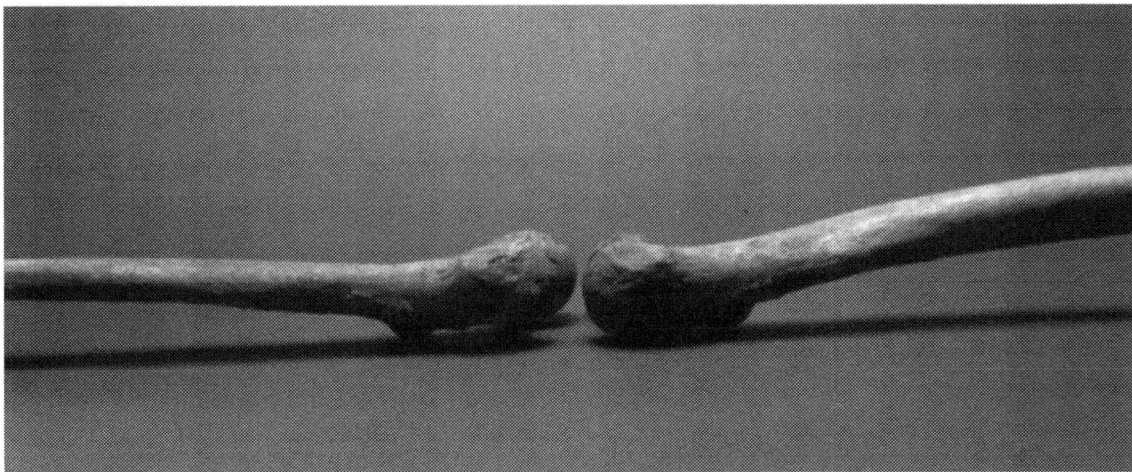

Figure 26. Detailed view of proximal femurs of the same individual. Note marked differences
in subtrochanteric and midshaft diameters.

In adults, skeletal evidence for infectious disease is seen in 4/28 (14.3%) females, and in 11/29 (37.9%) males. In females periostitis is recorded on the tibia in 4 individuals (4/22 females with recovered tibias), and on the fibula in one individual (1/16). In males, periostitis is recorded on the endocranial surface of the frontal and right parietal bone (healed and mild in expression) in a 16-20 year old male, on the femur in one individual (1/26), on the tibia in 11 individuals (11/25), and on the fibula in 4 individuals (4/18).

Skeletal evidence for healed fractures is present only in adults. The fractures are recorded in the cranium and postcranium. Cranial fractures are recorded in 2 males (2/14 males with preserved crania), and one female (1/13). All three fractures are well healed depression fractures located on the frontal

bone. All have rounded margins and smooth floors. None penetrated the inner table of the skull and none show evidence of infection. Postcranial fractures are noted on the clavicle, in 1/21 (4.8%) males with preserved clavicles, humerus, in 1/25 (4.0%) males with preserved humerii, radius, in 1/21 (4.8%) females with preserved radii and 4/23 (17.4%) males, and ulna, in 1/23 (4.3%) females, and 4/23 (17.4%) males.

As in the Privlaka series there is one possible case of postparalytic deformity. The case is recorded in a 25-30 years old female recovered from grave number 138. Apart from the female, the grave contained the remains of a neonatal subadult, buried by the right side of the female. The deformity is located in the left leg. The left femur, tibia and fibula are lighter, and considerably more gracile than the ones on the

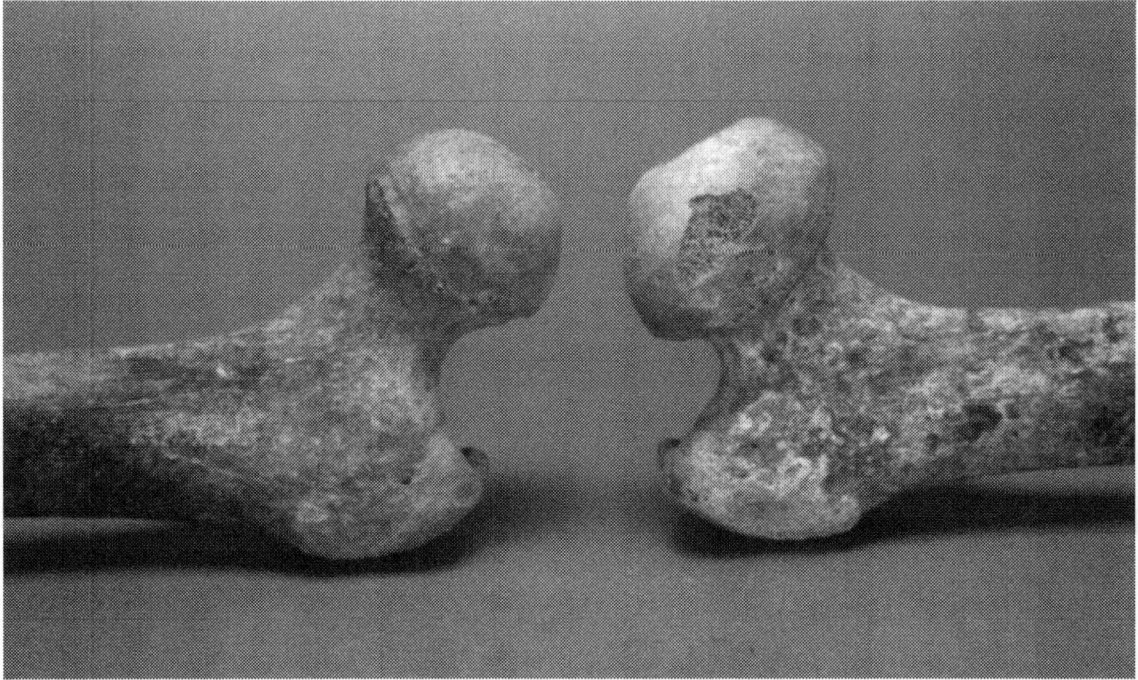

Figure 27. Possible case of slipped femoral capital epiphysis in the right femur of an adult female from Stenjevac.
Note flattened femoral head and the considerably shorter and thicker neck of the right femur.

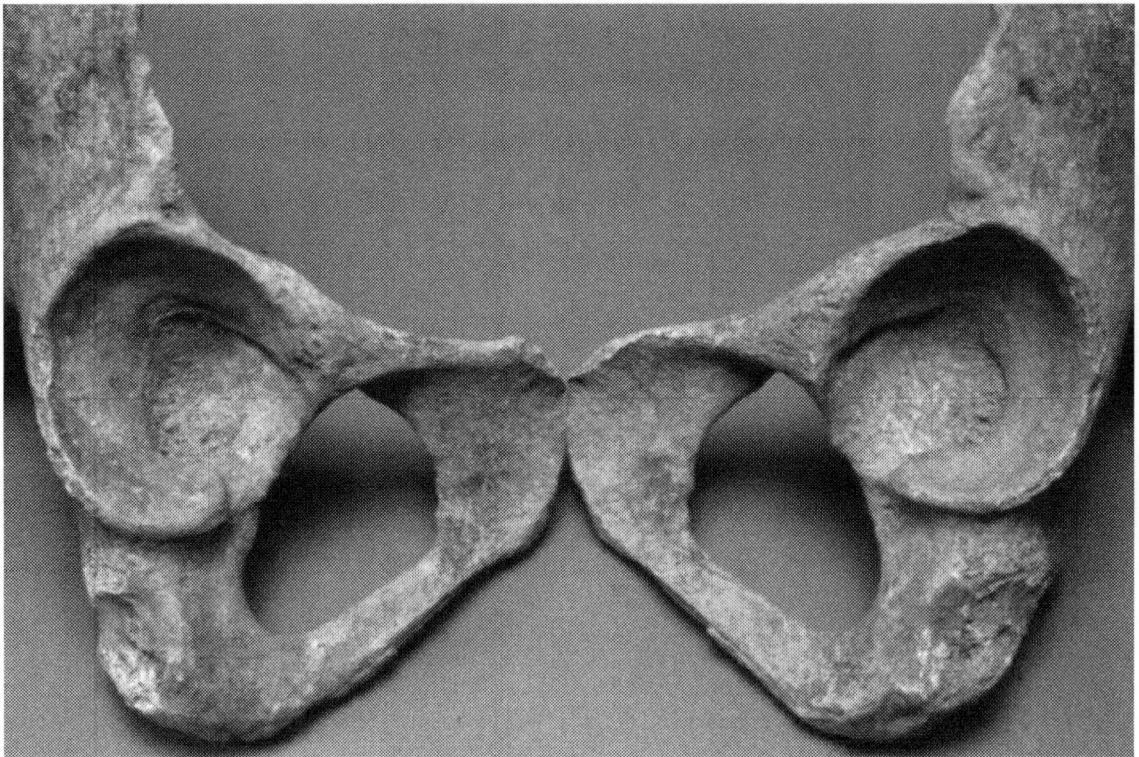

Figure 28. Comparison of innominates from the same individual.
The right acetabulum is shallower and slightly elongated.

right side (Figure 25). The bones from the left side are slightly damaged preventing accurate length measurements, but there appear to be no significant differences in the lengths of the bones. The primary differences are present in the sagittal diameters. The sagittal diameters in the subtrochanteric regions of the femurs are 24 mm on the right, and 18 mm on the left (Figure 26). The sagittal diameter at midshaft is 28.5 mm on the right, and 17.5 mm on the left femur. This is slightly compensated by a somewhat larger transverse midshaft diameter on the left side (27.5 mm compared to 25 mm on the right). The circumference at the midshaft of the right femur is 83 mm, compared to 74 mm on the left. The same pattern is observed on the tibia (maximum diameter at nutritium foramen on right side is 33.5 mm, on left 20 mm, circumference at nutritium foramen is 89 mm on right compared to 57.5 mm on left side), and on the fibula (maximum diameter on right side is 17 mm, compared to 15 mm on left side). The left innominate is not preserved. The observed changes are consistent with some type of post-adolescent neuromuscular paralysis.

A possible case of slipped femoral capital epiphysis is present in the right femur of a young adult female. This individual, aged between 17-20 years, exhibits a flattened femoral head, much greater in diameter than the left, with a poorly defined fovea capitis (Figure 27). The maximum length of the right femur is 12 mm shorter than that of the left (420 mm compared to 432 mm), but this is misleading due to the inferior displacement of the right femoral head. The right diaphysis shows a slight degree of anteroposterior flattening (sagittal diameter on right side is 23 mm, on left 25 mm, circumference at midshaft is 75 mm on right side, 80 mm on left), which may have been caused by the abnormal gait induced by the defective femoral head. The right femoral head is displaced inferiorly. It's maximum diameter is 47 mm, compared to 42 mm on the left side. The right femoral neck is considerably shorter and thicker than the left. There is no porosity on either the right femoral head or acetabulum. The right acetabulum does, however, appear to be slightly shallower, and more elongated, than the left (Figure 28).

Enthesophytes are recorded mostly in males and are present in one individual on the left humerus, in one individual on the right femurs, in 5 individuals on the right fibulae, and in 3 individuals on the calcaneus. In females enthesophytes are recorded in 8 individuals, in 2 cases on the distal fibula, and in 6 on the calcaneus.

Spondylolysis is present in the fifth lumbar vertebra of one male (in 1/21 or 4.8% of males with complete lumbar spines). No cases are noted in the female sample.

Osteoarthritis frequencies in the series are summarized in Table 140. Of the four major joints in the skeleton, osteoarthritis is in both sexes most frequently recorded in the knee. In females this is followed by the shoulder, elbow and hip, and in males by the elbow, shoulder and hip. Osteoarthritis frequencies are similar between males and females and more common in the old adult than the young adult age group.

The overall frequency of vertebral osteoarthritis in the series is 16.5% (125/756). The different regions of the spine show similar frequencies of osteoarthritis (Table 141). Greatest involvement occurs in the lumbar region (39/208 or 18.7%), followed by the cervical (18/150 or 18.0%) and thoracic (59/398 or 14.8%) regions. No sex differences are present in the total, and young adult age categories, but females older than 36 years exhibit significantly higher total frequencies of vertebral osteoarthritis than males (50.6% compared to 26.0%, $\chi^2 = 6.44$; P < .02). This, statistically significant, difference appears to be primarily related to higher female frequencies of vertebral osteoarthritis in the thoracic spine (20.7% compared to 9.5%), a difference which is also statistically significant ($\chi^2 = 6.58$; P < .02).

The frequencies of Schmorl's depressions in the series are summarized in Table 142. The overall frequency of Schmorl's depressions in the sample is 20.0% (121/606). Frequencies of Schmorl's depressions in the thoracic and lumbar spine

TABLE 140: Frequency of occurrence of osteoarthritis at major joints in the Stenjevac series

	Shoulder		Elbow		Hip		Knee	
	A[1]/O[2]	%	A/O	%	A/O	%	A/O	%
Female								
Young adult[3]	6/15	40.0	3/16	18.7	0/18	0.0	6/16	37.5
Old adult	3/6	50.0	6/7	85.7	3/7	42.8	5/7	71.4
Total	9/21	42.9	9/23	39.1	3/25	12.0	11/23	47.8
Male								
Young adult	2/11	18.2	4/12	33.3	0/14	0.0	5/13	38.5
Old adult	9/12	75.0	9/14	64.3	4/12	33.3	11/13	84.6
Total	11/23	47.8	13/26	50.0	4/26	15.4	16/26	61.5

[1] A = number of joints affected with osteoarthritis. Osteoarthritis was scored as present if at least one joint element showed evidence of osteoarthritic change.
[2] O = number of joints observed. A joint was scored as present if at least one joint element was completely present, or if two or three elements were partially present.
[3] Young adult = individuals aged between 16 to 35 years; Old adult = individuals older than 36 years.

TABLE 141: Frequency of occurrence of vertebral osteoarthritis in the Stenjevac series

	Cervical		Thoracic		Lumbar		Total	
	A[1]/O[2]	%	A/O	%	A/O	%	A/O	%
Female								
Young adult[3]	4/57	7.0	16/147	10.9	6/75	8.0	26/279	9.3
Old adult	8/19	42.1	23/41	56.1	8/17	47.1	39/77	50.6
Total	12/76	15.8	39/188	20.7	14/92	15.2	65/356	18.2
Male								
Young adult	0/31	0.0	1/115	0.9	8/58	13.8	9/204	4.4
Old adult	15/43	34.9	19/95	20.0	17/58	29.3	51/196	26.0
Total	15/74	20.3	20/210	9.5	25/116	21.5	60/400	15.0

[1] A = number of vertebrae affected with osteoarthritis or osteophytosis.
[2] O = number of vertebrae observed.
[3] Young adult = individuals aged between 16 to 35 years; Old adult = individuals older than 36 years.

are similar (19.8 % in the thoracic, and 20.2% in the lumbar spine). The total male frequency (23.6%) is higher than that recorded in females (15.7%). This difference is marginally not significant ($\chi^2 = 3.56$; P < .06).

TABLE 142: Frequency of occurrence of Schmorl's depressions in the Stenjevac series

	Thoracic		Lumbar		Total	
	A[1]/O[2]	%	A/O	%	A/O	%
Female						
Young adult[3]	24/147	16.3	12/75	16.0	36/222	16.2
Old adult	5/41	12.2	3/17	17.6	8/58	13.8
Total	29/188	15.4	15/92	16.3	44/280	15.7
Male						
Young adult	25/115	21.7	16/58	27.6	41/173	23.7
Old adult	25/95	26.3	11/58	19.0	36/153	23.5
Total	50/210	23.8	27/116	23.3	77/326	23.6

[1] A = number of vertebrae with Schmorl's depressions.

[2] O = number of vertebrae observed.

[3] Young adult = individuals aged between 16 to 35 years; Old adult = individuals older than 36 years.

5.7. CHARACTERISTICS OF THE COMPOSITE LATE MEDIEVAL SERIES

The Late medieval composite series is comprised of six skeletal series collected from sites evenly distributed throughout continental Croatia. In terms of temporal span it is very homogenous, covering the period from the 11th to the 13th century. Four of the six skeletal series are smaller, with the range of recovered individuals from 11 in Lobor to 19 in Đelekovec, while two, Đakovo phase I, and Stenjevac, are larger. The total number of recovered individuals (175) is larger than that in the Prehistoric and Antique composite series, but smaller than in the Early medieval composite series.

Croatian skeletal series from the Late medieval period have so far received little attention. Some biological data has been published for the Đakovo phase I series, but the primary concern in that report was craniometric differentiation between the two burial phases (Šlaus and Filipec, 1998). The osteochondroma from the adult male in Lobor has also been published as a case report of a bone tumor recovered from an archaeological series (Šlaus et al., 2000). Apart from these two limited reports, little is known

about the skeletal biology of the Late medieval period in continental Croatia.

Historical sources are, as already mentioned, conflicting and confusing. From the archaeological point of view, the period from the 10th to the 13th century is known as the Bijelo Brdo Culture. This is, in effect, a professional term which has been used for over 70 years to designate different types of material remains with common characteristics found in medieval graves from Slovakia, Hungary, Slovenia, continental Croatia, Vojvodina and western Rumania. The name of the culture derives from the eponymous site near Osijek in Croatia. The question of who the originators, and main bearers of this culture were, aroused much debate in archaeological circles. Only recently have we come to understand that the development of the Bijelo Brdo culture was a complex process influenced by numerous elements including the cultural heritage of previous periods, Byzantine influences, ethnic migrations, and the development of medieval states. The bearers of the Bijelo Brdo Culture have now been identified as Slavs and Hungarians, with the understanding that the Slav component was heterogeneous and consisted of Slovaks, Bulgars, and Croats (Demo, 1996).

The age and sex distribution in the Late medieval composite series is presented in Table 143. Subadults comprise 30.3% of the total sample, the highest frequency recorded in a composite series so far. Despite this, representation in the youngest age categories (birth-5 years) remains poor.

TABLE 143: Age and sex distribution in the Late medieval composite series

Age category	Subadult N[1]	%[2]	Female N	%	Male N	%	Total N	%
Birth -1	7	13.2					7	4.0
2- 5	13	24.5					13	7.4
6-10	16	30.2					16	9.1
11-15	17	32.1					17	9.7
16-20			3	4.8	2	3.3	5	2.9
21-25			11	17.7	13	21.8	24	13.7
26-30			10	16.2	3	5.0	13	7.4
31-35			15	24.3	16	26.7	31	17.8
36-40			5	8.1	8	13.3	13	7.4
41-45			4	6.4	11	18.3	15	8.6
46-50			4	6.4	2	3.3	6	3.4
51-55			6	9.7	2	3.3	8	4.6
56-60			1	1.6	1	1.7	2	1.1
60+			3	4.8	2	3.3	5	2.9
Total	53	100.0	62	100.0	60	100.0	175	100.0

Mean age at death[3]   x = 35.60   x = 35.23
                        sd = 12.23   sd = 10.69

[1] N = number of individuals dying.

[2] % = % of individuals dying.

[3] Mean age at death is calculated using median values of each age category (for example, 23 for the age category 21-25), and 65 for the age category 60+.

TABLE 144: Frequency of alveolar bone disease in the Late medieval composite series

Age category	Subadult A[1]/O[2]	%[3]	Female A/O	%	Male A/O	%
Young adult[4]			37/616	6.0	25/598	4.2
Old adult			136/392	34.7	74/428	17.3
Total	5/599	0.8	173/1008	17.2	99/1026	9.6

[1] A = number of tooth sockets with periodontal or periapical abscess, or antemortem tooth loss.
[2] O = number of tooth sockets observed.
[3] % = % of tooth sockets with periodontal or periapical abscess, or antemortem tooth loss.
[4] Young adult = individuals aged between 16 to 35 years; Old adult = individuals older than 36 years.

TABLE 145: Frequency of carious lesions in the Late medieval composite series

Age category	Subadult A[1]/O[2]	%[3]	Female A/O	%	Male A/O	%
Young adult[4]			29/521	5.6	44/492	8.9
Old adult			34/190	17.9	48/279	17.2
Total	14/438	3.2	63/711	8.9	92/771	11.9

[1] A = number of teeth with carious lesions.
[2] O = number of teeth observed.
[3] % = % of teeth with carious lesions.
[4] Young adult = individuals aged between 16 to 35 years; Old adult = individuals older than 36 years.

Subadults from these two categories comprise only 11.4% of the total sample, and less than half (37.7%) of the subadult sample. Subadult mortality in the series is highest from 6-10 years (30.2% of the subadult sample).

Males and females are evenly represented in the adult sample (60 and 62 individuals respectively). The average age at death of adults over 15 years is 35.6 years for females, and 35.2 years for males. These, almost identical values in average life-spans are reflected in similar mortality profiles. Both sexes exhibit high mortality between 21-35 years (58.2% of all adult female deaths, and 53.5% of all adult male deaths), with highest mortality between 31-35 years (24.3% of female, and 26.7% of all male deaths). Few individuals (10 females or 16.1% of all adult female deaths, and 5 males or 8.3% of all adult male deaths) live to be older than 50 years.

The frequencies of alveolar bone disease in the Late medieval composite series are summarized in Table 144. Alveolar bone disease is present in only 5 of the 599 (0.8%) subadult tooth sockets available for inspection. The total frequency in adults is 13.4% (272/2034) with an uneven distribution between males and females. The total frequency of alveolar bone disease in females (17.2%) is considerably higher than the frequency recorded in males (9.6%). This difference is statistically significant (χ^2=18.38, P< .01). The difference appears to be the result of differences in the old adult age category where females exhibit significantly higher frequencies of alveolar bone disease than males (34.7% compared to 17.3%, χ^2=18.57, P< .01). Frequencies in the young adult age categories are similar.

The pattern of higher frequencies of alveolar bone disease in females has already been noted in the Antique and Early medieval composite series. As the mortality distributions and mean ages at death are very similar in both sexes, it is likely that differences in the frequencies of alveolar bone disease result from one, or a combination of the factors, previously discussed. Once again, however, ethnographic and historical documentation of dietary practices and food preparation are not available for these populations.

The overall frequency of carious lesions (Table 145) in the Late medieval composite series is 8.8% (169/1920). Subadults contribute little with only 14 lesions (14/438 or 3.2%). The

total adult frequency is 10.4% (155/1482) with similar frequencies recorded in males and females (11.9% and 8.9% respectively).

Both subadults and adults display the same modal category, grade 2, for severity of carious lesion. In subadults, caries are most frequently noted on the interproximal surfaces of teeth (in 11/14 lesions), followed by root (2/14), and buccal (1/14) lesions.

In adults, carious lesions are most frequently located interproximally (in 33/63 or 52.4% of all carious lesions in females, and in 42/92 or 45.6% of all carious lesions in males). In both sexes this is followed by occlusal (15/63 or 23.8% in females, and 24/92 or 26.1% in males), root (10/63 or 15.9% in females, and 21/92 or 22.8% in males) and buccal caries (5/63 or 7.9% in females, and 4/92 or 4.3% in males). Males also exhibit one (1/92) lingually located carious lesion.

Enamel hypoplasia frequencies are summarized in Tables 146-149. In this series hypoplasias are most frequently recorded in the maxillary central incisors - 55.8%, followed by mandibular - 47.5%, and maxillary canines - 45.6% (Table 146). Slightly less than half (93/189 or 49.2%) of the analyzed teeth exhibit hypoplastic defects.

The total number of teeth available for analysis (189) is less than in the Early medieval (286), but similar to that recorded in the Antique composite series (193). Subadults are represented with 34 teeth (13 central maxillary incisors, 8 maxillary and 13 mandibular canines). In this series, hypoplastic defects in subadults are most frequently recorded on maxillary central incisors and mandibular canines (Table 147). Hypoplasias in the adult sample are most often noted

TABLE 146: Hypoplasia frequencies by individual in the Late medieval composite series

Tooth	N[1]	NwLEH	%wLEH
Maxillary I1[2]	52	29	55.8
Maxillary C	57	26	45.6
Mandibular C	80	38	47.5

[1] N = number of teeth observed; NwLEH = number of teeth with one or more LEH; %wLEH = % of N with one or more LEH.
[2] I = incisor; C = canine.

TABLE 147: Hypoplasia frequencies in the Late medieval composite series for subadults and adults

Tooth	Subadults		All adults		Females		Males	
	Nw/N[1]	%wLEH[2]	Nw/N	%wLEH	Nw/N	%wLEH	Nw/N	%wLEH
Maxillary I1[3]	9/13	69.2	20/39	51.3	8/17	47.1	12/22	54.5
Maxillary C	4/8	50.0	22/49	44.9	8/22	36.4	14/27	51.8
Mandibular C	9/13	69.2	29/67	43.3	8/32	25.0	21/35	60.0

[1] Nw = number of individuals with one or more LEH; N = number of individuals observed.
[2] %wLEH = % of N with one or more LEH.
[3] I = incisors; C = canines.

TABLE 148: Mean number of hypoplasias in incisors and canines in the Late medieval composite series

Tooth	Subadults			All adults			Females			Males		
	Mean	N	S.D.	Mean	N	S.D.	Mean	N	S.D.	Mean	N	S.D.
Maxillary I1[1]	0.92	13	0.83	0.72	39	0.78	0.65	17	0.76	0.77	22	0.79
Maxillary C	0.62	8	0.70	0.53	49	0.64	0.41	22	0.58	0.63	27	0.67
Mandibular C	1.00	13	0.78	0.58	67	0.74	0.28	32	0.51	0.86	35	0.80

[1] I = incisors; C = canines.

on maxillary central incisors, followed by maxillary, and mandibular canines. Subadults consistently exhibit higher frequencies of hypoplastic defects in all teeth analyzed than adults.

A breakdown of the adult sample by sex shows that males consistently exhibit slightly higher frequencies of hypoplastic defects than females. None of the differences is, however, statistically significant. The mean number of hypoplasias per tooth (Table 148), also shows slightly higher levels of subadult stress in males. As in the Early medieval composite series, subadults consistently exhibit a higher number of defects in all of the teeth affected than individuals who lived into adulthood.

Controlling for age (Table 149), males in the young adult age category exhibit higher frequencies of hypoplastic defects than

young adult females. In adults older than 36 years, males exhibit higher frequencies of hypoplastic defects in maxillary and mandibular canines, while females exhibit higher frequencies in central maxillary incisors.

Cribra orbitalia frequencies are summarized in Table 150. In the Late medieval composite series the expression of this condition ranges from slight pitting to severe sievelike lesions with considerable diplotic expansion.

Cribra orbitalia is observed in 48 of the 112 crania (42.9%) with intact orbits. The overall subadult frequency is 70.3% with the majority of lesions (19/26 or 73.1%) active at time of death. In adults, the lesion has a frequency of 29.3% with all of the lesions exhibiting some degree of healing. No sex differences in healing lesion frequencies are noted.

TABLE 149: Hypoplasia frequencies in adult dentition in the Late medieval composite series

Sex/age	Maxillary I1[1]		Maxillary C		Mandibular C	
	Nw/N[2]	%wLEH[3]	Nw/N	%wLEH	Nw/N	%wLEH
Female						
Young adult[4]	6/13	46.1	6/16	37.5	5/23	21.7
Old adult	2/4	50.0	2/6	33.3	3/9	33.3
Male						
Young adult	8/13	61.5	8/16	50.0	13/22	59.1
Old adult	4/9	44.4	6/11	54.5	8/13	61.5

[1] I = incisors; C = canines.
[2] Nw = number of individuals with one or more LEH; N = number of individuals observed.
[3] %wLEH = % of N with one or more LEH.
[4] Young adult = individuals aged between 16 to 35 years; Old adult = individuals older than 36 years.

Skeletal evidence for infectious disease is present in subadults and adults. Because of differential bone preservation, and the need to compare results with the other composite series, periostitis frequencies are presented not "by individual" but by bone.

Subadults exhibit endocranial periostitis on 5 frontal (5/37 recovered subadult frontal bones or 13.5%), 11 parietal (11/83 or 13.2%), and 3 occipital bones (3/41 or 7.3%). Periostitis is also recorded on one temporal bone (1/76), and one mandible (1/40). In the subadult postcranial skeleton, periostitis is recorded on one clavicle (1/44), 10 ribs

TABLE 150: Frequency of occurrence of cribra orbitalia in the Late medieval composite series

Age/sex	Cribra orbitalia			Active lesions	
	O[1]	A1[2]	%	A2[3]	% of A1
0 - 0.9	7	3	42.9	3	100.0
1 - 3.9	7	4	57.1	3	75.0
4 - 9.9	15	13	86.7	10	76.9
10 - 14.9	8	6	75.0	3	50.0
All subadults	37	26	70.3	19	73.1
Adult females	36	10	27.8	0	0.0
Adult males	39	12	30.8	0	0.0
All adults	75	22	29.3	0	0.0

[1] O = number of frontal bones observed.

[2] A1 = number of frontal bones in which at least one orbit shows evidence of cribra orbitalia.

[3] A2 = number of frontal bones in which cribra orbitalia is active at time of death.

TABLE 151: Frequency of occurrence of active periosteal lesions in the Late medieval composite series

Sex	Periosteal lesions		
	A1[1]	A2[2]	% of A1
Subadults	78	59	75.6
Adult females	15	4	26.7
Adult males	35	15	42.9
All adults	50	19	38.0
Total	128	78	60.9

[1] A1 = number of bones with periostitis.

[2] A2 = number of bones with periostitis active at time of death.

(10/193 or 5.2%), 4 humerii (4/66 or 6.1%), one radius (1/43), 3 femurs (3/69 or 4.3%), 30 tibiae (30/63 or 47.6%), and 8 fibulae (8/45 or 17.8%).

The most common location for endocranial periostitis in the adult sample are the parietals (in 2/86 or 2.3% of female, and 1/88 or 1.1% of male parietals). Endocranial periostitis is also noted on one (1/38) male occipital bone. In the adult postcranial skeleton, periostitis is noted on the femurs, tibiae and fibulae. In the female sample, 8/80 (10.0%) recovered tibiae, and 5/60 (8.3%) recovered fibulae exhibit periostitis. In males, periostitis is noted on 3/80 (3.7%) recovered femurs, 23/72 (31.9%) tibiae, and 7/49 (14.3%) fibulae.

As in the other composite series, subadults show less resistance to infectious disease than adults. Furthermore, most subadult lesions (75.6%) show no evidence of healing, while the same is true for 38.0% of adult lesions (Table 151). This difference is statistically significant (χ^2=4.1; P < .05).

margins and slightly porous floors. None penetrated the inner table of the skull and none exhibit evidence of subsequent infection. The high frequency of cranial fractures in adult males is indicative for their participation in violent activities. The distribution of other types of fractures in the series supports this hypothesis. Most of the long bone fractures are recorded in males, as is the only clavicle fracture. Males also exhibit high frequencies of defensive "parry" fractures on the midshaft of the ulna.

In the female sample, long bone fractures are recorded on the radius (2/65 recovered radii or 3.1%), and on the ulna (1/71 or 1.4%). In males, postcranial fractures are noted on the clavicle (1/66 recovered clavicles or 1.5%), humerus (1/72 or 1.4%), radius (4/67 or 6.0%), and ulna (7/70 or 10.0%).

Males also exhibit higher frequencies of enthesophytes. In the male sample, enthesophytes are recorded on one humerus (1/72 recovered male humerii or 1.4%), one femur (1/80 or 1.2%), 5 fibulae (1/49 or 10.2%), and 3 calcanei (3/41 or 7.3%). In females, enthesophytes are noted on 2 fibulae (2/60 or 3.3%), and on 6 calcanei (6/50 or 12.0%).

One case of spondylolysis is noted in the fifth lumbar vertebra of a 30-35 year old male (in 1/33 or 3.0% of males with

No cases of osteomyelitis are noted in the series.

The series is characterized by high frequencies of trauma. Skeletal evidence of healed fractures in the cranium and postcranium are present in subadults and adults,. In the subadult sample only one fracture is noted, a well healed rib fracture in a 12.5-14.5 year old individual from Sčitarjevo. In adults, cranial fractures are present in 9/79 (11.4%) complete crania. The sex distribution is uneven with 6 fractures noted in males (6/40 preserved crania or 15.0%), and 3 (3/39 or 7.7%) noted in females. All of the fractures are healed depression fractures with smooth

TABLE 152: Frequency of occurrence of osteoarthritis at major joints in the Late medieval composite series

	Shoulder		Elbow		Hip		Knee	
	A[1]/O[2]	%	A/O	%	A/O	%	A/O	%
Female								
Young adult[3]	6/21	28.6	3/22	13.6	0/29	0.0	6/25	24.0
Old adult	5/12	41.7	8/14	57.1	4/16	25.0	7/15	46.7
Total	11/33	33.3	11/36	30.6	4/45	8.9	13/40	32.5
Male								
Young adult	2/19	10.5	4/21	19.0	0/27	0.0	5/22	22.7
Old adult	9/14	64.3	9/16	56.2	4/15	26.7	11/15	73.3
Total	11/33	33.3	13/37	35.1	4/42	9.5	16/37	43.2

[1] A = number of joints affected with osteoarthritis. Osteoarthritis was scored as present if at least one joint element showed evidence of osteoarthritic change.

[2] O = number of joints observed. A joint was scored as present if at least one joint element was completely present, or if two or three elements were partially present.

[3] Young adult = individuals aged between 16 to 35 years; Old adult = individuals older than 36 years.

TABLE 153: Frequency of occurrence of vertebral osteoarthritis in the Late medieval composite series

	Cervical		Thoracic		Lumbar		Total	
	A^1/O^2	%	A/O	%	A/O	%	A/O	%
Female								
Young adult[3]	4/83	4.8	16/187	8.6	6/100	6.0	26/370	7.0
Old adult	15/51	29.4	40/92	43.5	30/42	71.4	85/185	45.9
Total	19/134	14.2	56/279	20.1	36/142	25.3	111/555	20.0
Male								
Young adult	0/51	0.0	1/139	0.7	9/74	12.2	10/264	3.8
Old adult	16/57	28.1	24/131	18.3	20/78	25.6	60/266	22.6
Total	16/108	14.8	25/270	9.3	29/152	19.1	70/530	13.2

[1] A = number of vertebrae affected with osteoarthritis or osteophytosis.

[2] O = number of vertebrae observed.

[3] Young adult = individuals aged between 16 to 35 years; Old adult = individuals older than 36 years.

complete lumbar spines). No cases are noted in the female sample.

Osteoarthritis frequencies in the series are summarized in Table 152. In the female sample osteoarthritis is most frequently recorded on the shoulder, in the male sample on the knee. No sex differences are noted. Osteoarthritis is, once again, more common in the old adult age category than in individuals who died before 35 years.

The overall frequency of vertebral osteoarthritis in the series (181/1085 or 16.7%) is slightly higher than the frequency recorded in the Early medieval composite series. Comparing the different regions of the spine (Table 153), greatest involvement occurs in the lumbar spine (65/294 or 22.1%), followed by the thoracic (81/549 or 14.7%) and cervical (35/242 or 14.5%) regions. Females exhibit a significantly higher total vertebral osteoarthritis frequency (20.0% compared to 13.2%, $\chi^2 = 6.04$; P < .02). The difference

appears to be caused by differences in the old adult age category where females exhibit a higher total frequency of vertebral osteoarthritis (45.9% compared to 22.6%, $\chi^2 = 13.02$; P < .01). Analysis by comparing the different regions of the spine show that the primary difference between males and females is located in the thoracic region where females exhibit significantly higher frequencies of vertebral osteoarthritis in the young adult ($\chi^2 = 7.58$; P < .01), old adult ($\chi^2 = 8.04$; P < .01), and total osteoarthritis categories ($\chi^2 = 8.79$; P < .01).

Frequencies of Schmorl's depressions in the series are summarized in Table 154. The overall frequency of Schmorl's depressions in the sample, 20.2% (171/845) is the highest recorded so far in a composite series. Frequencies of Schmorl's depressions in the thoracic and lumbar spine are similar (19.6 % and 21.4% respectively). The total frequency of Schmorl's lesions is significantly higher in males (26.8% compared to 13.6%, $\chi^2 = 14.65$; P < .01). This difference appears to result from differences in the old adult age category where males exhibit a significantly higher frequency of lesions (32.1% compared to 10.6%, $\chi^2 = 13.87$; P < .01). Statistically significant differences are also present in the total frequencies of lesions in the lumbar spine (27.6% compared to 14.8%, $\chi^2 = 4.10$; P < .05), and the total frequencies of lesions in the thoracic spine (26.4% compared to 12.9%, $\chi^2 = 9.93$; P < .01).

TABLE 154: Frequency of occurrence of Schmorl's depressions in the Late medieval composite series

	Thoracic		Lumbar		Total	
	A^1/O^2	%	A/O	%	A/O	%
Female						
Young adult[3]	27/179	15.1	14/90	15.6	41/269	15.2
Old adult	9/99	9.1	7/52	13.5	16/151	10.6
Total	36/278	12.9	21/142	14.8	57/420	13.6
Male						
Young adult	28/139	20.1	18/74	24.3	46/213	21.6
Old adult	44/134	32.8	24/78	30.8	68/212	32.1
Total	72/273	26.4	42/152	27.6	114/425	26.8

[1] A = number of vertebrae with Schmorl's depressions.

[2] O = number of vertebrae observed.

[3] Young adult = individuals aged between 16 to 35 years; Old adult = individuals older than 36 years.

6. BIOARCHAEOLOGY OF THE HISTORIC PERIOD

For the purposes of this analysis the historic period is defined as the period from the 14th-18th century. This period is characterized by the development of trade and manufacture, and the gradual dissolution of the feudal system. On the political front, the Hungarian Arpad dynasty was replaced in the beginning of the 14th century by the Angevins of Naples. Their reign is characterized by weakening of the old aristocracy, and the emergence of a lower layer of nobility which shared power with the king. In Slavonija this process was led by Ban Mikac, elected by Charles I in 1325. During the reign of the Angevins noble courts were developed, higher taxes on trade and manufacture were introduced as well as monetary reforms, all of which gave the aristocracy total autonomy.

The most important political event of this period is, however, the emergence, and after the battle of Sisak in 1593, the gradual decline in power of the Ottoman Turkish Empire. In the wake of their destruction of the Byzantine empire and the conquest of Constantinopolis, the Ottoman Turks penetrated southeastern Europe. Macedonia was conquered in 1371 after the decisive Battle of Marica, Serbia in 1389 after the destruction of the Serbian army in the Battle of Kosovo, and Bosnia in 1463.

From 1468 to 1483 the Turks organized massive raiding parties which penetrated deep into Croatia and neighboring Slovenia. The magnitude of these raids is evident in the number of prisoners taken. Historical sources estimate that approximately 60 000 prisoners were taken in the raid from 1469, and 30 000 in the raid from 1471 (Macan, 1992). In 1493, returning from a similar raid, the Turkish general Jakub-paša decisively beat the Croatian army in the battle on Krbavsko polje. In 1526 the Turks captured Osijek, and in the same year beat the Hungarian army at the battle of Mohacs. The Hungarian king Ludwig II was killed in this conflict and, hoping for support in their fight against the Turks, the Croatian nobility elected Ferdinand the Habsburg as their ruler. The Turks continued, however, to advance and captured Đakovo in 1536, Čazma in 1552, and Kostajnica in 1556. The turning point was the sea battle at Lepant, in which the Ottoman fleet was defeated and the myth of Turkish invincibility was destroyed, and, as already mentioned, the Battle of Sisak (1593) in which the Croatian Ban Thomas Erdödy defeated the Turkish general Hasan-paša. This defeat marks the end of Turkish expansion into Europe. The consequences for continental Croatia were severe. Trade with the East Adriatic towns was interrupted, established trade routes were abandoned, many towns lost their autonomy to local nobles, and money depreciated. Serfs suffered the most and attempted several uprisings, the largest of which occurred in 1573 in the Stubica region, 20 km north of Zagreb. Not surprisingly, the uprisings were brutally suppressed.

This period is represented by four skeletal series recovered from the sites of Đakovo, Tomaš, Nova Rača, and Kamengrad. The geographic position of the sites is shown in Figure 29.

6.1. THE ĐAKOVO PHASE II SKELETAL SERIES

As already discussed, use of the second phase of the Đakovo cemetery is dated from the 14th-16th century, more precisely to 1536 when Đakovo was captured by the Turks. Similar to the first phase, bone preservation and completeness of the skeletons is poor to average.

The age and sex distribution in the series is presented in Table 155. As in the first phase, subadults are poorly represented. They are completely absent in the youngest (0-1 year) age category, and represented by only 8 individuals in all other remaining subadult age categories. Subadults comprise 19.0% of the total sample. Subadult mortality in the series is highest between 2-5 years.

Peak mortality for females is between 21-25 years (33.2% of all adult females). Males exhibit highest mortality between 26-35 years (52.6%). This difference is reflected in different mean ages at death. The average age at death for adult females is 31.3 years (SD = 9.25), for adult males 35.4 years (SD = 12.1).

Frequencies of alveolar bone disease are presented in Table 156. Alveolar bone disease is not present in subadults, and has a low (12.4% or 82/661) overall frequency in adults. Males exhibit a considerably higher total frequency (17.4%) than females (5.7%). This difference is statistically significant (χ^2 = 15.14; P < 0.01). The difference appears to be caused by differences in the old adult age category in which males exhibit considerably higher frequencies of alveolar bone disease than females (30.2% compared to 10.3%, $\chi^2 = 8.81$; P < 0.01). As no differences are noted in the young adult age category, differences in alveolar bone disease frequencies may be related to the 4.1 years longer average male life-span.

Total caries frequencies (Table 157) are, however, similar in males and females (12.8% and 9.9% respectively), and are not significantly different in either the young adult, or old adult age categories.

Figure 29. The geographical locations of the Historic sites: 1. Đakovo, 2. Tomaš, 3. Nova Rača, 4. Kamengrad.

TABLE 155: Age and sex distribution in the Đakovo, burial phase II, series

Age category	Subadult N[1]	%[2]	Female N	%	Male N	%	Total N	%
Birth -1	0						0	
2- 5	4	50.0					4	9.5
6-10	2	25.0					2	4.8
11-15	2	25.0					2	4.8
16-20			1	6.7	1	5.3	2	4.8
21-25			5	33.2	2	10.5	7	16.6
26-30			1	6.7	5	26.3	6	14.3
31-35			3	20.0	5	26.3	8	19.0
36-40			3	20.0	1	5.3	4	9.5
41-45			1	6.7	1	5.3	2	4.8
46-50			0		0		0	
51-55			1	6.7	2	10.5	3	7.1
56-60			0		2	10.5	2	4.8
60+			0		0		0	
Total	8	100.0	15	100.0	19	100.0	42	100.0

Mean age at death[3] x = 31.33   x = 35.37
                      sd = 9.25   sd = 12.06

[1] N = number of individuals dying.

[2] % = % of individuals dying.

[3] Mean age at death is calculated using median values of each age category (for example, 23 for the age category 21-25), and 65 for the age category 60+.

TABLE 156: Frequency of alveolar bone disease in the Đakovo, burial phase II, series

Age category	Subadult A[1]/O[2]	%[3]	Female A/O	%	Male A/O	%
Young adult[4]			5/174	2.9	18/221	8.1
Old adult			11/107	10.3	48/159	30.2
Total	0/81	0.0	16/281	5.7	66/380	17.4

[1] A = number of tooth sockets with periodontal or periapical abscess, or antemortem tooth loss.

[2] O = number of tooth sockets observed.

[3] % = % of tooth sockets with periodontal or periapical abscess, or antemortem tooth loss.

[4] Young adult = individuals aged between 16 to 35 years; Old adult = individuals older than 36 years.

TABLE 157: Frequency of carious lesions in the Đakovo, burial phase II, series

Age category	Subadult A[1]/O[2]	%[3]	Female A/O	%	Male A/O	%
Young adult[4]			13/170	7.6	17/205	8.3
Old adult			12/83	14.5	23/107	21.5
Total	0/62	0.0	25/253	9.9	40/312	12.8

[1] A = number of teeth with carious lesions.

[2] O = number of teeth observed.

[3] % = % of teeth with carious lesions.

[4] Young adult = individuals aged between 16 to 35 years; Old adult = individuals older than 36 years.

No lesions are recorded in subadult teeth. In both sexes the majority of the observed lesions are located interproximally. In females these lesions are noted in 14/25 or 56.0% cases, in males, in 24/40 or 60.0%. Females also exhibit occlusal (10/25, or 40.0%), and root caries (1/25 or 4.0%), while males exhibit occlusal (11/40, or 27.5%), buccal (3/40 or 7.5%), lingual (1/40 or 2.5%), and root (1/40 or 2.5%) lesions. The modal category for severity of lesions is grade 2 in females, and grade 4 in males.

Enamel hypoplasia frequencies are presented in Table 158. Hypoplasias are most frequent in maxillary canines (54.5%), followed by mandibular canines (52.0%) and maxillary central incisors (42.1%). Similar to material from the first phase of the cemetery, subadult dentition is poorly preserved. Only 3 subadult teeth (one central incisor, one maxillary, and one mandibular canine) were available for analysis. Two deep hypoplastic defects are present on the mandibualr canine. In adults, hypoplastic defects are recorded in 32/63 (50.8%) of the teeth available for analysis (Table 159). The highest frequency is recorded in maxillary canines (57.1%), followed by mandibular canines (50.0%), and maxillary central incisors (44.4%). Males in the analyzed sample exhibit slightly higher frequencies of hypoplastic defects in all three tooth categories. None of the differences is, however, statistically significant. Controlling for age, females exhibit similar frequencies of hypoplastic defects in both age categories. In the male sample individuals who died before 35 years exhibit higher frequencies of hypolasia inducing stress (in 19/26 or 73.1% of analyzed teeth from this age category) than individuals who lived longer than 36 years (1/7 or 14.3%).

The series is characterized by relatively high frequencies of adult cribra orbitalia. Cribra orbitalia (Table 160) is recorded in one of the 4 subadults recovered with intact orbits. The lesion was healed and mild in expression. In adults it's presence is observed in 40.7% (11/27) of recovered frontal bones. The sex distribution is uneven with females exhibiting

TABLE 158: Hypoplasia frequencies by individual in the Đakovo, burial phase II, series

Tooth	N[1]	NwLEH	%wLEH
Maxillary I1[2]	19	8	42.1
Maxillary C	22	12	54.5
Mandibular C	25	13	52.0

[1] N = number of teeth observed; NwLEH = number of teeth with one or more LEH; %wLEH = % of N with one or more LEH.

[2] I = incisor; C = canine.

TABLE 159: Hypoplasia frequencies in the Đakovo, burial phase II, series for subadults and adults

Tooth	Subadults		All adults		Females		Males	
	Nw/N[1]	%wLEH[2]	Nw/N	%wLEH	Nw/N	%wLEH	Nw/N	%wLEH
Maxillary I1[3]	0/1	0.0	8/18	44.4	3/9	33.3	5/9	55.5
Maxillary C	0/1	0.0	12/21	57.1	5/11	45.4	7/10	70.0
Mandibular C	1/1	100.0	12/24	50.0	4/10	40.0	8/14	57.1

[1] Nw = number of individuals with one or more LEH; N = number of individuals observed.
[2] %wLEH = % of N with one or more LEH.
[3] I = incisors; C = canines.

higher frequencies (50.0%) than males (20.0%). The difference is not, however, statistically significant.

Skeletal evidence for infectious disease is recorded in 3/8 subadults, and 4/34 adults. In subadults, healed, mild in expression, endocranial periostitis is recorded on the parietals of a subadult aged between 3-5 years. Two subadults also exhibit bilateral, active, periostitis on the medial surfaces of the tibias. In the adult sample, one female exhibits mild, healed periostitis on the distal left tibia, and one exhibits active periostitis on the distal right femur as well as healed periostitis on the proximal right tibia. Two males exhibit mild, healed periostitis on the left tibia.

Healed fractures are recorded only in males. Cranial fractures are recorded in 2 individuals. One is recorded in an individual aged between 26-30 years. The fracture is located in the midline of the frontal bone, approximately 62 mm superior of nasion,. The fracture is a healed depression fracture, oval in shape, with rounded margins and a porous floor. The dimension of the fracture are 32x22 mm. There is no evidence of infection. The blow which caused it was evidently of considerable force as bone on the endocranial surface of the fracture projects into the endocranium. A healed depression fracture is also noted on the occipital bone of a 26-30 year old male. The fracture is irregular in shape, located 28 mm superior of the superior nuchal crest. There is no evidence of

infection. In the postcranium, 2 males exhibit rib fractures, both on the right side, one on the sternal end of the third right rib, and one on the sternal end of the fifth right rib. One male exhibits a well healed spiral fracture of the distal right radius, and one a well healed fracture on the proximal joint surface of the right tibia.

Osteoarthritis frequencies in major joints are low in the series and restricted to individuals older than 36 years. Two females exhibits mild osteoarthritis on the left hip. In males, osteoarthritis is recorded in 2/10 shoulders, 1/13 elbows, 1/15 hips, and 3/14 knees.

Females exhibit no evidence of vertebral osteoarthritis on any of the 78 vertebra available for analysis. Males exhibit a very low overall frequency with only 16/212 (7.5%) vertebra affected. Highest involvement is recorded in the lumbar spine (4/42 or 9.5%).

The frequencies of Schmorl's depressions in the series are summarized in Table 161. The overall frequency of Schmorl's depressions in the sample is relatively high (72/220 or 32.7%). Frequencies of Schmorl's depressions are slightly higher in the thoracic spine (35.3% or 54/153) than in the lumbar (26.9% or 18/67). The total male frequency is significantly higher than the total female frequency (39.3% compared to 16.9%, $\chi^2 = 5.02$; P < .03).

TABLE 160: Frequency of occurrence of cribra orbitalia in the Đakovo, burial phase II, series

Age/sex	Cribra orbitalia			Active lesions	
	O[1]	A1[2]	%	A2[3]	% of A1
0 - 0.9	0	0	0.0	0	0.0
1 - 3.9	0	0	0.0	0	0.0
4 - 9.9	2	1	50.0	0	0.0
10 - 14.9	2	0	0.0	0	0.0
All subadults	4	1	25.0	0	0.0
Adult females	12	6	50.0	0	0.0
Adult males	15	3	20.0	0	0.0
All adults	27	11	40.7	0	0.0

[1] O = number of frontal bones observed.
[2] A1 = number of frontal bones in which at least one orbit shows evidence of cribra orbitalia.
[3] A2 = number of frontal bones in which cribra orbitalia is active at time of death.

TABLE 161: Frequency of occurrence of Schmorl's depressions in the Đakovo, burial phase II, series

	Thoracic		Lumbar		Total	
	A[1]/O[2]	%	A/O	%	A/O	%
Female						
Young adult[3]	7/39	17.9	3/18	16.7	10/57	17.5
Old adult	1/1	100.0	0/7	0.0	1/8	12.5
Total	8/40	20.0	3/25	12.0	11/65	16.9
Male						
Young adult	25/64	39.1	8/24	33.3	33/88	37.5
Old adult	21/49	42.9	7/18	38.9	28/67	41.8
Total	46/113	40.7	15/42	35.7	61/155	39.3

[1] A = number of vertebrae with Schmorl's depressions.
[2] O = number of vertebrae observed.
[3] Young adult = individuals aged between 16 to 35 years; Old adult = individuals older than 36 years.

6.2. THE TOMAŠ SKELETAL SERIES

This is a small skeletal series in which subadults dominate. The remains were recovered in 1997 from a church cemetery in the village of Tomaš, approximately 70 km east of Zagreb. Use of the cemetery is dated to the 16th century (Jakovljević, 1999). Bone preservation and completeness of the remains is poor to moderate.

The age and sex distribution of the series is presented in Table 162. Subadults comprise 45.0% of the total sample (9/20), but are still obviously underrepresented in the youngest (birth-1 year) age category. Males and females are evenly represented with 5 females and 6 males in the adult sample. Peak mortality for adults appears to be between 21-25 years. The average age at death for adult females is 38.4 years (SD=20.0), for adult males it is 28.0 years (SD=8.9).

Alveolar bone disease is not recorded in subadults (0/104), and has a moderate (35/121 or 28.9%) overall frequency in adults. Females exhibit higher frequencies (34/60 or 56.7%) than males (1/61 or 1.6%). This difference is statistically significant ($\chi^2 = 23.69$; P < .01), and may reflect the longer average female life-span.

Surprisingly, no carious lesions are recorded in adults (0/24 teeth in females, and 0/48 teeth in males). Subadults exhibit

TABLE 162: Age and sex distribution in the Tomaš series

Age category	Subadult N[1]	%[2]	Female N	%	Male N	%	Total N	%
Birth -1	1	11.2					1	5.0
2- 5	4	44.4					4	20.0
6-10	4	44.4					4	20.0
11-15	0						0	
16-20			1	20.0	1	16.7	2	10.0
21-25			1	20.0	2	33.2	3	15.0
26-30			0		1	16.7	1	5.0
31-35			1	20.0	1	16.7	2	10.0
36-40			0		0		0	
41-45			0		1	16.7	1	5.0
46-50			0		0		0	
51-55			1	20.0	0		1	5.0
56-60			0		0		0	
60+			1	20.0	0		1	5.0
Total	9	100.0	5	100.0	6	100.0	20	100.0

Mean age at death[3]   x = 38.40   x = 28.00
                          sd = 20.01   sd = 8.94

[1] N = number of individuals dying.
[2] % = % of individuals dying.
[3] Mean age at death is calculated using median values of each age category (for example, 23 for the age category 21-25), and 65 for the age category 60+.

TABLE 163: Frequency of occurrence of cribra orbitalia in the Tomaš series

Age/sex	Cribra orbitalia O[1]	A1[2]	%	Active lesions A2[3]	% of A1
0 - 0.9	1	0	0.0	0	0.0
1 - 3.9	3	2	66.7	1	50.0
4 - 9.9	2	2	100.0	1	50.0
10 - 14.9	0	0	0.0	0	0.0
All subadults	6	4	66.7	2	50.0
Adult females	3	1	33.3	0	0.0
Adult males	2	1	50.0	0	0.0
All adults	5	2	40.0	0	0.0

[1] O = number of frontal bones observed.
[2] A1 = number of frontal bones in which at least one orbit shows evidence of cribra orbitalia.
[3] A2 = number of frontal bones in which cribra orbitalia is active at time of death.

6/75 (8.0%) carious lesions, 4 located occlusally, and 2 interproximally. The modal category for severity of lesions is grade 1.

Enamel hypoplasia is recorded in 7/10 available teeth (1/3 maxillary central incisors, 3/3 maxillary canines, and 3/4 mandibualr canines). Only one subadult tooth is available for analysis, a mandibular canine which exhibits two deep hypoplastic defects. In the adult sample, females exhibit one hypoplastic defect on a maxillary canine. Males exhibit hypoplasias on one central incisor, 2 maxillary canines, and 2 mandibular canines.

Cribra orbitalia is observed in 4 of the 6 subadult frontals with preserved orbits (Table 163). Two cases were active at time of death. In the adult sample, one female, and one male exhibit healing cribra orbitalia lesions.

Skeletal evidence for infectious disease is present in one adult, a male aged between 31-35 years who exhibits bilateral, mild, healed periostitis on the medial surfaces of the tibiae.

Skeletal evidence for trauma is present in one subadult and 2 adults. The subadult, aged between 5-7 years, exhibits a healed fracture of the left femur (Figure 30). The fracture is located on the proximal third of the diaphysis where a large callus, approximately 60 mm long, is visible on the medial side. The fracture resulted in mild lateral angulation, and a slight (10 mm) shortening of the

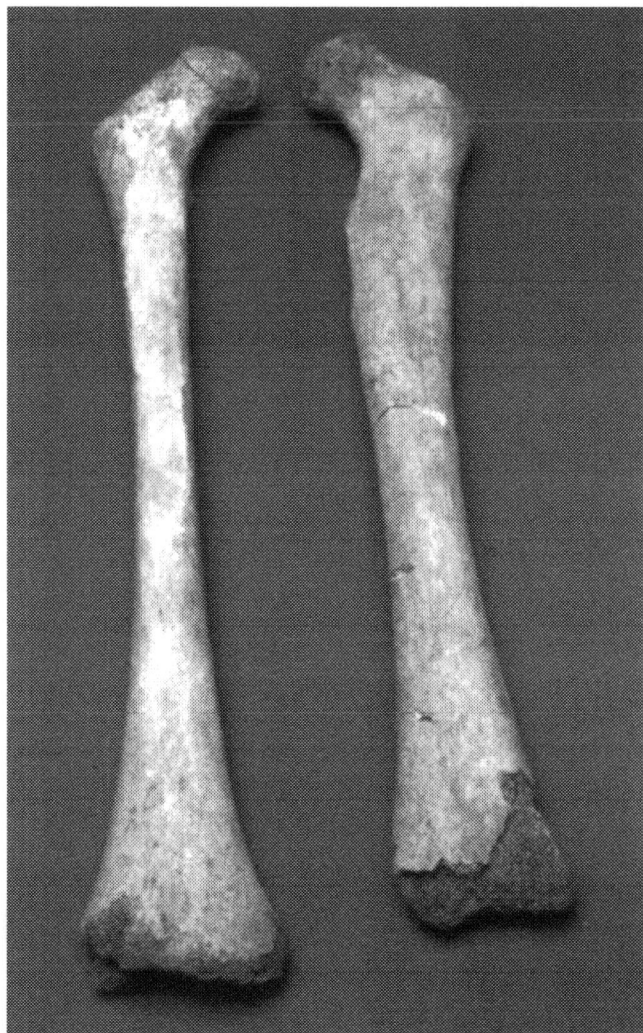

Figure 30. Healed fracture of the left femur in a subadult from Tomaš. The bone is swollen in the proximal and middle thirds of the diaphysis indicating probable post-traumatic infection..

diaphysis. The left bone is swollen in the proximal and middle thirds of the diaphysis indicating probable post-traumatic infection. One healed femoral fracture is also present in an adult male. This individual, aged between 26-30 years, exhibits a large callus (approximately 85 mm long) on the anterior side of the proximal right femur. There is no angulation or shortening of the diaphysis, and no evidence of infection. A depression fracture is also noted on the left parietal of a 51-55 year old female. The fracture is oval in shape (25x9 mm), with rounded margins and a slightly porous floor. The fracture did not penetrate the inner table of the skull, and there is no evidence of infection.

Osteoarthritis is not recorded in the series.

Vertebral osteoarthritis is recorded in only 2 female cervical vertebra (2/9 available female vertebra). None of the 22 available male vertebra show evidence of osteoarthritis.

Schmorl's lesion are recorded in 2/4 female, and 10/16 available male vertebra.

6.3. THE NOVA RAČA SKELETAL SERIES

This is the largest skeletal series from the Historic period. It was recovered during systematic excavations (1986-1995) of the parish church the "Assumption of the Holy Virgin Mary" in Nova Rača approximately 75 km east of Zagreb. Historic records indicate that the Nova Rača church was built in 1312 (Jakovljević, 1986). There is some evidence (Dobronić, 1984) that it may have been commissioned by the Knights Templars, a military priestly order which held land in this area during the 14th century. Recovered artifacts date the use of the cemetery to the period between the 14th-18th centuries (Medar, 1987; Jakovljević, 1988).

The age and sex distribution of the series is presented in Table 164. Subadults are better represented than in most of the series analyzed so far. They comprise 34.6% of the total sample but are, once again, underrepresented in the youngest (birth-1 year) age category (10 individuals or 9.6% of the total series). Five fetal skeletons, ranging in age from 37-41 weeks old, are recorded in this age category. Four were buried in individual graves while one was recovered from the pelvic area of an adult female. Subadult mortality in the series is highest from 6-10 years (33.3% of the subadult sample).

Males and females are evenly represented in the adult sample (35 and 33 individuals respectively). The average age at death of adults over 15 years is 29.9 years for females, and 34.1 years for males. This difference (4.2 years) in average lifespans is reflected in different mortality profiles. Peak female mortality is between 21-30 years (57.6% of all adult females died during this interval), with the highest mortality between 21-25 years. Males show an equally well defined peak mortality between 31-40 years (45.7% of all adult male deaths), with the highest mortality from 31-35 years. In both sexes only two individuals (2/33 or 6.1% of all adult female deaths, and 2/35 or 5.7% of all adult male deaths) lived to be older than 50 years.

The frequencies of alveolar bone disease are summarized in Table 165. Alveolar bone disease is not recorded in any of the 345 available subadult tooth sockets. The total frequency of alveolar bone disease in adults is 10.9% (94/864) with an uneven distribution between males and females. The total male frequency (13.5%) is considerably higher than the total female frequency (7.6%). This difference is statistically significant (χ^2=5.64, P< .02). Controlling for age, the frequency of alveolar bone disease is considerably higher in young adult males (11.2%) than in young adult females (4.7%). These frequencies are also significantly different (χ^2=6.63, P<.01).

The overall frequency of carious lesions is 10.0% (112/1119). Caries frequencies (Table 166) are similar in subadults (8.5%) and adults (10.7%). No significant sex differences are noted in total frequencies. When, however, age is controlled, caries frequencies are, once again, significantly higher in young adult males (11.5%) than in young adult females (5.4%). This difference is also statistically significant (χ^2=5.18, P< .03). Females from the old adult age category exhibit higher frequencies of carious lesions than males (25.4% compared to 14.2%) but this difference is not statistically significant.

TABLE 164: Age and sex distribution in the Nova Rača series

Age category	Subadult N[1]	%[2]	Female N	%	Male N	%	Total N	%
Birth -1	10	27.8					10	9.6
2- 5	8	22.2					8	7.7
6-10	12	33.3					12	11.5
11-15	6	16.7					6	5.8
16-20			3	9.1	2	5.6	5	4.8
21-25			12	36.4	5	14.3	17	16.4
26-30			7	21.2	5	14.3	12	11.5
31-35			4	12.1	9	25.7	13	12.5
36-40			2	6.1	7	20.0	9	8.7
41-45			2	6.1	4	11.4	6	5.8
46-50			1	3.0	1	2.9	2	1.9
51-55			1	3.0	1	2.9	2	1.9
56-60			0		0		0	
60+			1	3.0	1	2.9	2	1.9
Total	36	100.0	33	100.0	35	100.0	104	100.0

Mean age at death[3]
x = 29.87   x = 34.06
sd = 10.48   sd = 9.65

[1] N = number of individuals dying.
[2] % = % of individuals dying.
[3] Mean age at death is calculated using median values of each age category (for example, 23 for the age category 21-25), and 65 for the age category 60+.

TABLE 165: Frequency of alveolar bone disease in the Nova Rača series

Age category	Subadult A[1]/O[2]	%[3]	Female A/O	%	Male A/O	%
Young adult[4]			14/296	4.7	36/321	11.2
Old adult			15/86	17.4	29/161	18.0
Total	0/345	0.0	29/382	7.6	65/482	13.5

[1] A = number of tooth sockets with periodontal or periapical abscess, or antemortem tooth loss.
[2] O = number of tooth sockets observed.
[3] % = % of tooth sockets with periodontal or periapical abscess, or antemortem tooth loss.
[4] Young adult = individuals aged between 16 to 35 years; Old adult = individuals older than 36 years.

TABLE 166: Frequency of carious lesions in the Nova Rača series

Age category	Subadult A[1]/O[2]	%[3]	Female A/O	%	Male A/O	%
Young adult[4]			16/298	5.4	31/270	11.5
Old adult			16/63	25.4	19/134	14.2
Total	30/354	8.5	32/361	8.9	50/404	12.4

[1] A = number of teeth with carious lesions.
[2] O = number of teeth observed.
[3] % = % of teeth with carious lesions.
[4] Young adult = individuals aged between 16 to 35 years; Old adult = individuals older than 36 years.

Both subadults and adults display the same modal category, grade 2, for severity of carious lesion. The distribution of carious lesions is also similar. In subadults, carious lesions are most frequently located interproximally (in 24/30 or 80.0% of all carious lesions), followed by occlusal (5/30, 16.7%), and buccal (1/30, 3.3%) lesions. In females carious lesions are most often recorded interproximally (25/32, 78.1%), followed by occlusal (4/32, 12.5%), buccal (2/32, 6.2%), and lingual (1/32, 3.2%) lesions. Adult males also exhibit a high frequency of interproximal (25/50, 50%) and occlusal (13/50, 26.0%) lesions, but differ from females in their higher frequencies of root (7/50, 14.0%) and buccal (5/50 10.0%) lesions.

Enamel hypoplasia frequencies are summarized in Tables 167-170. The total frequency of hypoplasias in the available sample is 35.6% (79/222). Hypoplasias are most frequent in mandibular canines - 36.5%, followed by maxillary canines - 36.0, and maxillary central incisors - 34.2%.

Subadults are represented with 42 teeth (Table 168), 29 of which exhibit hypoplastic defects (69.0%). In this series, hypoplasia in subadults is most frequently recorded in maxillary central incisors (76.9%).

Adults consistently exhibit lower frequencies of hypoplasia inducing stress in all three tooth categories analyzed. The greatest difference is noted in hypoplasia frequencies in maxillary incisors (76.9% in subadults compared to 25.0% in adults, $\chi^2=3.94$, P< .05). A breakdown of the adult sample by sex shows that adult females consistently exhibit higher frequencies of hypoplasias than males. Of the 87 female teeth available for analysis 38 (43.7%) exhibit hypoplastic defects. In the male sample, 12/93 (12.9%) teeth exhibit hypoplastic defects. The greatest difference is noted in maxillary canines (48.2% in females compared to 9.7% in males, $\chi^2=4.91$, P< .03).

The mean number of hypoplasias per tooth (Table 169) is consistent with this pattern. Subadults exhibit a higher number of defects per tooth, in all three tooth categories than adults, while adult females exhibit a greater number of defects per tooth than adult males.

TABLE 167: Hypoplasia frequencies by individual in the Nova Rača series

Tooth	N[1]	NwLEH	%wLEH
Maxillary I1[2]	73	25	34.2
Maxillary C	75	27	36.0
Mandibular C	74	27	36.5

[1] N = number of teeth observed; NwLEH = number of teeth with one or more LEH; %wLEH = % of N with one or more LEH.
[2] I = incisor; C = canine.

TABLE 168: Hypoplasia frequencies in the Nova Rača series for subadults and adults

	Subadults		All adults		Females		Males	
Tooth	Nw/N[1]	%wLEH[2]	Nw/N	%wLEH	Nw/N	%wLEH	Nw/N	%wLEH
Maxillary I1[3]	10/13	76.9	15/60	25.0	10/29	34.5	5/31	16.1
Maxillary C	10/15	66.7	17/60	28.3	14/29	48.2	3/31	9.7
Mandibular C	9/14	64.4	18/60	30.0	14/29	48.2	4/31	12.9

[1] Nw = number of individuals with one or more LEH; N = number of individuals observed.
[2] %wLEH = % of N with one or more LEH.
[3] I = incisors; C = canines.

TABLE 169: Mean number of hypoplasias in incisors and canines in the Nova Rača series

	Subadults			All adults			Females			Males		
Tooth	Mean	N	S.D.	Mean	N	S.D.	Mean	N	S.D.	Mean	N	S.D.
MaxillaryI1[1]	0.92	13	0.61	0.33	60	0.62	0.44	29	0.67	0.22	31	0.55
Maxillary C	0.80	15	0.65	0.37	60	0.63	0.55	29	0.62	0.19	31	0.59
Mandibular C	0.71	14	0.59	0.42	60	0.69	0.59	29	0.67	0.26	31	0.67

[1] I = incisors; C = canines.

Controlling for age, young adult females have consistently higher frequencies of hypoplastic teeth than young adult males (Table 170). These differences are significantly different in maxillary canines (54.2% compared to 9.5%, χ^2=3.97, P< .05), and marginally not significant in mandibular canines (56.5% compared to 10.5%, χ^2=3.56, P< .06).

Cribra orbitalia frequencies are summarized in Table 171. In the Nova Rača series the expression of this condition ranges from slight pitting to severe sievelike lesions with considerable diplotic expansion. Cribra orbitalia is observed in 29 of the 73 crania (39.7%) with intact orbits. The overall subadult frequency is 58.6% with most of the lesions (10/17 or 58.8%) active at time of death. In adults the lesion has a frequency of 27.3% with all of the lesions exhibiting some degree of healing. While no significant sex differences in healing lesion frequencies are present, it is worth noting that the frequency of cribra orbitalia in adult females (36.4%), is twice as high

TABLE 171: Frequency of occurrence of cribra orbitalia in the Nova Rača series

	Cribra orbitalia			Active lesions	
Age/sex	O[1]	A1[2]	%	A2[3]	% of A1
0 - 0.9	10	2	20.0	2	100.0
1 - 3.9	5	3	60.0	3	100.0
4 - 9.9	7	6	85.7	3	50.0
10 - 14.9	7	6	85.7	2	33.3
All subadults	29	17	58.6	10	58.8
Adult females	22	8	36.4	0	0.0
Adult males	22	4	18.2	0	0.0
All adults	44	12	27.3	0	0.0

[1] O = number of frontal bones observed.
[2] A1 = number of frontal bones in which at least one orbit shows evidence of cribra orbitalia.
[3] A2 = number of frontal bones in which cribra orbitalia is active at time of death.

as that recorded in males (18.2%). An age breakdown of lesions shows that most of the lesions in males (3/4) are present in individuals older than 25 years, while in females most of the lesions (5/8) are recorded in individuals aged between 16-25 years.

Skeletal evidence for infectious disease is present in subadults and adults. In comparison to adults, subadults show less resistance to infectious disease. Slightly less than 60% of all subadults (21/36) exhibit at least one periosteal lesion on any bone. The majority of these lesions show no evidence of healing. Half of the

TABLE 170: Hypoplasia frequencies in adult dentition in the Nova Rača series

	Maxillary I1[1]		Maxillary C		Mandibular C	
Sex/age	Nw/N[2]	%wLEH[3]	Nw/N	%wLEH	Nw/N	%wLEH
Female						
Young adult[4]	9/24	37.5	13/24	54.2	13/23	56.5
Old adult	1/5	20.0	1/5	20.0	1/6	16.7
Male						
Young adult	4/21	19.0	2/21	9.5	2/19	10.5
Old adult	1/10	10.0	1/10	10.0	2/12	16.7

[1] I = incisors; C = canines.
[2] Nw = number of individuals with one or more LEH; N = number of individuals observed.
[3] %wLEH = % of N with one or more LEH.
[4] Young adult = individuals aged between 16 to 35 years; Old adult = individuals older than 36 years.

subadults in the sample exhibit at least one lesion active at time of death. Four skeletons buried in individual graves are aged to younger than birth and may have been premature stillborns. Each of these exhibits active systemic periostitis including severe, generalized, active endocranial periostitis possibly reflecting uterine infections which may be implicated in the premature births. Similarly, fetal remains with a gestation age of approximately 39 weeks, recovered from the abdomino-pelvic cavity of an adult female also exhibit severe, active, widespread periostitis on the endocranial surfaces of the frontal, parietal and occipital bones, on both mandibular rami, on the left clavicle, right ulna and both femurs and tibias. Of the remaining 16 subadults with periosteal lesions, 9 (4 aged from birth to 6 months, 4 from 2-5 years, and 1 from 6-10 years) exhibit both postcranial and endocranial periostitis, presumably reflecting systemic bacterial infections. In 7 subadults (5 aged from 6-10 years, and 2 from 11-15 years), periosteal lesions are localized on the tibia and fibula.

Skeletal indications of infectious disease in adults consist primarily of elevated periosteal lesions with linear striations and pitting along the shaft of long bones, most frequently the tibia, fibula and femur. Although some cases of localized infection were noted, the majority of lesions involve a larger area of bone, typically most of the medial surface of the tibia or a large area of bone along the linea asperea of the femur. In 7 of the 12 adults with periostitis the lesions are healed (3 males and 4 females), while in five individuals (1 male and 4 females) the lesions are active at time of death. Two cases of chronic osteomyelitis are also noted. The first, resulting from a healed fracture of the proximal right tibia, is present in an adult female. The second, caused by a fracture to the left distal femur, is present in an adult male. Sex differences in the frequencies of periosteal lesions are not statistically significant. The distribution of lesions is, however, consistent with the pattern observed in cribra orbitalia frequencies. Female lesion frequencies (8/33 individuals or 24.2%) are more than twice as high as male frequencies (4/35 individuals or 11.4%). Females also have a higher percentage of lesions active at time of death.

Healed fractures are common in the Nova Rača skeletal series. Two individuals, both male, have multiple fractures: one a rib and femur fracture, and one an ulnar and metatarsal fracture. Four individuals show evidence of cranial trauma. Three males have fractures of the outer table of the cranial vault (8.6% of male crania): two are small depressions in the parietal bone, and one is a transverse fracture of both nasal bones, made with a sharp-edged instrument. A small, circular depression fracture is also present in the frontal bone of one female.

In the upper part of the body, healed midshaft fractures of the left ulna are present in two males (6.3% of male ulnae). One subadult, aged between 11 to 13 years, has a healed midshaft fracture of the right clavicle. In the lower limb, there is a single femoral fracture, in a male, which has healed but was complicated by extensive infection. Two healed fractures of the tibia are also noted, one in a female, that resulted in chronic osteomyelitis, and one in a male. One male has a healed fracture of the fifth metatarsal of the right foot.

Enthesophytes are recorded only in males. Two individuals exhibit enthesophytes on the distal tibia, one on the distal fibula, and 2 on the posterior calcaneus.

Osteoarthritis frequencies in the series are summarized in Table 172. Of the four major joints in the skeleton, osteoarthritis is, in both sexes, most frequently recorded in the elbow. In females this is followed by the shoulder, knee, and hip. In males by the hip, shoulder and knee. In all four joints osteoarthritis is more common in males than in females although none of the differences is statistically significant. Controlling for age, young adult male frequencies are higher in all four joints than young adult female frequencies, although once again, none of the differences is statistically significant.

The overall frequency of vertebral osteoarthritis in the series is 11.6% (49/422). Comparing the different regions of the spine (Table 173), greatest involvement occurs in the thoracic region (30/179 or 16.8%), followed by the cervical (17/141 or 12.1%), and lumbar (2/102 or 2.0%) regions. The total male frequency (16.7%) is considerably higher than the total female frequency (5.6%). This difference is statistically significant ($\chi^2 = 9.12$; P < .01). Controlling for age, young adult males exhibit considerably higher total frequencies of vertebral osteoarthritis than young adult females (10.6% compared to 0.8%, $\chi^2 = 8.34$; P < .01). Significant differences are also present in the frequencies of young adult thoracic vertebral osteoarthritis (20.0% in males compared to none in females, $\chi^2 = 6.44$; P < .02), and in total cervical osteoarthritis frequencies (19.7% compared to 4.3%, $\chi^2 = 5.02$; P < .03).

The frequencies of Schmorl's depressions in the series are summarized in Table 174. The overall frequency of Schmorl's

TABLE 172: Frequency of occurrence of osteoarthritis at major joints in the Nova Rača series

	Shoulder		Elbow		Hip		Knee	
	A[1]/O[2]	%	A/O	%	A/O	%	A/O	%
Female								
Young adult[3]	0/14	0.0	1/14	7.1	0/18	0.0	0/11	0.0
Old adult	3/6	50.0	4/9	44.4	3/8	37.5	2/4	50.0
Total	3/20	15.0	5/23	21.7	3/26	11.5	2/15	13.3
Male								
Young adult	4/15	26.7	8/22	36.4	4/24	16.7	1/24	4.2
Old adult	2/8	25.0	3/10	30.0	6/9	66.7	6/9	66.7
Total	6/23	26.1	11/32	34.4	10/33	30.3	7/33	21.2

[1] A = number of joints affected with osteoarthritis. Osteoarthritis was scored as present if at least one joint element showed evidence of osteoarthritic change.
[2] O = number of joints observed. A joint was scored as present if at least one joint element was completely present, or if two or three elements were partially present.
[3] Young adult = individuals aged between 16 to 35 years; Old adult = individuals older than 36 years.

TABLE 173: Frequency of occurrence of vertebral osteoarthritis in the Nova
Rača series

	Cervical		Thoracic		Lumbar		Total	
	A[1]/O[2]	%	A/O	%	A/O	%	A/O	%
Female								
Young adult[3]	1/48	2.0	0/43	0.0	0/31	0.0	1/122	0.8
Old adult	2/22	9.0	7/35	20.0	1/16	6.3	10/73	13.7
Total	3/70	4.3	7/78	9.0	1/47	2.1	11/195	5.6
Male								
Young adult	2/44	4.5	14/70	20.0	0/37	0.0	16/151	10.6
Old adult	12/27	44.4	9/31	29.0	1/18	5.5	22/76	28.9
Total	14/71	19.7	23/101	22.8	1/55	1.8	38/227	16.7

[1] A = number of vertebrae affected with osteoarthritis or osteophytosis.
[2] O = number of vertebrae observed.
[3] Young adult = individuals aged between 16 to 35 years; Old adult = individuals older than 36 years.

TABLE 174: Frequency of occurrence of Schmorl's
depressions in the Nova Rača series

	Thoracic		Lumbar		Total	
	A[1]/O[2]	%	A/O	%	A/O	%
Female						
Young adult[3]	1/43	2.3	2/31	6.4	3/74	4.0
Old adult	4/35	11.4	4/16	25.0	8/51	15.7
Total	5/78	6.4	6/47	12.7	11/125	8.8
Male						
Young adult	15/70	21.4	3/37	8.1	18/107	16.8
Old adult	11/31	35.5	4/18	22.2	15/49	30.6
Total	26/101	25.7	7/55	12.7	33/156	21.1

[1] A = number of vertebrae with Schmorl's depressions.
[2] O = number of vertebrae observed.
[3] Young adult = individuals aged between 16 to 35 years; Old adult = individuals older than 36 years.

depressions in the sample is 15.6% (44/281). Schmorl's depressions are slightly more common in the thoracic (17.3%) than in the lumbar (12.7%) spine. Total male frequencies are significantly higher than female frequencies (21.1% compared to 8.8%, $\chi^2=5.16$; P < .03). This difference appears to be the result of differences in the young adult age category where males exhibit significantly higher total frequencies of Schmorl's defects than females (16.8% compared to 4.0%, $\chi^2=4.57$; P < .04). Significant differences are also present in the total frequencies of Schmorl's depressions in thoracic vertebra (25.7% compared to 6.4%, $\chi^2=7.21$; P < .01), and in the frequencies of Schmorl's depressions in young adult thoracic vertebra (21.4% compared to 2.3%, $\chi^2=4.97$; P < .03).

6.4. THE KAMENGRAD SKELETAL SERIES

The Kamengrad skeletal series was recovered in 1983 during systematic excavations of the Kamengrad site. Kamengrad is a historic fortress located on a low hill, approximately 7 km south of Koprivnica. It is fist mentioned in historical sources in 1272, and later in 1353, as the fortress of *Keukapronka* or Kamengrad (Stonefort) in Croatian. In 1446 during a conflict between the Croatian-Hungarian court and the Counts of Celje, Kamengrad was destroyed by Janos Hunyadi. Archaeological artifacts recovered from the site attest to the violent nature of the times. Among the recovered material are numerous weapons including iron arrowheads, an iron mace head, knives and spurs (Demo, 1984). The skeletal remains were recovered from the cemetery of the parish church "Saint Emericus". Artifacts from the graves date the use of the cemetery from the second half of the 14th to the 15th century (Demo, 1984). Preservation and completeness of the recovered skeletons was good to excellent.

The age and sex distribution of the series is presented in Table 175. Subadults comprise 20.0% of the sample, and are, as in most series, underrepresented in the youngest (birth-5 years) age categories. These categories are represented by only one individual or 2.8% of the complete sample. Males and females are unevenly distributed (16 females and 12 males), and exhibit considerably different mortality profiles. Females in the series appear to be at greater risk during young adulthood. More than two thirds (68.8%) of the female sample died before 40 years. In comparison, only 25.0% of males died during this interval. Peak mortality in females is between 36-40 years, for males between 41-45 years. These differences are reflected in different average ages at death. For females this is 38.4 years (SD=11.2), for males 47.3 years (SD=10.5).

The frequencies of alveolar bone disease are presented in Table 176. Alveolar bone disease is not present in subadults, and has a low (10.5%) overall frequency in adults. Females exhibit slightly higher frequencies (12.0%) than males (9.8%). More pronounced differences are recorded in the young adult age category but neither are statistically significant.

Adult caries frequencies are also low - 10.1% in females, 11.9% in males, and 11.3% overall (Table 177). Subadults exhibit only 4 carious lesions (4/81 or 4.9%). No sex differences are noted when controlling for age. The modal category for severity of lesion is grade 1 in females and grade 2 in males. Both sexes show a similar distribution of carious lesions. Carious lesions are most frequently located interproximally (in 6/9 of all carious lesions in females, and in 16/20 of all carious lesions in males). In males carious lesions are also recorded on the root of the tooth (2/20), and on the occlusal surface (2/20), while in females lesions are recorded on the root (2/9), and buccal surface of the tooth (1/9).

Enamel hypoplasia frequencies are summarized in Table 178. Slightly less than half (14/31 or 45.2%) of the teeth available

TABLE 175: Age and sex distribution in the Kamengrad series

Age category	Subadult N[1]	%[2]	Female N	%	Male N	%	Total N	%
Birth -1	1	14.3					1	2.8
2- 5	0						0	
6-10	3	42.8					3	8.6
11-15	3	42.9					3	8.6
16-20			0		0		0	
21-25			2	12.5	0		2	5.7
26-30			2	12.5	1	8.3	3	8.6
31-35			1	6.2	0		1	2.8
36-40			6	37.6	2	16.7	8	22.9
41-45			3	18.8	3	25.0	6	17.2
46-50			0		1	8.3	1	2.8
51-55			0		2	16.7	2	5.7
56-60			1	6.2	2	16.7	3	8.6
60+			1	6.2	1	8.3	2	5.7
Total	7	100.0	16	100.0	12	100.0	35	100.0

Mean age at death[3]   x = 38.43   x = 47.33
                        sd = 11.18   sd = 10.48

[1] N = number of individuals dying.

[2] % = % of individuals dying.

[3] Mean age at death is calculated using median values of each age category (for example, 23 for the age category 21-25), and 65 for the age category 60+.

TABLE 176: Frequency of alveolar bone disease in the Kamengrad series

Age category	Subadult A[1]/O[2]	%[3]	Female A/O	%	Male A/O	%
Young adult[4]			4/16	25.0	0/16	0.0
Old adult			11/109	10.1	24/229	10.5
Total	0/87	0.0	15/125	12.0	24/245	9.8

[1] A = number of tooth sockets with periodontal or periapical abscess, or antemortem tooth loss.

[2] O = number of tooth sockets observed.

[3] % = % of tooth sockets with periodontal or periapical abscess, or antemortem tooth loss.

[4] Young adult = individuals aged between 16 to 35 years; Old adult = individuals older than 36 years.

TABLE 177: Frequency of carious lesions in the Kamengrad series

Age category	Subadult A[1]/O[2]	%[3]	Female A/O	%	Male A/O	%
Young adult[4]			1/22	4.5	0/15	0.0
Old adult			8/67	11.9	20/153	13.1
Total	4/81	4.9	9/89	10.1	20/168	11.9

[1] A = number of teeth with carious lesions.

[2] O = number of teeth observed.

[3] % = % of teeth with carious lesions.

[4] Young adult = individuals aged between 16 to 35 years; Old adult = individuals older than 36 years.

for analysis exhibit hypoplastic defects. Hypoplasias are most frequently recorded in mandibular canines - 66.7%, followed by maxillary central incisors - 37.5%, and maxillary canines - 12.5%.

Subadults are poorly represented in the series. Only 10 teeth are available for analysis (4 central maxillary incisors, 2 maxillary, and 4 mandibular canines). One incisor, and 3 mandibualr canines exhibit hypoplastic lines. Male and female frequencies are similar: 5/9 available female, and 5/12 available male teeth exhibit hypoplastic defects.

Cribra orbitalia is recorded in 2/4 subadults with intact orbits (in both cases active at time of death), and in 1/16 adults (in an adult female).

Skeletal evidence for infectious disease is noted in subadults and adults. Two subadults exhibit periostitis on the medial shaft of the tibia, one active and one healed at time of death. Three adults (2 females and 1 male) exhibit healed periostitis on the medial surface of the tibia.

TABLE 178: Hypoplasia frequencies by individual in the Kamengrad series

Tooth	N[1]	NwLEH	%wLEH
Maxillary I1[2]	8	3	37.5
Maxillary C	8	1	12.5
Mandibular C	15	10	66.7

[1] N = number of teeth observed; NwLEH = number of teeth with one or more LEH; %wLEH = % of N with one or more LEH.

[2] I = incisor; C = canine.

One fracture is noted in the series. A compression fracture of the superior end plate of the ninth thoracic vertebra is present in a 56-60 year old female. The fracture resulted in bony union between the eighth and ninth thoracic vertebrae, and moderate kyphosis.

Enthesophytes are recorded in 2 males and 2 females, in all cases on the posterior calcaneus.

Osteoarthritis frequencies are low in the series and restricted to individuals older than 36 years. In females, osteoarthritis is recorded on two acetabuli (2/9). In males, moderate osteoarthritis of the elbow is noted in two (2/9), of the hip in one (1/10), and of the knee in one (1/7) individual.

The overall frequency of vertebral osteoarthritis in the series is low (6.2 % or 16/257). Comparing the different regions of the spine (Table 179), greatest involvement occurs in the thoracic spine (8.9%; 12/135), followed by the lumbar spine (7.4%; 4/54). None of the 68 available adult cervical vertebra

TABLE 179: Frequency of occurrence of vertebral osteoarthritis in the Kamengrad series

	Cervical A[1]/O[2]	%	Thoracic A/O	%	Lumbar A/O	%	Total A/O	%
Female								
Young adult[3]	0/13	0.0	2/30	6.7	3/15	20.0	5/58	8.6
Old adult	0/25	0.0	6/40	15.0	0/18	0.0	6/83	7.2
Total	0/38	0.0	8/70	11.4	3/33	9.1	11/141	7.8
Male								
Young adult	0/5	0.0	0/5	0.0	0/0	0.0	0/10	0.0
Old adult	0/25	0.0	4/60	6.7	1/21	4.8	5/106	4.7
Total	0/30	0.0	4/65	6.1	1/21	4.8	5/116	4.3

[1] A = number of vertebrae affected with osteoarthritis or osteophytosis.
[2] O = number of vertebrae observed.
[3] Young adult = individuals aged between 16 to 35 years; Old adult = individuals older than 36 years.

TABLE 180: Frequency of occurrence of Schmorl's depressions in the Kamengrad series

	Thoracic A[1]/O[2]	%	Lumbar A/O	%	Total A/O	%
Female						
Young adult[3]	3/30	10.0	0/15	0.0	3/45	6.7
Old adult	7/41	17.1	2/18	11.1	9/59	15.2
Total	10/71	14.1	2/33	6.1	12/104	11.5
Male						
Young adult	0/5	0.0	0/0	0.0	0/5	0.0
Old adult	11/60	18.3	3/21	14.3	14/81	17.3
Total	11/65	16.9	3/21	14.3	14/86	16.3

[1] A = number of vertebrae with Schmorl's depressions.
[2] O = number of vertebrae observed.
[3] Young adult = individuals aged between 16 to 35 years; Old adult = individuals older than 36 years.

exhibits evidence of osteoarthritis. No sex differences are noted in the series.

The frequencies of Schmorl's depressions in the series are summarized in Table 180. The overall frequency of Schmorl's depressions in the sample is 13.7% (26/190). Schmorl's depressions are more common in thoracic (21/136; 15.4%), than in lumbar (5/54; 9.3%) vertebrae. Males exhibit higher frequencies of Schmorl's defects in both segments of the spine but these differences are not statistically significant.

6.5. CHARACTERISTICS OF THE COMPOSITE HISTORIC SERIES

This is the second largest composite series with 201 recovered skeletons. It is comprised of four skeletal series located in central and western continental Croatia. Historical sources indicate that this was a violent period. Three of the four analyzed sites are linked with specific episodes of violence. The Kamengrad fortress was destroyed and abandoned in 1446 during conflicts between the Croatian-Hungarian court and the Counts of Celje. Đakovo was captured by Turks in 1536, ending the second burial phase of the medieval cemetery. The inhabitants of Nova Rača were frequently under attack from marauding Turkish war parties. One such episode, which occurred in 1540, is historically documented and relates of a massacre which Turkish raiders committed on the inhabitants of Nova Rača in front of the parish church. The number of casualties is not known but the incident was severe enough to be mentioned in a letter from the local magistrate to the military commander of the area (Medar, 1987).

The age and sex distribution of the series is presented in Table 181. Subadults comprise 29.8% of the total sample which is very similar to the 30.3% frequency recorded in the Late medieval composite series. Representation in the two youngest age categories is, however, slightly better. Subadults younger than 6 years account for 14.0% of the total sample, or 46.7% of the total subadult sample. As in all composite series except the Antique series, subadult mortality is highest from 6-10 years (35.0% of the subadult sample or 10.4% of the complete sample).

Males and females are evenly represented (72 and 69 individuals respectively). The average age at death of adults over 15 years is 32.8 years for females, and 36.1 years for males. This relatively small difference (3.3 years) in average life-spans is reflected, however, in noticeable differences in mortality profiles. The highest mortality rates for females are recorded from 21-30 years (30 individuals or 43.5%), for males from 26-35 years (27 individuals or 37.5%). The difference is additionally highlighted when the number of adults who died before 31 years is compared. Slightly more than half (50.7%) of the females in the series did not live to 31 years, compared to approximately a third (34.8%) of the males. Few individuals (7 females or 10.2% of all adult female deaths, and 11 males or 15.2% of all adult male deaths) lived to be older than 50 years.

The frequencies of alveolar bone disease and carious lesions are summarized in Tables 182 and 183. Alveolar bone disease is not present in any of the 617 subadult tooth sockets available for inspection. The total adult frequency is 12.4% (250/2016) with similar total frequencies for males and females (13.4% and 11.1% respectively). Frequencies in the old adult age category are also similar, but young males exhibit significantly more alveolar bone disease than young females (8.9% compared to 4.9%, $\chi^2=5.47$, P< .02).

The overall frequency of carious lesions in the Historic composite series is 9.7% (216/2231). Subadults exhibit a 7.0%

TABLE 181: Age and sex distribution in the Historic period composite series

Age category	Subadult N[1]	%[2]	Female N	%	Male N	%	Total N	%
Birth -1	12	20.0					12	6.0
2- 5	16	26.7					16	8.0
6-10	21	35.0					21	10.4
11-15	11	18.3					11	5.5
16-20			5	7.2	4	5.5	9	4.5
21-25			20	29.0	9	12.6	29	14.4
26-30			10	14.5	12	16.7	22	10.9
31-35			9	13.1	15	20.8	24	11.9
36-40			11	15.9	10	13.9	21	10.4
41-45			6	8.7	9	12.5	15	7.5
46-50			1	1.4	2	2.8	3	1.5
51-55			3	4.4	5	6.9	8	4.0
56-60			1	1.4	4	5.5	5	2.5
60+			3	4.4	2	2.8	5	2.5
Total	60	100.0	69	100.0	72	100.0	201	100.0

Mean age at death[3]   x = 32.80   x = 36.11
                        sd = 11.74   sd = 11.60

[1] N = number of individuals dying.

[2] % = % of individuals dying.

[3] Mean age at death is calculated using median values of each age category (for example, 23 for the age category 21-25), and 65 for the age category 60+.

TABLE 182: Frequency of alveolar bone disease in the Historic period composite series

Age category	Subadult A[1]/O[2]	%[3]	Female A/O	%	Male A/O	%
Young adult[4]			25/514	4.9	55/619	8.9
Old adult			69/334	20.7	101/549	18.4
Total	0/617	0.0	94/848	11.1	156/1168	13.4

[1] A = number of tooth sockets with periodontal or periapical abscess, or antemortem tooth loss.

[2] O = number of tooth sockets observed.

[3] % = % of tooth sockets with periodontal or periapical abscess, or antemortem tooth loss.

[4] Young adult = individuals aged between 16 to 35 years; Old adult = individuals older than 36 years.

TABLE 183: Frequency of carious lesions in the Historic period composite series

Age category	Subadult A[1]/O[2]	%[3]	Female A/O	%	Male A/O	%
Young adult[4]			30/514	5.8	48/538	8.9
Old adult			36/213	16.9	62/394	15.7
Total	40/572	7.0	66/727	9.1	110/932	11.8

[1] A = number of teeth with carious lesions.

[2] O = number of teeth observed.

[3] % = % of teeth with carious lesions.

[4] Young adult = individuals aged between 16 to 35 years; Old adult = individuals older than 36 years.

frequency, the highest frequency recorded in a composite series. The total adult frequency is 10.6% (176/1659). Adult male and female total frequencies are similar (11.8% and 9.1% respectively), as are frequencies in both adult age groups.

Both subadults and adults display the same modal category, grade 2, for severity of carious lesion. The distribution of carious lesions is also similar. Carious lesions in subadults are most frequently located interproximally (in 30/40 or 75.0% of all carious lesions), followed by occlusal (9/40, 22.5%) and buccal (1/40, 2.5%) lesions. In the adult sample carious lesions are in both sexes most frequently located interproximally (45/66 or 68.2% in females, and 65/110 or 59.1% of all carious lesions in males). In both sexes this is followed by occlusal (14/66 or 21.2% in females, and 26/110 or 23.6% in males), root (3/66 or 4.5% in females, 10/110 or 9.1% in males), buccal (3/66 or 4.5% in females, 8/110 or 7.3 % in males), and lingual (1/66 or 1.5 in females, 1/110 or 0.9% in males) caries.

Enamel hypoplasia frequencies are summarized in Tables 184-187. Hypoplastic defects are recorded in 133 of the 329 (40.4%) teeth available for analysis. Hypoplasias are most frequent in the mandibular canines - 44.9%, followed by maxillary canines - 39.8% and maxillary central incisors - 35.9%.

The Historic composite series has the highest number (56) of subadult teeth available for analysis (18 central maxillary incisors, 18 maxillary and 20 mandibular canines). The total subadult hypolasia frequency is 62.5% (35/56). In this series, hypoplasia in subadults is most frequently recorded in mandibular canines (70.0%), followed by maxillary central incisors (61.1%), and maxillary canines (55.5%).

Comparison with hypoplasia frequencies in the adult sample shows that subadults exhibit higher frequencies of hypoplastic defects in all three tooth categories analyzed than adults. The difference between total subadult (62.5%) and total adult (35.9%) hypoplasia frequencies is statistically significant (χ^2 = 4.60; P < .04).

TABLE 184: Hypoplasia frequencies by individual in the Historic period composite series

Tooth	N[1]	NwLEH	%wLEH
Maxillary I1[2]	103	37	35.9
Maxillary C	108	43	39.8
Mandibular C	118	53	44.9

[1] N = number of teeth observed; NwLEH = number of teeth with one or more LEH; %wLEH = % of N with one or more LEH.

[2] I = incisor; C = canine.

TABLE 185: Hypoplasia frequencies in the Historic period composite series for subadults and adults

Tooth	Subadults		All adults		Females		Males	
	Nw/N[1]	%wLEH[2]	Nw/N	%wLEH	Nw/N	%wLEH	Nw/N	%wLEH
Maxillary I1[3]	11/18	61.1	26/85	30.6	14/41	34.1	12/44	27.3
Maxillary C	10/18	55.5	33/90	36.7	21/43	48.8	12/47	25.5
Mandibular C	14/20	70.0	39/98	39.8	21/45	46.7	18/53	34.0

[1] Nw = number of individuals with one or more LEH; N = number of individuals observed.
[2] %wLEH = % of N with one or more LEH.
[3] I = incisors; C = canines.

TABLE 186: Mean number of hypoplasias in incisors and canines in the Historic period composite series

Tooth	Subadults			All adults			Females			Males		
	Mean	N	S.D.	Mean	N	S.D.	Mean	N	S.D.	Mean	N	S.D.
MaxillaryI1[1]	0.83	18	0.69	0.36	85	0.59	0.41	41	0.62	0.32	44	0.55
Maxillary C	0.67	18	0.67	0.50	90	0.73	0.63	43	0.72	0.38	47	0.73
Mandibular C	0.90	20	0.70	0.58	98	0.79	0.67	45	0.82	0.51	53	0.77

[1] I = incisors; C = canines.

TABLE 187: Hypoplasia frequencies in adult dentition in the Historic period composite series

Sex/age	Maxillary I1[1]		Maxillary C		Mandibular C	
	Nw/N[2]	%wLEH[3]	Nw/N	%wLEH	Nw/N	%wLEH
Female						
Young adult[4]	12/33	36.4	17/34	50.0	16/32	50.0
Old adult	2/8	25.0	4/9	44.4	5/13	38.5
Male						
Young adult	10/31	32.3	11/32	34.3	12/31	38.7
Old adult	2/13	15.4	1/15	6.7	6/22	27.3

[1] I = incisors; C = canines.
[2] Nw = number of individuals with one or more LEH; N = number of individuals observed.
[3] %wLEH = % of N with one or more LEH.
[4] Young adult = individuals aged between 16 to 35 years; Old adult = individuals older than 36 years.

individuals who died before 35 years consistently exhibit higher frequencies of hypoplastic defects than individuals who lived to be older than 36 years.

Cribra orbitalia frequencies are summarized in Table 188. In the Historic composite series the expression of this condition ranges from slight pitting to severe sievelike lesions with some diplotic expansion.

Cribra orbitalia is observed in 48 of the 135 crania (35.5%) with intact orbits. The overall subadult frequency is 55.8% with more than half of the lesions (14/

The highest frequency of hypoplastic defects in the adult sample (Table 185) is recorded in mandibular canines (39.8%), followed by maxillary canines (36.7%), and maxillary central incisors (30.6%). A breakdown of the adult sample by sex shows that females exhibit slightly higher frequencies of hypoplastic defects in all three tooth categories. None of the differences is, however, statistically significant. The difference between total female (56/129 or 43.4%) and total male (42/144 or 29.2%) hypoplasia frequencies is, similarly, not significant.

The observed pattern of higher frequencies of hypoplasia inducing stress in subadults is further supported by comparing the mean number of hypoplastic defects in the analyzed teeth (Table 186). Subadults exhibit a higher number of defects in all three tooth categories than individuals who lived into adulthood. Males and females exhibit similar values. Controlling for age (Table 187) in the adult sample,

TABLE 188: Frequency of occurrence of cribra orbitalia in the Historic period composite series

Age/sex	Cribra orbitalia			Active lesions	
	O[1]	A1[2]	%	A2[3]	% of A1
0 - 0.9	11	2	18.2	2	100.0
1 - 3.9	8	5	62.5	4	80.0
4 - 9.9	13	10	76.9	5	50.0
10 - 14.9	11	7	63.6	3	42.8
All subadults	43	24	55.8	14	58.3
Adult females	44	16	36.4	0	0.0
Adult males	48	8	16.7	0	0.0
All adults	92	24	26.1	0	0.0

[1] O = number of frontal bones observed.
[2] A1 = number of frontal bones in which at least one orbit shows evidence of cribra orbitalia.
[3] A2 = number of frontal bones in which cribra orbitalia is active at time of death.

24) active at time of death. The lesion first appears in subadults at approximately 6 months of age and increases in frequency to a maximum of 76.9% between ages 4 to 9.9. In adults the lesion has a frequency of 26.1% with all of the lesions exhibiting some degree of healing. Subadult and adult frequencies are significantly different ($\chi^2 = 4.27$; P < .04). No significant sex differences are present in cribra orbitalia frequencies in adults.

Skeletal evidence for infectious disease is present in subadults and adults. Because of differential bone preservation, periostitis frequencies are, once again, presented by bone.

TABLE 190: Frequency of occurrence of osteoarthritis at major joints in the Historic period composite series

	Shoulder		Elbow		Hip		Knee	
	A^1/O^2	%	A/O	%	A/O	%	A/O	%
Female								
Young adult[3]	0/24	0.0	1/24	4.2	0/27	0.0	0/20	0.0
Old adult	3/11	27.3	4/15	26.7	7/19	36.8	2/15	13.3
Total	3/35	8.6	5/39	12.8	7/46	15.2	2/35	5.7
Male								
Young adult	4/23	17.4	8/32	25.0	4/38	10.5	1/38	2.6
Old adult	4/19	21.0	6/23	26.1	8/24	33.3	10/20	50.0
Total	8/42	19.0	14/55	25.4	12/62	19.3	11/58	19.0

[1] A = number of joints affected with osteoarthritis. Osteoarthritis was scored as present if at least one joint element showed evidence of osteoarthritic change.

[2] O = number of joints observed. A joint was scored as present if at least one joint element was completely present, or if two or three elements were partially present.

[3] Young adult = individuals aged between 16 to 35 years; Old adult = individuals older than 36 years.

Subadults exhibit endocranial periostitis on 8 frontal (8/43 recovered subadult frontal bones or 18.6%), 17 parietal (17/90 or 18.9%), 10 occipital (10/48 or 20.8%), and 8 temporal (8/84 or 9.5%) bones. Periostitis is also recorded on 6 mandibulae (6/45 or 13.3%). In the subadult postcranial skeleton, periostitis is recorded on 4 clavicles (4/51, 7.8%), 7 ribs (7/165, 4.2%), 4 humerii (4/63 or 6.3%), 3 radii (3/49, 6.1%), 14 femora (14/72, 19.4%), 29 tibiae (29/69 or 42.0%), and 6 fibulae (6/43, 13.9%).

Adults exhibit periostitis only in the postcranial skeleton. Periostitis in females is recorded on one humerus (1/68 recovered female humerii or 1.5%), one radius (1/54, 1.8%), one ulna (1/59, 1.7%) 2 femurs (2/75, 2.7%), 12 tibiae (12/70, 17.1%) and 2 fibulae (2/45, 4.4%). In males, periostitis is noted on the tibiae (9/82, 11.0%), and on one fibula (1/66, 1.5%).

As in the other composite series, subadults show less resistance to infectious disease than adults. Furthermore, most subadult lesions (70.6%) show no evidence of healing, while the same is true for only 25.0% of adult lesions (Table 189). This difference is statistically significant (χ^2=4.91; P < .03).

Three cases of osteomyelitis are noted in the series. All were caused by infections subsequent to fracture. One is located

on the proximal femur of a subadult, one in the proximal tibia of a female, and one in the distal femur of a male.

Healed fractures are recorded in subadults and adults. Most of the fractures are noted in adult males.

Skeletal evidence of healed fractures is noted in 2 subadults. One individual has a fracture of the proximal femur, complicated by subsequent osteomyelitis (1/35 or 2.8% of subadults with both femora recovered). One individual exhibits a healed fracture of the clavicle (1/24, 4.2%).

Four females exhibit evidence of skeletal trauma. Two individuals exhibit healed depression fractures on the cranium (2/49 or 4.1% of females with complete crania). One individual has a fracture on the proximal tibia, complicated by subsequent infection (1/34, 2.9%), while one exhibits a fracture of the ninth thoracic vertebra (1/16 or 6.2% of females with complete thoracic spines).

Adult males also exhibit cranial and postcranial fractures. Healed cranial fractures are recorded in 5 individuals (5/52 or 9.6% of males with complete crania). Postcranial fractures are recorded in the ribs, radius, ulna, femur, tibia and fifth metatarsal. Two individuals exhibit rib fractures (2/17 or 11.8% of males with intact rib cages). One individual exhibits a well healed fracture of the distal radius (1/35 or 2.8% of males with both radii recovered). Two individuals exhibit "parry" fractures on the midshaft of the ulnas (2/35 or 5.7%). Two individuals exhibit femoral fractures (2/49 or 4.1%), 2 exhibit tibial fractures (2/39 or 5.1%), and one exhibits a well healed fracture of the fifth metatarsal bone.

Enthesophytes are noted only in adults. Two females exhibit enthesophytes on the posterior calcanei (2/19 or 10.5% of females with both calcanei recovered). Males exhibit enthesophytes on the distal tibia (2/39 or 5.1% of males with both tibiae recovered), distal fibula (1/31 or 3.2%), and posterior calcaneus (2/21 or 9.5%).

TABLE 189: Frequency of occurrence of active periosteal lesions in the Historic period composite series

	Periosteal lesions		
Sex	$A1^1$	$A2^2$	% of A1
Subadults	119	84	70.6
Adult females	18	5	27.8
Adult males	10	2	20.0
All adults	28	7	25.0
Total	147	91	61.9

[1] A1 = number of bones with periostitis.

[2] A2 = number of bones with periostitis active at time of death.

TABLE 191: Frequency of occurrence of vertebral osteoarthritis in the Historic period composite series

	Cervical		Thoracic		Lumbar		Total	
	A^1/O^2	%	A/O	%	A/O	%	A/O	%
Female								
Young adult[3]	1/74	1.3	2/114	1.7	3/64	4.7	6/252	2.4
Old adult	4/52	7.7	13/78	16.7	1/41	2.4	18/171	10.5
Total	5/126	4.0	15/192	7.8	4/105	3.8	24/423	5.7
Male								
Young adult	2/87	2.3	15/151	9.9	0/65	0.0	17/303	5.6
Old adult	16/77	20.8	20/140	14.3	6/57	10.5	42/274	15.3
Total	18/164	11.0	35/291	12.0	6/122	4.9	59/577	10.2

[1] A = number of vertebrae affected with osteoarthritis or osteophytosis.
[2] O = number of vertebrae observed.
[3] Young adult = individuals aged between 16 to 35 years; Old adult = individuals older than 36 years.

TABLE 192: Frequency of occurrence of Schmorl's depressions in the Historic period composite series

	Thoracic		Lumbar		Total	
	A^1/O^2	%	A/O	%	A/O	%
Female						
Young adult[3]	13/114	11.4	5/64	7.8	18/178	10.1
Old adult	12/79	15.2	6/41	14.6	18/120	15.0
Total	25/193	12.9	11/105	10.5	36/298	12.1
Male						
Young adult	48/151	31.8	13/65	20.0	61/216	28.2
Old adult	43/140	30.7	14/57	24.6	57/197	28.9
Total	91/291	31.3	27/122	22.1	118/413	28.6

[1] A = number of vertebrae with Schmorl's depressions.
[2] O = number of vertebrae observed.
[3] Young adult = individuals aged between 16 to 35 years; Old adult = individuals older than 36 years.

There is no skeletal evidence of dislocation in the series.

Spondylolysis is not recorded in any of the 57 individuals (10 subadult and 47 adult) with complete lumbar spines.

Osteoarthritis frequencies in the series are summarized in Table 190. Osteoarthritis in females is most frequently recorded in the hip joint, followed by the elbow, shoulder, and knee. In males the highest frequency of osteoarthritis is noted in the elbow, followed by the hip, and shoulder and knee which exhibit identical frequencies. Males exhibit higher frequencies of osteoarthritis in all four joints analyzed but none of the differences are significant. Frequencies recorded in the old adult age category are similar in males and females. In the young adult age category males exhibit higher frequencies of osteoarthritis in all four joints. None of the differences is, however, significant.

The overall frequency of vertebral osteoarthritis in the series is 8.3% (83/1000). Comparing the different regions of the spine (Table 191), greatest involvement occurs in the thoracic region 10.3% (50/483), followed by the cervical 7.9% (23/290), and lumbar 4.4% (10/227) regions. The total male frequency (10.2%) is higher than the total female frequency (5.7%). This difference is statistically significant ($\chi^2 = 5.12$; P < .03).

The frequencies of Schmorl's depressions in the series are summarized in Table 192. The overall frequency of Schmorl's depressions in the sample is 21.7% (154/711). Frequencies of Schmorl's depressions are higher in the thoracic spine (24.0% or 116/484) than in the lumbar (16.7% or 38/227). The total male frequency is significantly higher than the total female frequency (28.6% compared to 12.1%, $\chi^2 = 17.57$; P < .01). This difference is noted in both young adult, and old adult age categories, in both of which males exhibit significantly higher frequencies of Schmorl's defects than females ($\chi^2 = 12.69$; P < .01 in the young adult, and $\chi^2 = 4.51$; P < .04 in the old adult age category). These differences appear to be primarily related to differences in the thoracic spine where total frequencies, and frequencies in the young adult age category are significantly higher in males ($\chi^2 = 12.80$; P < .01 in total frequencies, and $\chi^2 = 8.93$; P < .01 in the young adult age category).

7. SIMILARITIES AND DIFFERENCES BETWEEN THE COMPOSITE SERIES

Comparisons between the five composite series show both differences and similarities in demography and the frequency and distribution of disease categories. The similarities may reflect mortuary practices common to the inhabitants of continental Croatia from Prehistoric to Historic times, most noticeable in the biased exclusion of subadult burials in almost all of the skeletal series analyzed. They are also the result of similar levels of cariogenics in the diet, and similar physiological damage that results from suboptimal health in the fetus, infant and developing child, reflected in the skeleton by the presence of cribra orbitalia and enamel hypoplasia.

Differences in the frequencies of specific disease categories and trauma are of primary interest when evaluating changes in general health and the quality of life in successive temporal groups. These data reach their full potential when correlated with available historical and archaeological information. Using this approach specific processes such as migrations, wars, and changes in subsistence strategy can be documented in the biological data and tested in archaeological and historical contexts. Data derived in this manner can also be used to generate hypotheses explaining potential inconsistencies between biological and historical or archaeological data.

7.1. SIMILARITIES BETWEEN COMPOSITE SERIES

One of the most noticeable similarities in all five composite series is the consistent underrepresentation of subadults. Subadults comprise from 21.8% of the total sample in the Early medieval composite series, to 30.3% of the sample in the Late medieval composite series. The two youngest age categories (birth-1 year, and 2-5 years) are the most poorly represented age categories in all five composite series and consistently comprise less than 15.0% of the total sample. This problem is by no means specific only to continental Croatia. The underrepresentation of infants in cemetery samples is a ubiquitous problem. Contributing factors in skeletal series from Croatia include specific mortuary practices such as secondary inhumation, the absence of defined cemeteries in the Prehistoric composite series, and possible differential burial customs for infants and stillborns in the Antique and medieval composite series. Differential burial depths for adults and subadults may also have contributed. Graves dug for adults were, as a rule, deeper than those of children and thus more likely to remain undisturbed. There is some evidence that that this practice is present in continental Croatia (Jakovljević, personal communication), and it has been documented in neighboring Hungary in medieval cemeteries from Alattyan-Tulat and Kerpuszta (Acsádi and Nemeskéri, 1970). Whatever the reasons, the biased exclusion of subadult individuals in all five composite series precludes meaningful consideration of longevity, survivorship, and life expectancy from birth.

Paradoxically, cremated remains recovered from urns in urn cemeteries can sometimes give better approximations of subadult mortality than skeletal series. These series contain the cremated remains of adults and subadults, including infants and premature births, stored in urns generally buried at the same depth. Analysis of a Retz-Gajary culture (3500-3000 years B.C.) urn cemetery from neighboring Slovenia shows that 32 of the 113 recovered individuals (28.5% of the complete sample) died during the first two years of life (Šlaus, technical report 45-10/00, available at the Croatian Academy of Sciences and Arts).

Adult mortality appears to be similar in all five temporal groups. The mean ages at death for adults are: 35.8 years in the Prehistoric composite series, 38.4 years in the Antique composite series, 34.5 years in the Early medieval composite series, 35.4 years in the Late medieval composite series, and 34.5 in the Historic composite series. All five composite series show approximately equivalent rates of death for 16-25 year olds with a range from 16.6% in the Early and Late medieval series to 23.2% in the Prehistoric series. Slight differences are noted in rates of death for 26-40 year olds (range from 26.0% in the Prehistoric series to 42.7% in the Early medieval

series), and in rates of death for individuals older than 40 years (range from 18.0% in Historic series to 32.8% in Antique series) but no pattern is evident.

No significant sex differences in mortality patterns are noted. Adult males live slightly longer in the Prehistoric, Early medieval, and Historic composite series. Females live longer in the Antique and Late medieval composite series. Sex differences in the three series in which males live longer appear to be primarily related to differences in young adult mortality patterns. Female rates of death for 16-25 year olds are in all three series almost twice as high as those recorded in males. In theory, this difference in sex-related mortality could be attributed to complications in pregnancy and childbirth, an assumption which is supported by analysis of burial configuration. In cases of multiple interments within graves, the only consistent pattern noted in continental Croatia involves the pairing of infants with adult females. Unfortunately, antepartum complications such as toxemia and premature rupture of membranes, and postpartum complications such as hemorrhage, hypertensive disorders, and puerperal sepsis, do not affect the skeleton, precluding this hypothesis from being tested on skeletal collections. The only evidence for childbirth-related deaths that can be seen in skeletal material is the presence of fetal remains in the abdomino-pelvic cavity of an adult female. Such events are, however, rarely documented in an archaeological context on a worldwide basis (Acsádi and Nemeskéri, 1970; Owsley and Bradtmiller, 1983). In the five composite series from continental Croatia only one such case is noted. These incidents, furthermore do not reflect female deaths during the puerperal period, as well as the long-term effects of suboptimal health caused by maternal depletion, where female health is comprised due to repeated episodes of pregnancy and lactation. The role of these factors in developing differential male/female mortality profiles needs further investigation through comparative analyses of mortality distributions through time and across different geographical regions.

Low frequencies of dental disease characterize all five composite series. Alveolar bone disease is rare in subadults from all five temporal groups. The greatest recorded frequency is 0.8% noted in the Late medieval composite series. In three series (the Prehistoric, Early medieval, and Historic composite series), alveolar bone disease is not present in any of the available subadult tooth sockets.

Alveolar bone disease is also consistently rare in adults from all five temporal groups. Total adult frequencies range from 8.6% recorded in the Antique composite series, to 14.3% recorded in the Prehistoric series. The three youngest composite series (Early medieval, Late medieval, and Historic series) exhibit very similar frequencies with the range varying from 12.4% to 13.4%.

Caries frequencies are also uniformly low. Subadult frequencies range from 1.3% in the Early medieval series, to 7.0% recorded in the Historic series. Adult frequencies are slightly higher with a range from 7.6% in the Prehistoric, to 10.6% in the Historic composite series. Excluding the

Prehistoric series, the four remaining composite series exhibit an even smaller range with carious lesions present in from 9.5% to 10.6% of the recovered teeth.

The location of the carious lesions on the surface of the tooth, and the severity of the lesions is also similar. In four of the five composite series the modal category for severity of lesion is grade 2 - a lesion that is more than a pit, but less than half of the tooth surface destroyed. In the Prehistoric composite series the modal category for severity of lesion is grade 1- a lesion that is a pit or slight fissure.

Carious lesions are most frequently located interproximally. The range for this location in male dentition in the five temporal groups is from 40.2% to 73.3% of all lesions, in female dentition from 43.5% to 69.2%. The second most frequent location for carious lesions is on the occlusal surface of the tooth, and the third is on the root of the tooth. Buccal and lingual caries are rare in all five composite series.

The permanent dentition is one of the best preserved elements in all five composite series. The similar levels of dental disease noted in both adult and subadult dentitions suggest similar levels of cariogenics in the diet of the inhabitants of continental Croatia from Prehistoric to Historic times.

Undernutrition, infection, and stressors impair morphological development in children, and impact adult morbidity and mortality through metabolic imprinting and impaired immune response (Barker, 1994; Henry and Ulijaszek, 1996). A growing body of bioarchaeological literature links the prevalence of cribra orbitalia and enamel hypoplasia to decreased life expectancy in prehistoric populations (Cook and Buikstra, 1979; Duray, 1996; Goodman and Armelagos, 1988, 1989; Mittler and Van Gerven, 1994; Simpson et al. 1990; Stodder, 1997). Data from skeletal series recovered in continental Croatia clearly reflect these long-term effects in all five temporal groups. The prevalence of hypoplasias in subadult and adult dentitions is similar in all composite series. Subadults consistently exhibit higher frequencies of hypoplastic defects in all three tooth categories analyzed than adults. There is only one exception to this pattern - the frequency of hypoplasias in mandibular canines in the Antique composite series is slightly higher in adults (45.3%) than subadults (36.4%).

Total subadult hypoplasia frequencies range from 45.2% in the Antique composite series, to 64.7% recorded in the Late medieval series. Adult total frequencies are considerably lower, ranging from 35.9% in the Historic, to 45.8% in the Late medieval composite series. Differences are significant in the Historic composite series (χ^2=4.60; P < .04), and in the complete assemblage from continental Croatia (59.4% in subadults, compared to 41.1% in adults; χ^2=6.86; P < .01).

Subadults in all five composite series also exhibit a higher mean number of defects per tooth than adults. This is noted in all three tooth categories with, again, only one exception. The mean number of defects per tooth in mandibular canines in the Prehistoric series is slightly higher in adults (0.65),

than in subadults (0.50). However, it is worth noting that the sample of subadult teeth in the Prehistoric composite series is very small. Only 7 teeth, 2 of them mandibular canines were available for analysis.

A breakdown of the adult sample by age shows that young adults tend to have higher frequencies of hypoplastic defects than individuals who lived to be older than 36 years. This is, for instance, noted in both sexes, in all three tooth categories in the Antique and Historic composite series. The same pattern, but less strictly adhered to, is recorded in the Prehistoric and Early medieval composite series. The only clear exception is the Late medieval composite series in which hypoplasia frequencies in the young adult and old adult age categories are similar.

To summarize, in all five temporal groups the frequency of hypoplasias is lower in individuals who lived until adulthood than in subadults. Not only do adults have a lower incidence of hypoplasia, they also have a smaller number of defects in the teeth affected than individuals who died as children. Individuals older than 36 years also tend to have lower frequencies of hypoplasia than individuals who died before 35 years. These data are consistent with the pattern recorded in other skeletal series (Cook and Buikstra, 1979; Duray, 1996; Goodman and Armelagos, 1988, 1989; Rose et al, 1978; Simpson et al. 1990; Stodder, 1997; White, 1978), and strongly suggest that hypoplasias are related to age at death in the archaeological series from continental Croatia.

The same pattern of subadult and adult involvement is noted in cribra orbitalia frequencies. Cribra orbitalia frequencies in subadults range from 33.3% in the Antique composite series, to 70.3% in the Late medieval composite series. Adult frequencies are considerably lower with a range from 17.2% recorded in the Antique series, to 29.3% in the Late medieval series. Higher frequencies of cribra orbitalia are associated with infancy and childhood in all five composite series. Significant differences are noted in the Early medieval (χ^2=6.56; P < .02), Late medieval (χ^2=5.43; P < .02), and Historic (χ^2=4.27; P < .04) composite series, as well as in the complete assemblage from continental Croatia (56.4% in subadults compared to 23.0% in adults, χ^2=25.31; P < .01). This is consistent with the pattern recorded in other skeletal series (Cybulski, 1977; El-Najjar et al., 1976; Hengen, 1971; Mittler and Van Gerven, 1994, Stuart-Macadam, 1985; Walker, 1985). The implication of the age association is further supported by differentiating active from healed lesions. In all five temporal groups, the frequency of active lesions is highest in the two youngest (0-0.9, and 1-3.9 years) age categories. After 4 years the frequency of active lesions in subadults declines and is uniformly lowest in the 10-14.9 years age category. Together, these data support Stuart-Macadam's (1985) assertion that cribra orbitalia represents a childhood condition.

Subadults in all five temporal groups also exhibit a significantly higher percentage of periosteal lesions active at time of death than adults. The range for percentage of active periosteal lesions in subadults is from 60.0% in the Prehistoric composite series to 75.6% recorded in the Late medieval series. Adults show greater resistance to infectious disease. No active periosteal lesions are recorded in adults from the Prehistoric composite series. In the remaining four temporal groups the range for percentage of active periosteal lesions is from 11.1% recorded in the Antique and Early medieval series, to 38.0% in the Late medieval series. Significant differences between percentages of active lesions in subadults and adults are noted in the Early medieval ($\chi^2 = 7.62$; P < .01), Late medieval ($\chi^2 = 4.07$; P < .05), and Historic ($\chi^2 = 4.91$; P < .03) composite series, as well as in the complete assemblage from continental Croatia (70.9% of periosteal lesions are active in subadults compared to 24.4% in adults, $\chi^2 = 23.15$; P < .01).

The higher susceptibility to infectious disease noted in subadults may be related to greater iron deficiency as indicated by the significantly higher frequencies of cribra orbitalia in subadults. There is evidence that iron deficiency can contribute to decreased immunocompetence and a corresponding increased susceptibility to infectious disease (Basta et al., 1979; Bhaskaram, 1988; Sherman, 1984). Individuals who died as subadults also experienced greater level of subadult stress as seen in the higher frequencies of enamel hypoplasia recorded in subadults. It is therefore probable that the synergism of physiological stressors and impaired immune function increased susceptibility to infectious disease in subadults.

Skeletal markers of physical stress do not exhibit such well defined patterns of involvement. No significant sex differences are noted in the frequencies of osteoarthritis in the major joints in any of the temporal groups. The age-dependence of joint osteoarthritis is, however, clearly demonstrated in all five composite series. Individuals older than 36 years uniformly exhibit higher frequencies of osteoarthritis than individuals who died before 35 years. Only two exceptions are noted, both in the Antique composite series, one in females involving the frequency of osteoarthritis in the elbow, and one in males involving the frequency of osteoarthritis in the knee.

Total vertebral osteoarthritis frequencies are low in all five temporal groups with a range from 5.9% in the Prehistoric composite series to 16.7% recorded in the Late medieval series. In three composite series: the Antique, Early medieval and Historic, greatest involvement occurs in the thoracic spine. In two, the Prehistoric and Late medieval, greatest involvement occurs in the lumbar spine. The age-dependence of vertebral osteoarthritis is also clearly demonstrated. In all five temporal groups vertebral osteoarthritis is more frequent in the old adult age category.

Total frequencies of Schmorl's depressions range from 4.7% in the Prehistoric series to 21.7% recorded in the Historic composite series. No clear trend is noticed in the distribution of the lesions. In three series, the Prehistoric, Early medieval, and Historic, greatest involvement occurs in the thoracic spine, in two, the Antique and Late medieval, in the lumbar spine. Unlike the other analyzed indicators of physical stress, no clear age-dependence is noted in the distribution of Schmorl's lesions.

7.2. DIFFERENCES IN, AND BETWEEN COMPOSITE SERIES

Individuals from the five temporal groups also exhibit significant differences in the distribution and frequencies of specific disease categories. These differences include sex differences within individual composite series, as well as temporal differences in the frequencies of specific disease categories.

7.2.1. Sex differences in composite series

Significant sex differences in the frequencies of alveolar bone disease are noted in all five temporal groups. In two series, the Prehistoric and Historic, males exhibit significantly higher frequencies of alveolar bone disease. In the Prehistoric series the differences are noted in total frequencies and frequencies in the old adult age category. These differences may reflect differences in the age distribution as males in the sample on average live 6.7 years longer than females. In the Historic composite series the difference is noted in the young adult age categories and is, therefore, not related to the age distribution.

Females exhibit significantly higher frequencies of alveolar bone disease in three temporal groups, the Antique, Early medieval, and Late medieval. In the Antique and Late medieval series differences are noted in total frequencies and frequencies in the old adult age categories. These differences do not, however, appear to be related to the age distribution as mortality patterns in these two composite series are very similar. In the Early medieval composite series the difference is noted in the young adult age category and is therefore clearly not related to differences in age distribution.

Sex differences, although less frequently, are also noted in the frequencies of carious lesions. Differences are noted in two series, in both cases in the young adult age category. In the Antique composite series young adult males exhibit higher frequencies of caries than females. In the Early medieval series females younger than 35 years have significantly more caries than males. Young adult females also exhibit higher frequencies of alveolar bone disease in this series. Similar to most of the differences in alveolar bone pathology, these differences do not appear to be related to mortality patterns and the age distribution in a series. Instead, the observed differences may reflect a number of conditions including differential susceptibility to dental disease, differential access to foodstuffs, differential physiological insults, and/or differential cultural behaviors which impacted dental health. Unfortunately, as already discussed, no ethno-historical data regarding food preparation or behavior that could affect dental health is available for these populations. The recovered teeth show no evidence of any type of cultural behavior that could affect dental health (e.g., dental modification, interproximal grooves). Further systematic analyses of dental disease frequencies in skeletal series from continental Croatia are, therefore, necessary to determine the causes of these differences.

Sex differences in the distribution of markers of subadult stress in adults are not significant. As a general observation, males tend to have higher frequencies of enamel hypoplasia, and a higher mean number of defects per tooth than females. None of the differences noted is, however, statistically significant and there is one exception. In the Historic period females exhibit both a higher frequency of enamel hypolasia, and a higher number of defects per tooth than males.

The same pattern is seen in the frequencies of cribra orbitalia. In four of the five composite series, the one exception again being the Historic composite series, males exhibit higher frequencies of healing cribra orbitalia lesions than females. In the Antique composite series this difference is marginally not significant ($\chi^2=3.40$; P < .07). These data imply higher rates of anemia in subadult males from Prehistoric to Late medieval times.

No sex differences are noted in the frequencies of periosteal lesions and joint osteoarthritis.

Females exhibit significantly higher frequencies of vertebral osteoarthritis in the Prehistoric (both in total frequencies and in the frequencies recorded in young adults), and Late medieval series (in total frequencies and frequencies in the old adult age category). Higher frequencies of vertebral osteoarthritis are recorded in males in the Antique (in the young adult age category), and the Historic series (in total frequencies).

Schmorl's defects are considerably more frequent in male vertebral columns. The differences are significant in the three youngest composite series. In the Early medieval series differences are noted in total frequencies and frequencies recorded in young adults, in the Late medieval series in total frequencies and frequencies recorded in the old adult age category, and in the Historic series in total frequencies, and frequencies recorded in both the young and old adult age categories. Females exhibit a significantly higher frequency of Schmorl's defects in the Prehistoric composite series.

No clear pattern is seen in sex differences related to stress on the vertebral column. The data does imply, however, that Schmorl's defects can result from factors not related to those responsible for the development of vertebral osteoarthritis. In two composite series, the Early medieval and Late medieval, males exhibit significantly higher total frequencies of Schmorl's defects than females. These differences are not, however, accompanied with higher male frequencies in vertebral osteoarthritis. No sex differences are noted in the Early medieval series, while in the Late medieval series females exhibit significantly higher frequencies of vertebral osteoarthritis than males.

7.2.2. Temporal differences between composite series

Comparing the frequencies of specific disease categories across the five temporal groups provides a, somewhat, surprising result. The frequencies of several skeletal indicators

of stress; enamel hypoplasia, cribra orbitalia, skeletal evidence of infectious disease, and trauma, imply that living conditions deteriorated significantly during the Late medieval period.

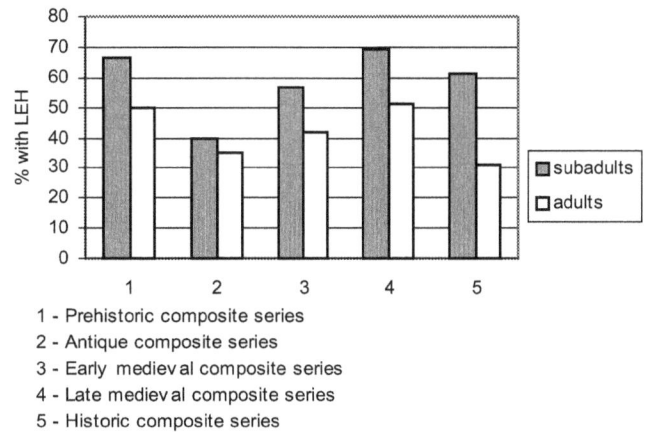

1 - Prehistoric composite series
2 - Antique composite series
3 - Early medieval composite series
4 - Late medieval composite series
5 - Historic composite series

Figure 31. The frequencies of enamel hypolasia in subadult and adult central maxillary incisors in the five temporal groups.

Total enamel hypoplasia frequencies are, for instance, highest in the Late medieval period (49.2% of all analyzed teeth from this period exhibit hypoplastic defects), as are frequencies recorded separately for subadults (64.7%), and adults (45.8%). In all five composite series hypoplasias are most frequently recorded on maxillary central incisors and mandibular canines. When the frequencies of hypoplastic defects in maxillary central incisors are compared across the five temporal groups, the highest frequency in both subadults and adults is recorded in the Late medieval series (Figure 31). The same pattern is noted when the mean number of defects in maxillary central incisors is analyzed in the five temporal groups (Figure 32).

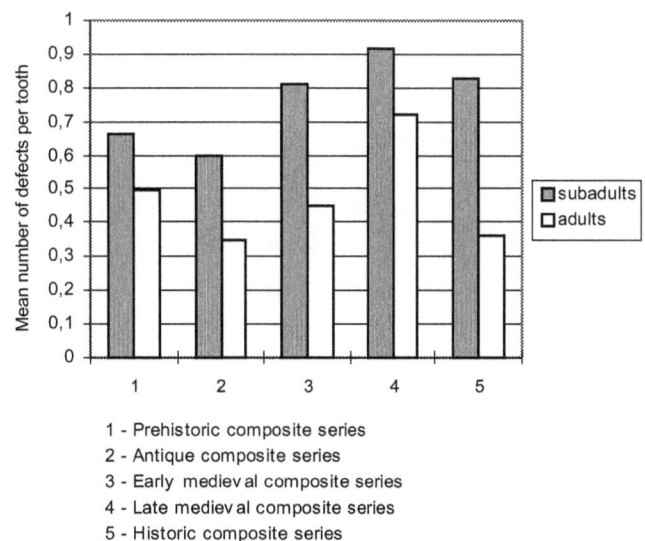

1 - Prehistoric composite series
2 - Antique composite series
3 - Early medieval composite series
4 - Late medieval composite series
5 - Historic composite series

Figure 32. The mean number of hypoplasias in subadult and adult central maxillary incisors in the five temporal groups.

Cribra orbitalia frequencies in subadults and adults are also highest in the Late medieval composite series (Figure 33). Furthermore, the percentage of cribra orbitalia lesions active at time of death in subadults is also highest (73.1%) in this temporal group.

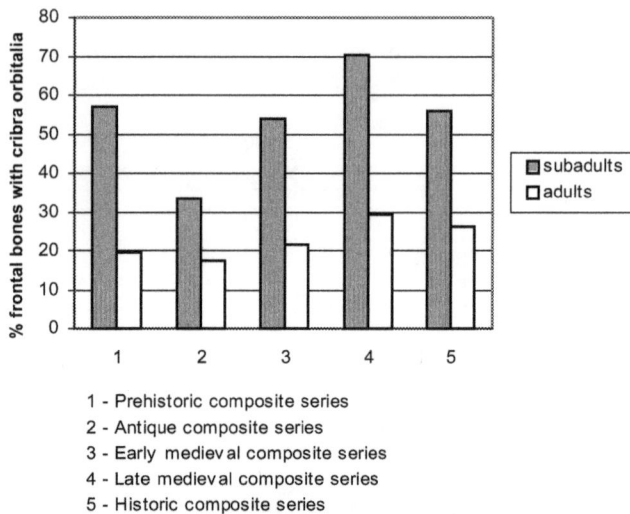

1 - Prehistoric composite series
2 - Antique composite series
3 - Early medieval composite series
4 - Late medieval composite series
5 - Historic composite series

Figure 33. The frequency of cribra orbitalia in subadults and adults in the five temporal groups.

Skeletal evidence for infectious disease is also most prevalent in the Late medieval composite series. Tibial periostitis frequencies in subadults and adults are highest in this series (Figure 34), as are the frequencies of subadult and adult periosteal lesions active at time of death (Figure 35).

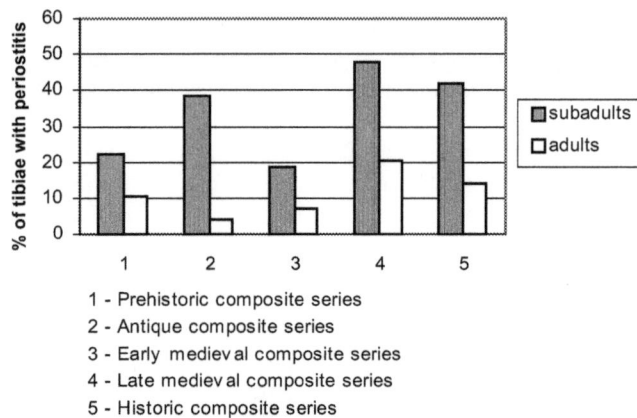

1 - Prehistoric composite series
2 - Antique composite series
3 - Early medieval composite series
4 - Late medieval composite series
5 - Historic composite series

Figure 34. The frequencies of tibial periostitis in subadults and adults in the five composite series.

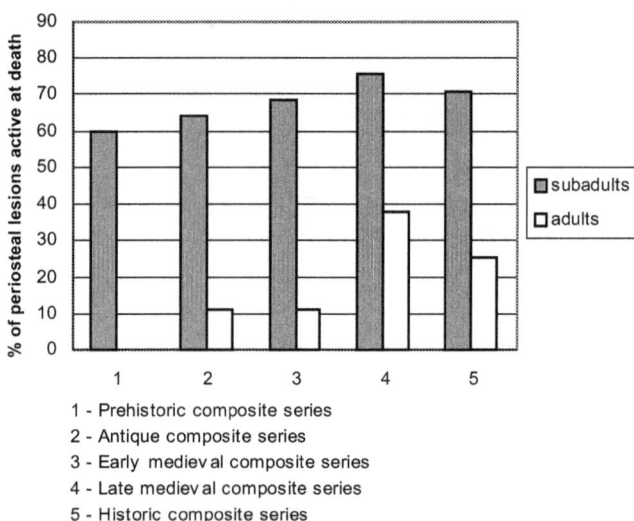

1 - Prehistoric composite series
2 - Antique composite series
3 - Early medieval composite series
4 - Late medieval composite series
5 - Historic composite series

Figure 35. The frequencies of periosteal lesions active at time of death in subadults and adults in the five temporal groups.

Defensive, midshaft fractures of the ulna in adults are also most frequent in the Late medieval period (Figure 36).

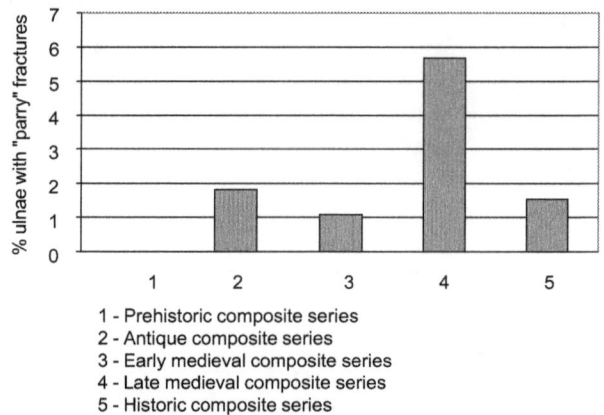

1 - Prehistoric composite series
2 - Antique composite series
3 - Early medieval composite series
4 - Late medieval composite series
5 - Historic composite series

Figure 36. The frequency of midshaft "parry" fractures of the ulna in adults in the five temporal groups.

Collectively these data, the high frequencies of subadult stress, infectious disease, and trauma, suggest a significant decline in general health and quality of life in the Late medieval period. There is, however, no indication of deteriorating living conditions in the available historical sources or the archaeological record. The Late medieval period is, with the exception of the violent but brief Mongol invasion in 1242, generally regarded as a period of relative stability and development. Certainly, based on historical sources it would appear to be more tranquil than the Early medieval period, characterized by the destruction of the short-lived Gepid and Avar kingdoms, and the Historic period, characterized by Turkish raids, invasion and long-term border conflicts. Even the Antique period, with it's frequent civil wars, barbarian intrusions and inherent socio-economic weaknesses which eventually led to the fall of the Western Roman Empire, could reasonably be viewed as a more hostile environment to the inhabiting populations. Yet in all of these periods, subadult stress, infectious disease, and trauma frequencies are lower than in the Late medieval period. Clearly, archaeological data and historic sources are not telling the whole story.

A different type of biological data than that discussed so far can supply a hypothesis to explain this apparent inconsistency. These data are metric data from crania.

8. CRANIOMETRIC RELATIONSHIPS BETWEEN MEDIEVAL POPULATIONS FROM CONTINENTAL CROATIA

Biological anthropology has a long tradition of taking measurements, particularly of the cranium. This tradition dates from the mid-nineteenth century and has since then undergone important theoretical and methodological changes. The two developments most responsible for the use of craniometric data in bioarchaeological investigations are the development of multivariate statistical procedures, and the development of computers and software programs which allow management of large data bases (Jantz, 1994). The basic principle of these analyses is that similar craniofacial morphology reflects genetic similarity.

Multivariate statistical analyses of craniometric data have successfully been used to infer historical relationships and migrations in numerous previous studies (for example, Jantz, 1973, 1974; Key, 1994; Owsley and Jantz, 1999; Rösing and Schwidetzky, 1977, 1981; Schwidetzky, 1967, 1972; Schwidetzky and Rösing, 1984, Šlaus 1998b, 2000b; Šlaus and Filipec, 1998). This type of investigation is particularly amenable to answering questions related to the origin of the first Croat populations that settled on the east coast of the Adriatic. This in turn may help to explain the apparent deterioration of living conditions in continental Croatia during the Late medieval period.

Historical sources are vague and inconsistent regarding both the origin of, and the time of arrival of the first Croatian populations on the east Adriatic coast (Katičić, 1997). Two similar, but slightly conflicting reports, are presented in the *"De Administrando Imperio"* written in the 10th century by the Byzantine Emperor Constantine VII. In the 29. and 31. chapters of this book, the Emperor states that Croats originate from an area north of Hungary. The Emperor Heraclius (610-641) invited them to live in Dalmatia. During their migration they defeated the Avars and settled in Dalmatia after which they were, again on the orders of Heraclius, christened by priests from Rome. The 30. chapter, written by an anonymous writer, states that Croats originate from an area north of Bavaria where they were subject to the Franks. Led by five brothers and two sisters they made their way south to Dalmatia where they settled after defeating the Avars.

TABLE 193: Sites included in principal components analysis

Site	Country	Datation	Reference
1. Vukovar-Lijeva Bara	Croatia	10-11 cent.	Pilarić and Schwidetzky, 1987
2. Bribir	Croatia	9-11 cent.	Pilarić and Schwidetzky, 1987
3. Mravinci	Croatia	9-10 cent.	Mikić, 1990
4. Nin-Ždrijac	Croatia	8-10 cent.	Štefančić, 1995
5. Danilo	Croatia	10-16 cent.	Šlaus, 1996
6. St. Jankovci	Croatia	7-8 cent.	Šlaus, 1993
7. Privlaka	Croatia	8-9 cent.	Šlaus, 1993
8. Bijelo Brdo	Croatia	10-11 cent.	Šlaus, 2000b
9. Bugojno	B and H	10-16 cent.	Klug, 1987
10. Gomjenica	B and H	10-11 cent.	Pilarić, 1969[2]
11. Tokod	Hungary	4-5 cent.	Éry, 1981
12. Baranja	Hungary	4-5 cent.	Éry, 1981
13. Kékesd	Hungary	8 cent.	Wenger, 1968
14. Kérpuszta-Kérektábla	Hungary	10-12 cent.	Liptak, 1953
15. Szekszárd-Palánk	Hungary	6-8 cent.	Liptak, 1974
16. Toponár-Örház	Hungary	8 cent.	Wenger, 1974
17. Alattyán-Tulát	Hungary	6-8 cent.	Wenger, 1957
18. Ártánd	Hungary	8 cent.	Éry, 1967
19. Homokmégy-Halom	Hungary	7-8 cent.	Liptak, 1957
20. Madaras	Hungary	6-8 cent.	Liptak and Marcsik, 1976
21. Sükösd-Ságod	Hungary	7 cent.	Kohegyi and Marcsik, 1971
22. Szeged-Fehértó A	Hungary	6-8 cent.	Liptak and Vamos, 1969
23. Szeged Kundomb	Hungary	6-8 cent.	Liptak and Marcsik, 1966
24. Szeged Makkoserdo	Hungary	6-8 cent.	Vamos, 1973
25. Szentes-Kaján	Hungary	7-8 cent.	Wenger, 1955
26. Üllo I	Hungary	7-8 cent.	Liptak 1955
27. Üllo II	Hungary	7-8 cent.	Liptak, 1955
28. Kecel I	Hungary	8 cent.	Liptak, 1954
29. Virt	Slovakia	7-8 cent.	Hanakova et al., 1976
30. Želovce	Slovakia	7-8 cent.	Stloukal and Hanakova, 1974
31. Nové Zámky I+II	Czech Rep.	8 cent.	Stloukal and Hanakova, 1966
32. Josefov	Czech Rep.	9 cent.	Hanakova and Stloukal, 1966
33. Mikulčice	Czech Rep.	9 cent.	Stloukal and Vyhnanek, 1976
34. Pitten-Kreuzackergasse	Austria	9 cent.	Fabrizii and Reuer, 1977
35. Ptuj	Slovenia	10-11 cent.	Ivaniček, 1951
36. Nadrljan-Salaš	Yugoslavia	6-7 cent.	Bartucz and Farkas, 1957
37. Cedynia	Poland	8-10 cent.	Wokroj, 1971
38. Wišlica	Poland	10-13 cent.	Wiercinski, 1971
39. Ostrów-Lednicki	Poland	9-12 cent.	Wokroj, 1953

Other medieval authors, writing in the 12th and 13th centuries disagree and state that Croats are of Germanic origin, one of them even equating the Croats with Goths.

Multivariate statistical analysis of craniometric data from 39 sites in Central Europe were used as an investigative procedure to elucidate historical relationships between Early medieval populations. The provenance and datations of the sites included in the analysis are presented in Table 193. The analyzed data set includes sites from Croatia, Bosnia and Herzegovina, Slovenia, Yugoslavia, Hungary, the Czech Republic, Slovakia, Austria, and Poland. Sample means for eight cranial measurements are shown in Table 194. The cranial measurements included in the analysis are: maximum cranial length (Martin-Saller No. 1), maximum cranial breadth

(Martin-Saller No. 8), minimum frontal breadth (Martin-Saller No. 9), basion-bregma height (Martin-Saller No. 17), bizygomatic breadth (Martin-Saller No. 45), upper facial height (Martin-Saller No. 48), orbital breadth (Martin-Saller No. 51), and orbital height (Martin-Saller No. 52). Only male skulls were used in the analysis.

The data was first analyzed by principal components analysis using the MULTIVARIATE - PRINCIPAL COMPONENTS subroutine in the Statgraphics 4.0 statistical software package. The procedure calculated 8 principal components, the first two of which account for more than 50.0% of the variability in the sample (Table 195). The distribution of the sites on the first two principal components is shown in Figure 37. If the Croatian and Bosnian and Herzegovinian sites are excluded

TABLE 194: Sample mean values for cranial variables

Site	Mean values for variables defined by Martin-Saller							
	1	8	9	17	45	48	51	52
1. Vukovar-Lijeva Bara	182.9	144.1	98.9	134.2	129.2	78.1	40.9	32.9
2. Bribir	185.8	135.1	98.1	136.5	119.0	67.7	40.0	32.9
3. Mravinci	186.1	138.3	97.9	136.3	131.3	68.9	38.1	30.3
4. Nin-Ždrijac	187.7	138.1	96.7	135.4	131.3	70.3	40.7	32.9
5. Danilo	187.2	145.5	97.2	139.4	134.0	67.0	40.2	31.5
6. St. Jankovci	181.8	140.3	97.2	131.4	135.5	70.7	40.0	32.2
7. Privlaka	184.6	139.5	96.8	133.7	130.6	70.6	39.4	33.0
8. Bijelo Brdo	187.5	140.5	99.3	137.1	134.2	73.1	39.8	33.3
9. Bugojno	192.6	141.8	98.3	138.8	133.0	69.7	41.8	32.4
10. Gomjenica	190.9	138.7	97.7	139.3	128.8	71.3	39.7	33.5
11. Tokod	183.1	141.9	96.2	132.0	132.5	66.5	42.4	33.2
12. Baranja	184.5	140.9	97.0	132.5	130.9	70.1	42.2	34.2
13. Kékesd	182.9	143.7	99.4	137.3	134.3	69.8	41.8	33.8
14. Kérpuszta-Kérektábla	183.4	142.6	99.1	135.1	133.7	69.3	36.3	32.6
15. Szekszárd-Palánk	184.1	146.1	99.3	137.1	134.7	70.7	40.5	33.1
16. Toponár-Orház	188.0	140.3	98.3	137.7	132.9	69.3	42.1	33.7
17. Alattyán-Tulát	185.4	147.7	98.5	130.5	136.4	69.4	42.3	34.0
18. Ártánd	186.3	146.2	98.1	134.4	137.8	70.1	43.0	33.3
19. Homokmégy-Halom	181.9	145.2	97.4	133.2	134.3	72.2	40.3	33.1
20. Madaras	181.0	142.8	94.3	130.8	138.1	76.3	40.1	33.7
21. Sükösd-Ságod	182.9	141.8	95.7	127.8	133.1	69.5	40.8	32.8
22. Szeged-Fehértó A	182.2	139.5	98.1	131.5	134.5	70.9	40.6	34.4
23. Szeged Kundomb	182.6	145.0	96.8	129.5	134.0	68.9	41.4	32.7
24. Szeged Makkoserdo	179.0	142.4	99.0	135.7	135.6	69.3	41.4	32.6
25. Szentes-Kaján	178.2	143.1	97.6	136.2	134.0	70.7	40.6	33.8
26. Üllo I	181.8	143.8	95.4	130.3	132.6	71.6	39.7	32.7
27. Üllo II	181.5	144.8	98.1	129.9	134.2	69.9	39.3	31.6
28. Kecel I	181.8	145.4	98.2	129.6	134.6	70.6	40.0	32.8
29. Virt	184.1	140.4	98.7	136.4	130.5	68.2	41.9	32.5
30. Želovce	185.5	142.2	99.3	136.2	133.0	70.6	41.8	31.9
31. Nové Zámky I+II	184.5	140.1	97.8	133.1	134.3	71.5	41.0	33.3
32. Josefov	188.6	137.8	99.3	137.1	133.4	72.3	42.6	33.0
33. Mikulčice	187.4	142.6	99.2	137.0	133.9	72.4	41.9	33.7
34. Pitten-Kreuzackergasse	187.6	140.0	98.1	137.2	132.8	71.0	42.2	33.5
35. Ptuj	189.3	143.6	99.5	136.5	133.2	70.6	41.7	32.9
36. Nadrljan-Salaš	181.9	145.0	96.0	127.1	133.5	69.4	39.0	32.6
37. Cedynia	189.0	139.3	97.6	134.7	132.5	68.1	40.1	32.9
38. Wišlica	189.5	139.1	96.1	135.0	131.5	70.0	41.9	32.6
39. Ostrów-Lednicki	185.2	140.9	97.3	136.0	132.4	65.0	40.8	31.8

TABLE 195: Principal components analysis

Component number	Percent of variance	Cumulative percentage
1	30.39	30.39
2	22.50	52.89
3	14.84	67.73
4	12.13	79.86
5	8.6	88.02
6	4.58	92.60
7	4.09	96.69
8	3.31	100.00

TABLE 196: Values for component weights in the first two principal components

Variable number according to Martin-Saller	Component weights on the 1. principal component	Component weights on the 2. principal component
1	0.496	0.112
8	-0.425	0.279
9	0.300	0.371
17	0.528	0.192
45	-0.390	0.350
48	-0.166	0.263
51	0.125	0.560
52	-0.084	0.476

from analysis, this distribution shows a clear pattern of intergroup relationships with four well defined clusters. The first cluster consists of samples from Avaroslav sites west of the Danube, the second of samples from Avaroslav sites east of the Danube, the third of samples from the Bijelo Brdo culture, and the fourth of samples from Polish sites (Figure 38).

The positions of the analyzed Croatian sites in relation to the observed clusters are the following. Samples from the Dalmatian sites: Bribir, Mravinci, Nin-Ždrijac and Danilo-Šematorij representing the nucleus of the Early medieval Croat state, are located in the lower right part of the plot in the cluster of Polish sites. Nin-Ždrijac, the most important early medieval Croatian site occupies almost the same position as Cedynia, an early medieval site from northern Poland approximately 75 km south of the Baltic sea. The two Croatian Avaroslav sites: Privlaka and Stari Jankovci are located in the cluster of Avaroslav sites west of the Danube. Bijelo Brdo is located in the cluster of Bijelo Brdo sites, while Vukovar, another Bijelo Brdo culture site, appears to be more similar to Avaroslav sites east of the Danube. The position of the two Bosnian sites is unclear. Gomjenica is closest to the cluster of Polish sites, while Bugojno appears to be closest to the Bijelo Brdo cluster.

These results seem to suggest that Early medieval Croat populations migrated to the east coast of the Adriatic from an area located in modern Poland. As the only fact in which all historical sources concur is that Croats are not autochthonous, but migrated to modern Croatia from an as yet unknown place of origin, this result is not unreasonable.

Values for the component weights in the first two principal components are shown in Table 196. The first principal component is dominated by measurements defining the neurocranium, and primarily differentiates between dolichocranic and brachycranic, and hypsicranic and chamaecranic skulls. Measurement defining the face are better represented in the second principal component which primarily differentiates skulls with wide faces and large orbits from skulls with narrow faces and small orbits.

In an attempt to confirm the hypothesis suggested by principal components analysis the same sites, minus the eight Croatian, and two Bosnian sites whose affiliation is now under investigation, were subjected to discriminant function analysis. The aim was to determine if the 29 analyzed sites could accurately be classified into the four large population groups suggested by Principal components analysis: Avaroslav populations west of the Danube, Avaroslav populations east of the Danube, Bijelo Brdo culture populations, and Polish populations. The analysis was carried out with the MULTIVARIATE - DISCRIMINANT FUNCTION subroutine in the Statgraphics 4.0 statistical software package. The procedure calculated two statistically significant discriminant functions (Table 197). The distribution of the analyzed sites and the four group centroids on the two discriminant functions is shown in Figure 39. The accuracy of the functions appears to be high. Only one of the 29 analyzed sites, Toponar-Orhaz an Avaroslav site west of the Danube, is classified into the wrong group.

Classification function coefficients for classifying new observations are presented in Table 198. The number of rows equals the number of variables plus one, the last row being a constant in each function. The number of columns equals the number of groups. A new case is classified by evaluating each function and assigning the case to the group corresponding to the highest function value.

Applying these coefficients to the Croatian and Bosnian samples gives the following results. The Dalmatian sites: Nin-Ždrijac, Mravinci, and Danilo-Šematorij are classified into the group of Polish populations, as are the two Bosnian sites, Bugojno and Gomjenica. Vukovar and Bijelo Brdo are classified into the group of Bijelo Brdo culture populations. The two Avaroslav sites, Privlaka and Stari Jankovci, are classified into the group of Avaroslav populations west of the Danube. Only Bribir appears to be wrongly classified. This Early medieval Croatian site is classified into the group of Bijelo Brdo culture populations.

These results support the hypothesis suggested by principal components analysis, and also tentatively suggest that Early medieval Croat populations were not limited to the eastern Adriatic coast, but expanded into modern Bosnia and Herzegovina.

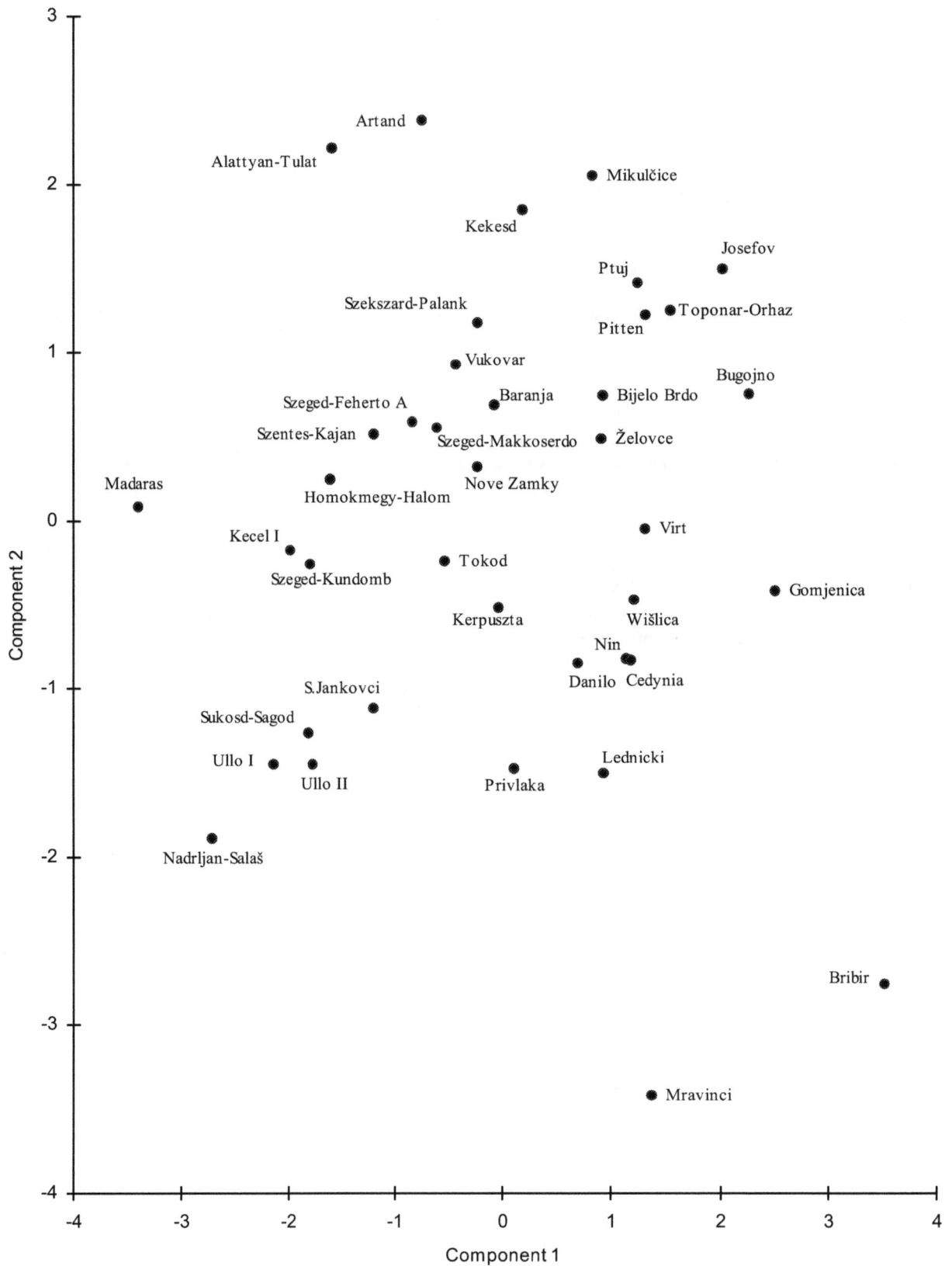

Figure 37. Plot of the sites on the first two principal components

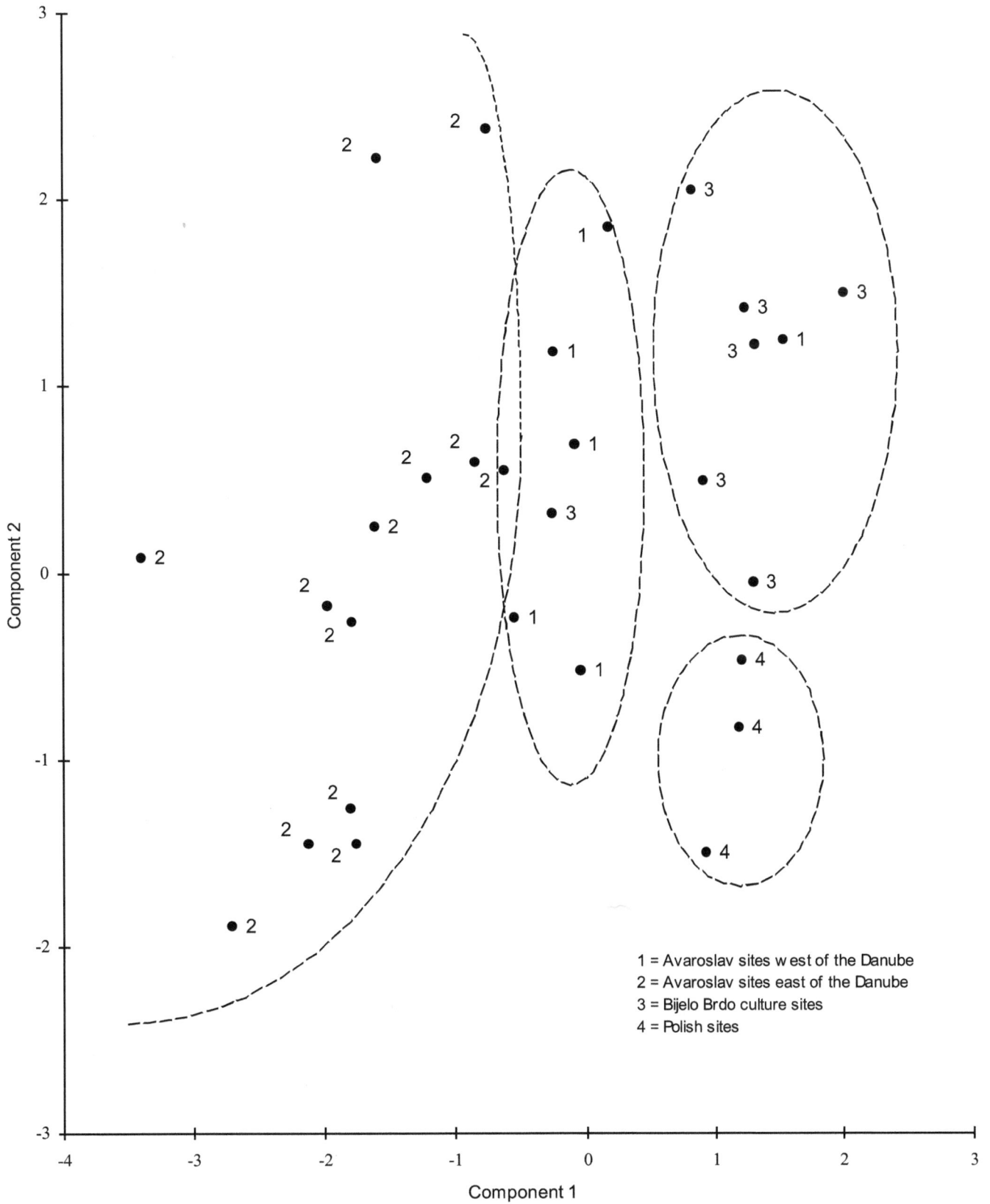

Figure 38. Distribution of sites on the first two principal components without Croatian and Bosnian sites

1 = Avaroslav sites w est of the Danube
2 = Avaroslav sites east of the Danube
3 = Bijelo Brdo culture sites
4 = Polish sites

TABLE 197: Discriminant analysis of Early medieval crania from Central Europe

Dis. function	Eigenvalue	Relative percentage	Cannonical correlation	Wilks λ	χ^2	DF	Sig. level
1	6.1786	73.45	0.9277	0.0341	74.29	24	0.0000
2	1.7511	20.82	0.7978	0.2451	30.93	14	0.0056

TABLE 198: Classification function coefficients

Variable number according to Martin-Saller	Population group[*]			
	1	2	3	4
1	28.55	27.34	28.99	30.87
8	22.38	22.62	21.62	21.11
9	51.39	52.28	53.08	48.06
17	1.73	0.21	1.39	3.40
45	19.35	20.45	18.71	20.30
48	14.73	15.78	16.39	12.59
51	-4.63	-2.97	-2.85	-8.09
52	50.66	49.49	46.57	47.77
Constant	-9418.35	-9367.12	-9483.89	-9313.95

[*] 1= Avaroslav populations west of the Danube
2 = Avaroslav populations east of the Danube
3 = Bijelo Brdo populations
4 = Polish populations

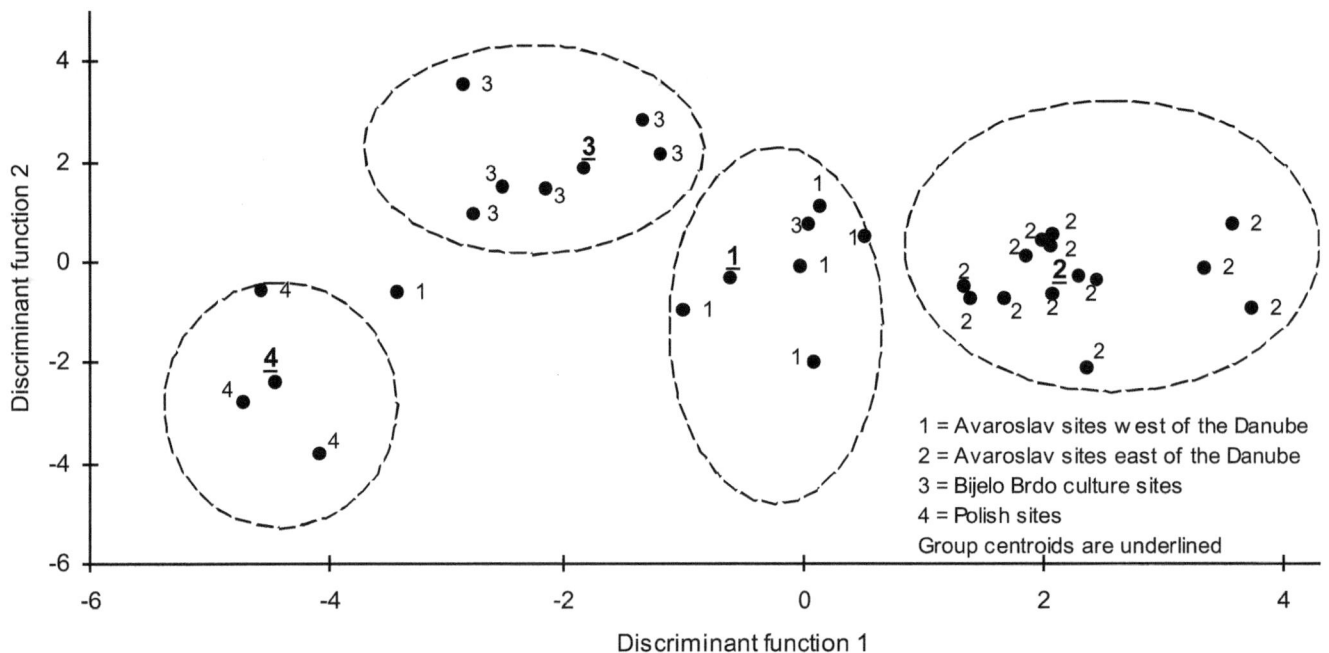

Figure 39. Plot of the analyzed sites and the four group centroids on the two discriminant functions

Following the publication of these discriminant functions (Šlaus, 1998b), a skeletal biology research project was developed at the Croatian Academy of Sciences and Arts. The purpose of this project was to collect craniometric data from two sources: 1) medieval skeletal series from Croatia not included in the previous analysis, and 2) published reports of medieval skeletal series from neighboring countries not included in the previous analysis. The collected data would be pooled and analyzed with the developed discriminant functions.

In two years craniometric data were collected from an additional 6 series in continental Croatia (including 4 series featured in this book: Stenjevac, Lobor, Đelekovec, and Đakovo phase I), and from 8 sites in Hungary, the Czech republic, and Slovakia. The provenance and datation of these sites is presented in Table 199. Sample means for eight cranial measurements from these series were pooled with sample means from 13 previously analyzed sites (Table 200) and analyzed with discriminant functions.

Figure 40 shows the samples plotted on the two discriminant functions. All of the analyzed samples fall into one of two groups: the Polish or Early medieval Croat population group, and the Bijelo Brdo culture population group. When the analyzed sites are separated into two temporal groups, an older group comprised of sites dated from the 8th to the 10th century, and a younger group comprised of sites younger than the 10th century, the following pictures appear.

Figure 41 shows the geographical positions of the older sites. As can be seen, only four of the analyzed sites are affiliated with the Polish or Early medieval Croat population group. These sites are placed in a, more or less, straight line, wedged between a cluster of Bijelo Brdo sites compactly placed to the north. This figure may depict one migration route taken by the early medieval Croat populations.

Figure 42 shows the geographical position of the younger sites. This is a more complex picture which appears to depict an expansion of early medieval Croat populations from the confines of their state on the east coast of the Adriatic, to the north into modern Bosnia and Herzegovina and what is today continental Croatia. Of the eight sites analyzed in continental Croatia, five (Stenjevac, Đelekovec, Zvonimirovo, Josipovo and Đakovo phase I) are affiliated with early medieval Croat populations, while three (Lobor, Bijelo Brdo and Vukovar) are affiliated with Bijelo Brdo culture populations.

It is possible that this northward expansion of Early medieval Croat populations is related to the significant deterioration of living conditions in continental Croatia during Late medieval times. The high frequency of defensive mid-shaft fractures of the ulna (more than three times as high as frequencies recorded in the other composite series, see Figure 36), argues that this expansion was characterized by violent confrontations.

TABLE 199: Sites included in discriminant function analysis

Site	Country	Datation	Reference
1. Nin-Ždrijac	Croatia	8-10 cent.	Štefančić, 1995
2. Danilo-Šematorij	Croatia	10-16 cent.	Šlaus, 1996
3. Mravinci	Croatia	9-10 cent.	Mikić, 1990
4. Bugojno-Čipulići	B and H	10-16 cent.	Klug, 1987
5. Gomjenica-Baltine Bare	B and H	10-11 cent.	Pilarić, 1969
6. Stenjevac-Župni voćnjak	Croatia	11-13 cent.	Šlaus, 2000b
7. Lobor	Croatia	11 cent.	Šlaus, 2000b
8. Ptuj-Grad	Slovenia	10-11 cent.	Ivaniček, 1951
9. Đelekovec-Ščapovo I	Croatia	12-13 cent.	Šlaus, 2000b
10. Zvonimirovo-Veliko polje	Croatia	11 cent.	Šlaus, 2000b
11. Josipovo-Ciganka	Croatia	11 cent.	Boljunčić, 1997b
12. Đakovo I	Croatia	11-13 cent.	Šlaus and Filipec, 1998
13. Bijelo Brdo-Ulica Venecija	Croatia	10-11 cent.	Šlaus, 1998
14. Vukovar-Lijeva Bara	Croatia	10-11 cent.	Pilarić and Schwidetzky, 1987
15. Alsórajk-Határi	Hungary	9 cent.	Éry, 1996
16. Zalaszabar-Dezsosziget	Hungary	9 cent.	Éry, 1992
17. Garabonc I	Hungary	9 cent.	Éry, 1992
18. Zalavár-Kápolna	Hungary	11-12 cent.	Wenger, 1970
19. Kaposvár-Fészerlakpuszta	Hungary	8 cent.	Wenger, 1975
20. Pitten-Kreuzackergasse	Austria	9 cent.	Fabrizii and Reuer, 1977
21. Rajhrad	Czech Rep.	9 cent.	Hanáková et al., 1986
22. Mikulčice I-IV	Czech Rep.	9 cent.	Stloukal and Vyhnanek, 1976
23. Abraham	Slovakia	11 cent.	Stloukal and Hanáková, 1971
24. Nitra-Lupka	Slovakia	9 cent.	Thurzo, 1969
25. Virt	Slovakia	7-8 cent.	Hanáková et al., 1976
26. Želovce	Slovakia	7-8 cent.	Stloukal and Hanáková, 1974

TABLE 200: Sample means for eight cranial variables analyzed by discriminant functions

Site	Mean values for variables defined by Martin-Saller							
	1	8	9	17	45	48	51	52
1. Nin-Ždrijac	187.7	138.1	96.7	135.4	131.3	70.3	40.7	32.9
2. Danilo	187.2	145.5	97.2	139.4	134.0	67.0	40.2	31.5
3. Mravinci	186.1	138.3	97.9	136.3	131.3	68.9	38.1	30.3
4. Bugojno	192.6	141.8	98.3	138.8	133.0	69.7	41.8	32.4
5. Gomjenica	190.9	138.7	97.7	139.3	128.8	71.3	39.7	33.5
6. Stenjevac	189.5	141.5	101.7	142.0	131.0	70.7	38.3	32.0
7. Lobor	187.0	142.0	101.0	130.0	129.0	66.0	37.0	30.0
8. Ptuj	189.3	143.6	99.5	136.5	133.2	70.6	41.7	32.9
9. Đelekovec	181.1	141.8	96.2	139.5	127.9	65.7	39.4	30.9
10. Zvonimirovo	193.0	140.0	100.0	140.0	138.0	74.0	41.0	34.0
11. Josipovo	193.0	143.0	98.3	142.0	130.0	74.6	38.4	33.9
12. Đakovo phase I	193.0	141.3	101.6	139.3	138.5	63.3	40.2	33.0
13. Bijelo Brdo	187.5	140.5	99.3	137.1	134.2	73.1	39.8	33.3
14. Vukovar	182.9	144.1	98.9	134.2	129.2	78.1	40.9	32.9
15. Alsórajk	184.9	139.2	97.8	135.7	130.4	70.4	41.7	32.5
16. Zalaszabar	189.7	137.7	98.6	138.8	133.2	69.4	42.5	32.6
17. Garabonc I	189.3	141.7	98.9	135.6	132.7	69.7	41.3	32.6
18. Zalavár	186.1	140.8	95.9	135.1	132.0	68.3	39.9	32.1
19. Kaposvár	187.4	139.2	101.6	139.2	134.8	68.4	42.8	33.7
20. Pitten	187.6	140.0	98.1	137.2	132.8	71.0	42.2	33.5
21. Rajhrad	186.5	141.5	97.7	135.0	132.1	68.3	41.7	32.8
22. Mikulčice I-IV	187.4	142.6	99.2	137.0	133.9	72.4	41.9	33.7
23. Abraham	187.0	142.0	98.0	135.5	135.3	71.9	41.4	33.5
24. Nitra	184.7	136.8	96.7	133.6	132.1	68.3	38.8	31.8
25. Virt	184.1	140.4	98.7	136.4	130.5	68.2	41.9	32.5
26. Želovce	185.5	142.2	99.3	136.2	133.0	70.6	41.8	31.9

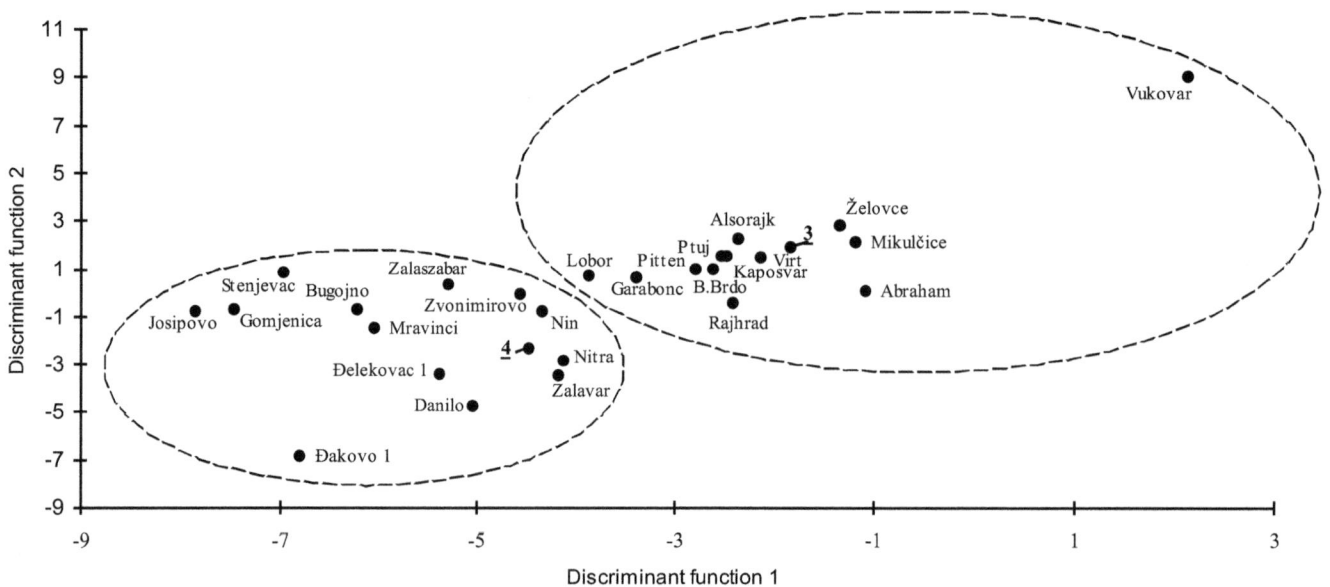

Figure 40. Plot of additionally analyzed sites on the two discriminant functions

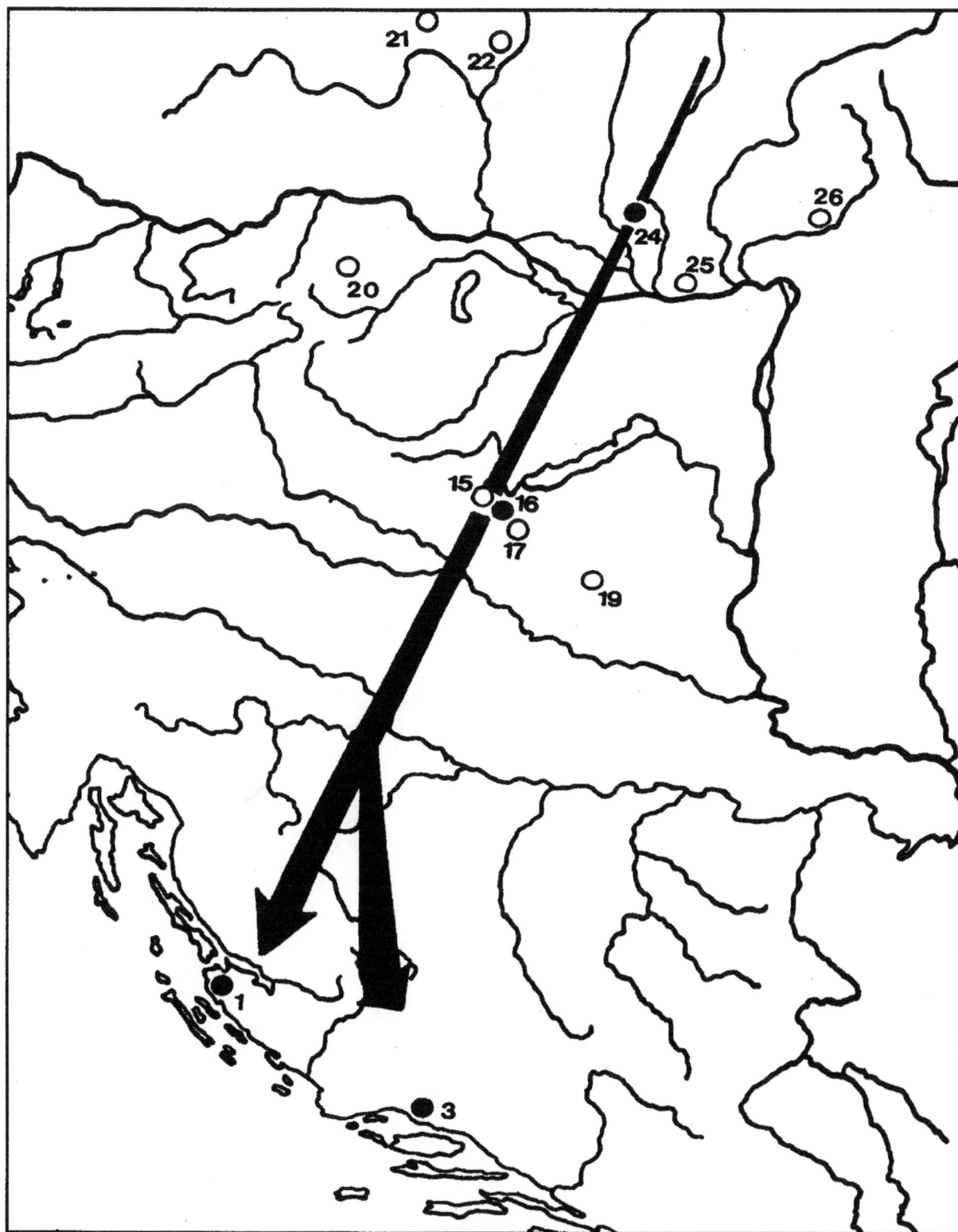

Figure 41. Geographical location of the 8th-10th century sites. Numbers correspond to site numbers in Table 199.

● Early medieval Croat
○ Bijelo Brdo Culture

It that is indeed the case, an obvious question that can be raised is how is it, and is it even possible, that this expansion was not recorded in historical sources? The answer to this question lies outside the province of this book. Certainly, based on the sketchy and conflicting reports regarding the arrival of the Croats on the east coast of the Adriatic, it would seem that a gradual northward expansion of Croat populations could go unnoticed in historical sources. It is important to keep in mind that the first history writers who mention the arrival of the Croats are not Croat, but Byzantine writers, who for their own political reasons took an interest into events taking place on their frontiers. During the Late medieval period the Byzantine Empire was in an unstoppable decline and could no longer take the time to record anything outside it's own borders.

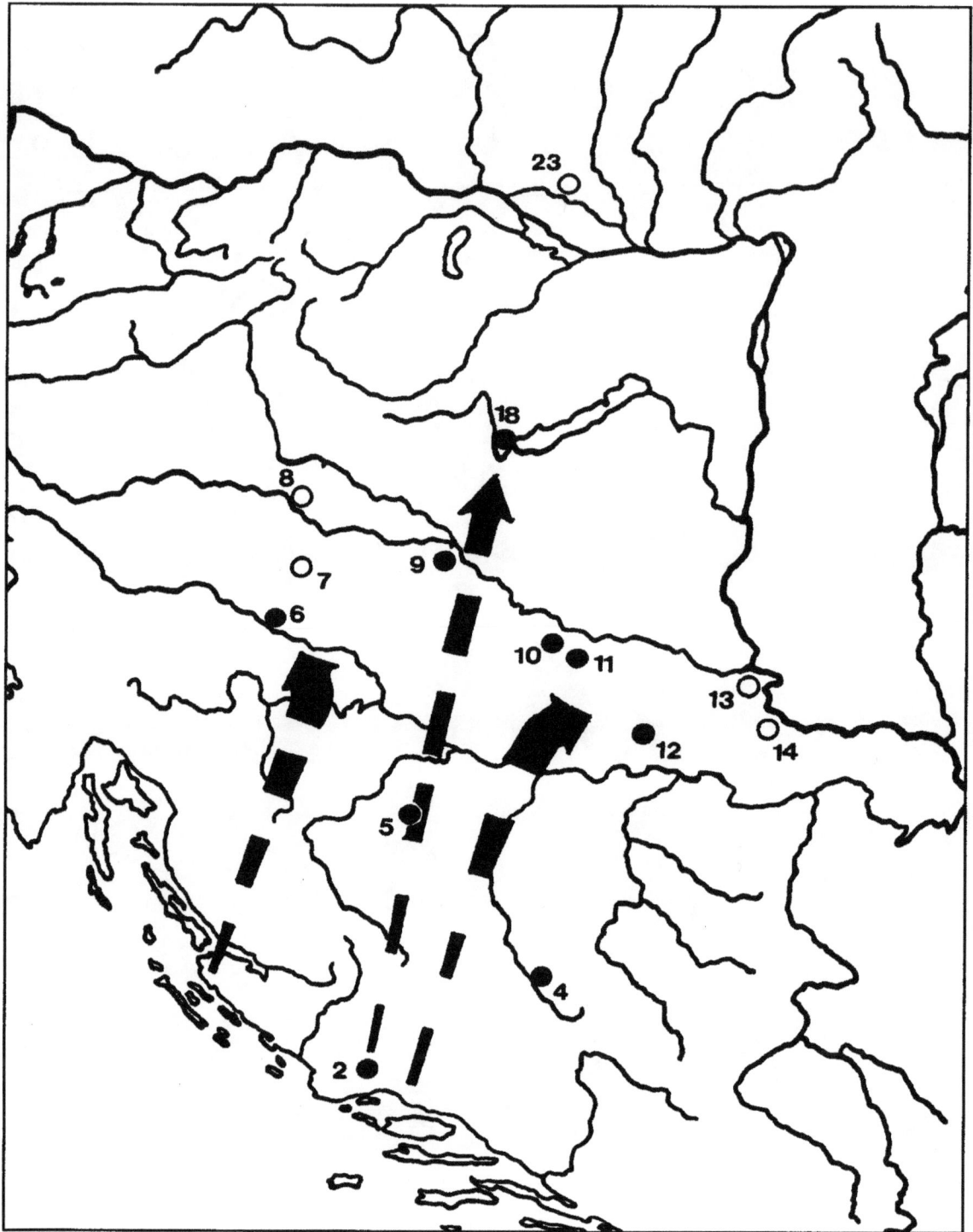

Figure 42. Geographical location of the sites younger than the 10th century.
Numbers correspond to site numbers in Table 199.

● Early medieval Croat
○ Bijelo Brdo Culture

9. CONCLUSIONS

Skeletal collections are, like historical documents, and artifacts recovered from archaeological sites, a record of the past and must be studied if that past is to be understood. The accomplishments of past researchers are numerous but there is still much that we do not know and, as this book demonstrates, important data that can be inferred only by bioarchaeological research. Future investigations of newly recovered and existing museum collections are therefore necessary. These investigations must take full advantage of recent technological advances, including DNA analyses, and more sophisticated research designs. Archaeological institutions must insure that bioarchaeological research is an integral part of any project dealing with recovered human skeletal remains, including cremated remains, and that the completed analysis is of high quality. Once this is recognized, and adequate funding for this type of research is made available, bioarchaeological data will become a primary source for elucidating the lives of the past inhabitants of Croatia.

This book examines the bioarchaeology of continental Croatia from Prehistoric to Historic times and offers a model for research applicable to future investigations. The data collected shows important similarities and differences in demography and disease frequencies between five temporal groups. Differences in the frequencies of subadult stress, infectious disease and trauma suggest a deterioration of living conditions during the Late medieval period. Multivariate craniometric analyses show that this coincides with an expansion of Early medieval Croat populations from the eastern coast of the Adriatic, into modern Bosnia and Herzegovina and continental Croatia. Further analyses of skeletal series from continental Croatia are necessary to see if data from these collections confirm this correlation.

Another future goal is to apply this research model to skeletal series from the east Adriatic coast. The eastern Adriatic coast is a very different environment from continental Croatia offering more opportunities for different subsistence strategies and easier access to trade. Comparing the frequencies of specific disease categories across the five temporal groups analyzed in this book will show to what extent these differences affected general health and quality of life.

ABBREVIATIONS FOR JOURNALS CITED

A. Ant. Arch.	Acta Antiqua et Archaeologica
Acta Arch. Acad. Sc. Hung.	Acta Archaeologica Academiae Scientarium Hungaricae
A. Biol.	Acta Biologica Universitatis Szegediensis
Am. Anthropol.	American Anthropologist
Am. J. Archaeol.	American Journal of Archaeology
Am. J. Clin. Nutr.	American Journal of Clinical Nutrition
Am. J. Phys. Anthropol.	Americam Journal of PhysicalAnthropology
Ann. HN	Annales Historico-naturalis Musei Nationalis Hungarici
Ann. N.Y. Acad. Sci.	Annales of the New York Academy of Science
Anthropol. Anz.	Anthropologischer Anzeiger
Anthropol. Közl.	Anthropologiai Közlemények
Anthropol. Hung.	Anthropologia Hungarica
AP	Arheološki pregled
ARR	Arheološki radovi i rasprave
Biol. Közl.	Biológiai Közlemények
CMJ	Croatian Medical Journal
Coll. Antropol.	Collegium Antropologicum
Cran. Hung.	Crania Hungarica
Curr. Anthropol.	Current Anthropology
GZM	Glasnik Zemaljskog Muzeja Sarajevo
Hum. Biol.	Human Biology
Hum. Evol.	Human Evolution
J. Amer. Dent. Assoc.	Jornal of the American Dental Association
J. Archaeol. Sci.	Journal of Archaeological Science
J. Bone Joint Surg.	Journal of Bone and Joint Surgery
J. Canad. Dent. Assoc.	Journal of the Canadian Dental Association
J. Dent. Res.	Journal of Dental Research
J. Forensic Sci.	Journal of Forensic Sciences
Mat. Prace Antrop.	Materialy i prace antropologiczne, Wroclaw
Med. Anthropol.	Medical Anthropology
Mitteil. Prähist. Komm.	Mitteilungen der Prähistorische Kommission
Muz.Vjes.	Muzejski vjesnik Varaždin
Obavijesti	Obavijesti Hrvatskog arheološkog društva
Odont. Rev.	Odontological Review
Opusc. Archaeol.	Opuscula Archaeologica
Pod. Zbor.	Podravski Zbornik
Pril. Inst. arheol.	Prilozi Instituta za arheologiju u Zagrebu
Rad HAZU	Radovi Hrvatske akademije znanosti i umjetnosti
Slov. Arch.	Slovenská Archeologia
SHP	Starohrvatska prosvjeta
SNM	Sborník Národního Muzea v Praze
VAHD	Vjesnik za arheologiju i historiju dalmatinsku
VAMZ	Vjesnik Arheološkog muzeja u Zagrebu
World Archaeol.	World Archaeology
Yearbook Phys. Anthropol.	Yearbook of Physical Anthropology

REFERENCES CITED

Acsádi G and Nemeskéri J (1970) History of Human Life Span and Mortality. Budapest: Akadémiai Kiadó.

Aufderheide AC and Rodriguez-Martin C (1998) The Cambridge Encyclopedia of Human Paleopathology. Cambridge: Cambridge University Press.

Barker DJP (1994) Mother, Babies, and Disease in Later Life. London: BMJ.

Bartucz L and Farkas Gy (1957) Zwei Adorjáner Gräberfelder der Awarenzeit aus anthropologischem Geschichtspunkte Betrachtet. A. Biol. 3: 315-347.

Bass WM (1987) Human Osteology. A Laboratory and Field Manual of the Human Skeleton. 3rd ed. Columbia, MO: Missouri Archaeological Society.

Basta SS, Karyadi D, and Scrimshaw NS (1979) Iron deficiency anemia and the productivity of adult males in Indonesia. Am. J. Clin. Nutr. 32: 916-925.

Bhaskar SN (1981) Synopsis of Oral pathology. 6th ed. St. Louis, Mo.: C.V. Mosby.

Bhaskaram P (1988) Immunology of iron-deficient subjects. In RK Chandra (ed.): Nutrition and Immunology. New York: Alan R. Liss, Inc. pp. 149-168.

Boljunčić J (1991) Anomalije na gornjim ljuskama zatiljnih kostiju dviju brončanodobnih čovječjih lubanja iz spilje Bezdanjače kod Vrhovina u Lici. Rad HAZU 458: 131-142.

Boljunčić J (1993) Antropološka analiza kosturnih ostataka iz srednjevjekovnog groblja Zvonimirovo kod Suhopolja (Hrvatska). Pril. Inst. arheol. 10: 131-148.

Boljunčić J (1997a) Antropološka analiza ranosrednjovjekovnog groblja Zvonimirovo-Veliko Polje. In Ž Tomičić (ed.): Zvonimirovo i Josipovo, groblja starohrvatskog doba u Virovitičko-podravskoj županiji. Zagreb-Virovitica: Institut za arheologiju u Zagrebu, pp. 53-61.

Boljunčić J (1997b) Antropološka analiza ranosrednjovjekovnog groblja Josipovo (Ciganka). In Ž Tomičić (ed.): Zvonimirovo i Josipovo, groblja starohrvatskog doba u Virovitičko-podravskoj županiji. Zagreb-Virovitica: Institut za arheologiju u Zagrebu, pp. 27-35.

Brandt M (1980) Opća povijest srednjeg vijeka. Zagreb: Školska knjiga.

Brooks S and Suchey JM (1990) Skeletal age determination based on the os pubis: A comparison of the Acsádi-Nemeskéri and Suchey-Brooks methods. Hum. Evol. 5: 227-238.

Cambi N (1988) Antički sarkofazi u Dalmaciji. Split: Književni krug.

Cook DC and Buikstra JE (1979) Health and differential survival in prehistoric populations: Prenatal dental defects. Am. J. Phys. Anthropol. 51: 649-664.

Cybulski JS (1977) Cribra orbitalia, a possible sign of anemia in early historic native populations of the British Columbia coast. Am. J. Phys. Anthropol. 47: 31-49.

Cyron GM, Hutton WC and Troup JDG (1976) Spondylolytic fractures. J. Bone Joint Surg. 58 B(4): 462-466.

Demo Ž (1984) Castrum Keukaproncha/Kuwar - počeci istraživanja. Pod. Zbor. 84: 320-360.

Demo Ž (1996) Vukovar Lijeva Bara. Zagreb: Arheološki muzej Zagreb.

Dimitrijević S, Težak-Gregl T and Majnarić-Pandžić N (1998) Prapovijest. Zagreb: Naprijed.

Dobronić L (1984) Viteški redovi: Templari i Ivanovci u Hrvatskoj. Zagreb: Kršćanska sadašnjost.

Drechsler-Bižić R (1979) Nekropola brončanog doba u pećini Bezdanjači kod Vrhovina. VAMZ 12/13: 27-78.

Duray SM (1996) Dental indicators of stress and reduced age at death in prehistoric Native Americans. Am. J. Phys. Anthropol. 99: 275-286.

Durman A (2000) The Vučedol Orion and the Oldest European Calendar - Exhibition catalogue. Zagreb: Arheološki muzej u Zagrebu, Gradski muzej Vinkovci, Gradski muzej Vukovar.

Durman A and Obelić B (1989) Radiocarbon dating of the Vučedol culture complex. Radiocarbon 31: 1003-1009.

El-Najjar MY (1976) Maize, malaria, and the anemias in the Pre-Columbian New World. Yearbook Phys. Anthropol. 20: 329-337.

El-Najjar MY, Ryan DJ Turner CG, and Lozoff B (1976) The etiology of porotic hyperostosis among the prehistoric and historic Anasazi Indians of southwestern United States. Am. J. Phys. Anthropol. 44: 477-488.

Éry K (1967) An anthropological study of the Late Avar period population of Ártánd. Ann. HN. 59: 465-484.

Éry K (1981) Anthropologische Analyse der Population von Tokod aus dem 5. Jahrhundert, In A. Mócsy (ed.): Die spätrömische Festung und das Gräberfeld von Tokod. Budapest: Akadémiai Kiadó, pp. 223-263.

Éry K (1992) Anthropologische Untersuchungen an drei Populationen aus dem 9. Jahrhundert in Westungarn. Antaeus 21: 337-375.

Éry K (1996) Anthropologische Untersuchungen an zwei frühgeschichtlichen Populationen des Hahóter Beckens (SW-Ungarn). Antaeus. 23: 147-165.

Fabrizii S and Reuer E (1977) Die Skelette aus dem frühmittelalterlichen Gräberfeld von Pitten, p.B. Neunkirchen. Mitteil. Prähist. Komm. 17/18: 175-233.

Fazekas IG and Kósa F (1978) Forensic Fetal Osteology. Budapest: Akadémiai Kiadó.

Filipec K (1996) Istraživanje srednjovjekovnog groblja u Đakovu 1995 i 1996 godine. Opusc. Archaeol. 20: 189-197.

Filipec K (1997) Đakovo-Župna Crkva, treća godina zaštitnih arheoloških iskopavanja. Opusc. Archaeol. 21: 239-242.

Filipec K (1999) Zaštitno arheološko iskapanje kod svetišta Majke Božije Gorske u Loboru. Obavijesti 31: 88-93.

Gilbert BM and McKern TW (1973) A method for aging the female os pubis. Am. J. Phys. Anthropol. 38: 31-38.

Goodman AH and Armelagos GJ (1985) Factors affecting the distribution of enamel hypoplasias within the human permanent dentition. Am. J. Phys. Anthropol. 68: 479-493.

Goodman AH and Armelagos GJ (1988) Childhood stress and decreased longevity in a prehistoric population. Am. Anthropol. *90:* 936-944.

Goodman AH and Armelagos GJ (1989) Infant and childhood morbidity and mortality risks in archaeological populations. World Archaeology *21:* 227-242.

Goodman AH and Rose JC (1990) Assessment of systemic physiological perturbations from dental enamel hypoplasias and associated histological structures. Yearbook Phys. Anthropol. *33:* 59-110.

Goodman AH and Rose JC (1991) Dental enamel hypoplasias as indicators of nutritional status. In M Kelley and C Larsen (eds.): Advances in Dental Anthropology. New York: Wiley-Liss. Inc., pp. 279-294.

Goodman AH, Armelagos GJ, and Rose JC (1980) Enamel hypoplasias as indicators of stress in three prehistoric populations from Illinois. Hum. Biol. *52:* 515-528.

Goodman AH, Martinez C, and Chavez A (1991) Nutritional supplementation and the development of linear enamel hypoplasia in children from Solis, Mexico. Am. J. Clin. Nutr. *53:* 773-781.

Goodman AH, Pelto GH, Allen LH, and Chavez A (1992) Socioeconomic and anthropometric correlates of linear enamel hypoplasia in children from Solis, Mexico. In AH Goodman and LL Capasso (eds.): Recent Contributions to the Study of Enamel Developmental Defects. Chieti, Italy: Journal of Paleopathology, Monographic Publication 2, pp. 373-380.

Göricke-Lukić H (1999) Osijek-trg Bana Josipa Jelačića 19, rezultati zaštitnog iskapanja istočne nekropole rimske Murse. Obavijesti *3:* 86-89.

Göricke-Lukić H (2000) Sjeveroistočna nekropola rimske Murse. Zagreb-Osijek: Hrvatska akademija znanosti i umjetnosti and Muzej Slavonije Osijek.

Gregl Z (1982) Zagreb - Stenjevac. VAMZ *(15):* 272-273.

Gregl Z (1994) Kasnoantička nekropola Štrbinci kod Đakova - istraživanja 1993 g. Opusc. archaeol. *18:* 181-190.

Gregl Z (1997) Rimske nekropole sjeverne Hrvatske. Zagreb: Arheološki muzej u Zagrebu.

Gustafson G and Koch G (1974) Age estimation up to 16 years of age based on dental development. Odont. Rev. *25:* 297-306.

Hanáková H and Stloukal M (1966) Staroslovanské pohřebiště v Josefove. Rozpravy Českoslov. Akad. Ved Ročnik 76, Seseit 9.

Hanáková H, Stloukal M and Vyhnánek L (1976) Kostry ze slovansko-avarkého pohřebiště ve Virtu, SNM *32:* 57-113.

Hanáková H, Stana Č and Stloukal M (1986) Velkomoravské pohřebiště v Rajhrade. Prague: Národni Muzeum v Praze.

Hengen OP (1971) Cribra orbitalia: Pathogenesis and probable etiology. Homo *22:* 57-75.

Henry CJK and Ulijaszek J (eds.) (1996) Long-term Consequences of Early Environment : Growth, Development and the Lifespan Developmental Perspective. Society for the Study of Human Biology Series No. 37. New York: Cambridge University Press.

Hildebolt CF, Molnar S, Elvin-Lewis M and McKee JK (1988) The effect of geochemical factors on prevalences of dental diseases for prehistoric inhabitants of the state of Missouri. Am. J. Phys. Anthropol. *75:* 1-14.

Huss-Ashmore R, Goodman AH, and Armelagos GJ (1982) Nutritional inference from paleopathology. In MB Schiffer (ed.): Advances in Archaeological Method and Theory, Vol. 5. New York: Academic Press, pp. 395-474.

Iscan MY, Loth SR, and Wright RK (1984) Age estimation from the rib by phase analysis: White males. J. Forensic Sci. *29:* 1094-1104.

Iscan MY, Loth SR, and Wright RK (1985) Age estimation from the rib by phase analysis: White females. J. Forensic Sci. *30:* 853-863.

Ivaniček F (1951) Staroslavenska nekropola u Ptuju-rezultati antropoloških istraživanja. Ljubljana: Slovenska akademija znanosti in umetnosti.

Jakovljević G (1986) Arheološka istraživanja u Novoj Rači. Obavijesti *18:* 18-19.

Jakovljević G (1988) Novi rezultati istraživanja župne crkve u Novoj Rači. Obavijesti *20:* 48-50.

Jakovljević G (1999) Zaštitna iskopavanja crkava u Đurđicu i Tomašu kraj Bjelovara. Muz. Vjes. *21/22:* 27-29.

Jantz RL (1973) Microevolutionary change in Arikara crania: A multivariate analysis. Am. J. Phys. Anthropol. *38:* 15-26.

Jantz RL (1974) The Redbird focus: Cranial evidence in tribal identification. Plains Anthropologist *19:* 5-13.

Jantz RL (1994) The Social, Historical, and Functional Dimensions of Skeletal Variation. In DW Owsley and RL Jantz (eds.): Skeletal Biology in the Great Plains: Migration, Warfare, Health, and Subsistence. Washington: Smithsonian Institution Press, pp. 175-178.

Katičić R (1997) O podrijetlu Hrvata. In I Supičić (ed.): Hrvatska i Europa: Kultura, Znanost i Umjetnost, Svezak I. Zagreb: Hrvatska akademija znanosti i umjetnosti and AGM, pp. 149-167.

Key PJ (1994) Relationships of the Woodland Period on the Northern and Central Plains: The Craniometric evidence. In DW Owsley and RL Jantz (eds.): Skeletal Biology in the Great Plains: Migration, Warfare, Health, and Subsistence. Washington: Smithsonian Institution Press, pp. 179-187.

Klaić N (1971) Povijest Hrvata u ranom srednjem vijeku. Zagreb: Školska knjiga.

Klaić N (1990) Povijest Hrvata u srednjem vijeku. Zagreb: Globus.

Klug S (1987) Čipulić-Bugojno. Ein Beitrag zur Anthropologie mittelalterlicher Südslawen. Homo *38:* 16-34.

Kohegyi M and Marcsik A (1971) The avar age cemetry at Sükösd. A. Ant. Arch. *14:* 87-94.

Kolar S (1976) Arheološki lokaliteti u općini Koprivnica. Pod. Zbor. *76:* 103-116.

Kovačević J (1963) Avari i zlato. Starinar *13-14:* 125-135.

Kreshover SJ (1960) Metabolic disturbances in tooth formation. Ann. N.Y. Acad. Sci. *85:* 161-167.

Krogman WM and Iscan MY (1986) The Human Skeleton in Forensic Medicine. 2nd ed. Springfield, IL: C.C. Thomas.

Larsen CS (1983) Behavioral implications of temporal change in cariogenesis. J. Archaeol. Sci. *10:* 1-8.

Lipták P (1953) L'analyse typologique de la population de Kérpuszta au moyen âge. Acta Arch. Acad. Sc. Hung. *3:* 303-370.

Lipták P (1954) Avars in the environs of Kecel. Biol. Közl. *2:* 159-180.

Lipták P (1955) Recherches anthropologiques sur les ossements avares des environs d' Üllo. Acta Arch. Acad. Sc. Hung. *6:* 231-316.

Lipták P (1957) The Avar age population of Homokmégy-Halom. Anthropol. Közl. *4:* 25-42.

Lipták P (1974) Anthropological analysis of the Avar-Period population of Szekszard-Palankpuszta. A. Biol. *20:* 199-211.

Lipták P (1983) Avars and Ancient Hungarians. Budapest: Akademiai Kiado.

Lipták P and Marcsik A (1966) An anthropological examination of the Avar-Age population of Szeged-Kundomb. Anthropol. Közl. *10:* 13-56.

Lipták P and Marcsik A (1976) An anthropological characterization of the skeletal remains of an Avar cemetery near Madars-Téglaveto. Cumania *4*: 115-140.

Lipták P and Vámos K (1969) An anthropological examination of the skeletal material of the Avar Age cemetery called "Fehérto-A". Anthropol. Közl. *13*: 3-30.

Lovejoy CO, Meindl RS, Pryzbeck TR, and Mensforth RP (1985) Chronological metamorphosis of the auricular surface of the ilium: A new method for the determination of age at death. Am. J. Phys. Anthropol. *68*: 15-28.

Lukacs JR (1992) Dental paleopathology and agricultural intensification in South Asia: New evidence from Bronza Age Harappa. Am. J. Phys. Anthropol. *87*: 133-150.

Lukacs JR and Pal JN (1993) Mesolithic subsistence in north India: Inferences from dental pathology and odontometry. Curr. Anthropol. *34*: 745-765.

Macan T (1992) Povijest Hrvatskoga Naroda. Zagreb: Školska Knjiga.

Majnarić-Pandžić N (2000) O pojavi novih tipova konjske opreme iz završnog starijeg željeznog doba u istočnoj Hrvatskoj. Opusc. archaeol. *23/24*: 27-38.

Malez M, Vekić P, Garašić M and Prebanić O (1988) Antropološko i arheološko značenje Jopićeve spilje na Kordunu (SR Hrvatska). Naš Krš *24/25*: 63-68.

Mann RW and Jantz RL (1988) Maxillary suture obliteration: Aging the human skeleton based on intact or fragmentary maxilla. J. Forensic Sci. *32*: 148-157.

Mann RW and Murphy SP (1990) Regional Atlas of Bone Disease. A Guide to Pathologic and Normal Variation in the Human Skeleton. Springfield IL.: C.C. Thomas.

McKern TW and Stewart TD (1957) Skeletal Age Changes in Young American Males. Analyzed from the Standpoint of Age Identification. Environmental Protection Research Division (Quarter-Master Research and Development Center, U.S. Army, Natick, Massachusetts), Technical Report EP-45.

Medar M (1987) Sažeti prikaz dosadašnjih rezultata arheoloških istraživanja prostora crkve Svete Marije u Novoj Rači kod Bjelovara. Obavijesti *19*: 46-49.

Meindl RS and Lovejoy CO (1985) Ectocranial suture closure: A revised method for the determination of skeletal age at death based on the lateral-anterior sutures. Am. J. Phys. Anthropol. *68*: 57-66.

Meindl RS, Lovejoy CO, Mensforth RP, and Don Carlos L (1985) Accuracy and direction of error in the sexing of the skeleton: Implications for paleodemography. Am. J. Phys. Anthropol. *68*: 79-85.

Mensforth RP, Lovejoy CO, Lallo JW, and Armelagos GJ (1978) The role of constitutional factors, diet and infectious disease in the etiology of porotic hyperostosis and periosteal reactions in prehistoric infants and children. Med. Anthropol. *2*: 1-59.

Merbs CF (1983) Patterns of activity-induced pathology in a Canadian Inuit poplation. Archaeological Survey of Canada Paper, Mercury Series 119. National Museum of Man, Ottawa, Ontario Canada.

Merbs CF (1989) Trauma. In MY Iscan and KAR Kennedy (eds.): Reconstruction of Life from the Skeleton. New York: A.R. Liss, pp. 161-190.

Migotti B (1997) Evidence for Christianity in Roman Southern Pannonia (Northern Croatia). Oxford: BAR 684.

Migotti B (1998) Accede Ad Certissiam - Antički i ranokršćanski horizont arheološkog nalazišta Štrbinci kod Đakova. Zagreb: Hrvatska akademija znanosti i umjetnosti, Odsjek za arheologiju.

Mikić Ž (1990) Antropološki profil srednjovekovne nekropole u Mravincima kod Splita. VAHD *83*: 225-232.

Mittler DM and Van Gerven DP (1994) Developmental, diachronic, and demographic analysis of cribra orbitalia in the medieval Christian populations of Kulubnarti. Am. J. Phys. Anthropol. *93*: 287-297.

Moorrees CFA, Fanning EA, and Hunt EE (1963) Age variation of formation stages for ten permanent teeth. J. Dent. Res. *42*: 1490-1502.

Ortner DJ and Putschar WGJ (1981) Identification of Pathological Conditions in Human Skeletal Remains. Smithsonian Contributions to Anthropology, No. 28. Washington, D.C.: Smithsonian Institution Press.

Owsley DW and Bradtmiller B (1983) Mortality of pregnant females in Arikara villages: Osteological evidence. Am. J. Phys. Anthropol. *61*: 331-336.

Owsley DW, Orser CE, Mann RW, Moore-Jansen PH, and Montgomery RL (1987) Demography and pathology of an urban slave population from New Orleans. Am. J. Phys. Anthropol. *74*: 185-197.

Owsley DW, Mann RW, and Murphy SP (1991) Injuries, surgical care and disease. In S Pfeiffer and RF Williamson (eds.): Snake Hill: An Investigation of a Military Cemetery from the War of 1812. Toronto: Dundurn Press, pp. 198-226.

Owsley DW and Jantz RL (1999) A Systematic approach to the Skeletal Biology of the Southern Plains. In JC Rose (ed.): Bioarchaeology of the South Central United States. Fayetteville, Arkansas: Arkansas Archaeological Survey Research Report No. 55, pp. 171-183.

Perinić Lj (1999) Istraživanje kasnoantičke nekropole Štrbinci kod Đakova godine 1999. Obavijesti *31*: 98-102.

Phenice TW (1969) A newly developed visual method of sexing the os pubis. Am. J. Phys. Anthropol. *30*: 297-301.

Philpott R (1991) Burial Practices in Roman Britain. Oxford: BAR 219.

Pilarić G (1967) Antropološka istraživanja starohrvatskog groblja u Daraž-Bošnjacima 1961. godine. ARR *4/5*: 419-443.

Pilarić G (1968) Fenotipske značajke bjelobrdskih lubanja iz ranog srednjeg vijeka. ARR *6*: 263-291.

Pilarić G (1969) Antropološka istraživanja slavenske populacije sa Baltinih Bara kod Gomjenice. GZM *24*: 185-211.

Pilarić G and Schwidetzky I (1987) Vukovar und Bribir: Beitrag zur Anthropologie mittelalterlicher Sudslawen. Homo *38*: 1-15.

Pindborg JJ (1970) Pathology of the dental hard tissues. Philadelphia: W.B. Saunders.

Pintarić T (2000) Arheološko i geofizikalno istraživanje u Sčitarjevu. Obavijesti *32*: 64-67.

Rose JC, Armelagos GJ and Lallo JW (1978) Histological enamel indicators of childhood stress in prehistoric skeletal samples. Am. J. Phys. Anthropol. *49*: 511-516.

Rösing FW and Schwidetzky I (1977) Vergleichend-statistische Untersuchungen zur Anthropologie des fruhen Mittelalters (500-1000 n.d. Z.). Homo *28*: 65-115.

Rösing FW and Schwidetzky I (1981) Vergleichend-statistische Untersuchungen zur Anthropologie des Hochmittelalters (1000-1500 n.d. Z.). Homo *32*: 211-251.

Sarnat BG and Schour IS (1941) Enamel hypoplasia (chronologic enamel aplasia) in relation to systemic disease: A chronologic, morphologic, and etiologic classsification. J. Amer. Dent. Assoc. *28*: 1989-2000.

Sarnat BG and Schour IS (1942) Enamel hypoplasia (chronologic enamel aplasia) in relation to systemic disease: A chronologic, morphologic, and etiologic classsification. J. Amer. Dent. Assoc. *29*: 67-75.

Schmorl G and Junghanns H (1971) The Human Spine in Health and Disease. 2nd ed. (American). New York: Grune and Stratton.

Schneider KN (1986) Dental caries, enamel composition, and subsistence among prehistoric Amerindians of Ohio. Am. J. Phys. Anthropol. 71: 95-102.

Schwidetzky I (1967) Vergleichend-statistische Untersuchungen zur Anthropologie des Neolithikums: Ergebnisse der Penrose-Analyse. Das Gesamtmaterial. Homo 18: 174-198.

Schwidetzky I (1972) Vergleichend-statistische Untersuchungen zur Anthropologie der Eisenzeit. Homo 23: 245-272.

Schwidetzky I and Rösing FW (1984) Vergleichend-statistische Untersuchungen zur Anthropologie der Neuzeit (nach 1500). Homo 35: 1-49.

Sherman AR (1984) Iron, infection and immunity. In RR Watson (ed.): Nutrition, Disease, Resistance and Immune function. New York: Marcel Dekker, Inc., pp. 251-266.

Simoni K (1988) Sondažna istraživanja ranosrednjovjekovnog groblja u Stenjevcu kraj Zagreba. VAMZ 21: 159-160.

Simpson S, Hutchinson DL, and Larsen CS (1990) Coping with stress: Tooth-size, dental defects, and age at death. In CS Larsen (ed.): The Archaeology of Mission Santa Catalina de Guale: 2. Biocultural Inerpretations of a Population in Transition. New York: Anthropological Papers of the American Museum of Natural History no. 68.

Smokvina M (1959) Kosti i zglobovi. Zagreb: Jugoslavenska akademija znanosti i umjetnosti.

Steinbock RT (1976) Paleopathological Diagnosis and Interpretation: Bone Diseases in Ancient Human Populations. Springfield, IL.: C.C. Thomas.

Stloukal M and Hanáková H (1966) Antropologie der Slawen aus dem Gräberfeld in Nové Zámky. Slov. Arch. 14: 167-204.

Stloukal M and Hanáková H (1971) Antropologie ranestredovekeho pohrebište v Ábrahámu. SNM 22B: 57-131.

Stloukal M and Hanáková H (1974) Antropologický vyzkum pohrebište 7.-8. stoleti v Želovcich. Slov. Arch. 22: 129-188.

Stloukal M and Vyhnanek L (1976) Slováné velkomoravských Mikulčic. Prague: Nár. Muz. Praze.

Stodder ALW (1997) Subadult stress, morbidity, and longevity in Latte Period populations on Guam, Mariana Islands. Am. J. Phys. Anthropol. 104: 363-380.

Stuart-Macadam P (1985) Porotic hyperostosis: Representative of a childhood condition. Am. J. Phys. Anthropol. 66: 391-398.

Šarić-Bužančić A (1999) Pregled arheoloških i antropoloških istraživanja kasnosrednjovjekovnog groblja na lokalitetu Sv. Vid. In E Marin (ed.): Sveti Vid. Split: Arheološki muzej Split, pp. 209-266.

Šimić J (1998) Otkriće rimskih grobova u Zmajevcu (Baranja). Obavijesti 30: 55-56.

Šišić F (1925) Povijest Hrvata u vrijeme narodnih vladara. Zagreb: Nakladni zavod Matice hrvatske (pretisak iz 1990.)

Šlaus M (1993) Cranial variation and microevolution in two early medieval populations from Croatia: Privlaka and Stari Jankovci. Opusc. archaeol. 17: 273-307.

Šlaus M (1994) Osteological evidence for perimortem trauma and occupational stress in two medieval skeletons from Croatia. Coll. Antropol. 18: 165-175.

Šlaus M (1996) Antropološka analiza kasnosrednjovjekovne populacije iz Danila Gornjeg kraj Šibenika. ARR 12: 343-364.

Šlaus M (1997a) Demography and disease in the early medieval site of Privlaka. Opusc. archaeol. 20: 141-149.

Šlaus M (1997b) Discriminant function sexing of fragmentary and complete femora from medieval sites in continental Croatia. Opusc. archaeol. 21: 167-175.

Šlaus M (1998a) Antropološka analiza osteološkog materijala. In B Migotti (ed.): Accede ad Certissiam; Antički i ranokršćanski horizont arheološkog nalazišta Štrbinci kod Đakova. Zagreb: Hrvatska akademija znanosti i umjetnosti, pp. 121-134.

Šlaus M (1998b) Kraniometrijska analiza srednjovjekovnih populacija središnje Europe s posebnim osvrtom na položaj hrvatskih nalazišta. SHP 25: 81-107.

Šlaus M (1999) Antropološka analiza kasnoantičke populacije s nalazišta Ad Basilicas Pictas. In F Oreb, T Rismondo and M Topić (eds.): Ad Basilicas Pictas. Split: Ministarstvo kulture Republike Hrvatske, pp. 60-65.

Šlaus M (2000a) Biocultural analysis of sex differences in mortality profiles and stress levels in the late Medieval population from Nova Rača, Croatia. Am. J. Phys. Anthropol. 111: 193-209.

Šlaus M (2000b) Kraniometrijska analiza srednjovjekovnih nalazišta središnje Europe: novi dokazi o ekspanziji hrvatskih populacija tijekom 10. do 13. stoljeća. Opusc. archaeol. 23/24: 273-284.

Šlaus M and Filipec K (1998) Bioarchaeology of the medieval Đakovo cemetery: Archaeological and anthropological evidence for ethnic affiliation and migration. Opusc. archaeol. 22: 129-139.

Šlaus M, Pećina-Hrnčević A and Jakovljević G (1997) Dental disease in the late medieval population from Nova Rača, Croatia. Coll. Antropol. 21: 561-572.

Šlaus M, Orlić D and Pećina M (2000) Osteochondroma in a skeleton from an 11th century Croatian cemetery. CMJ 41: 336-340.

Šmalcelj M (1973) Privlaka - "Gole Njive" (općina Vinkovci) - Nekropola 7. do 9. stoljeća, sistematska iskopavanja. AP 15: 117-119.

Šmalcelj M (1976) Privlaka - "Gole Njive", Vinkovci - nekropola 8. do 9. stoljeća. AP 18: 127-128.

Šmalcelj M (1986) Srednjevjekovno groblje u Đelekovcu kraj Koprivnice. Obavijesti 18: 18.

Štefančič M (1995) Antropološka obdelava zgodnjesrednjeveških okostij iz grobišča Nin-Ždrijac (severna Dalmacija). Arheološki vestnik 46: 291-325.

Teschler-Nicola M and Berner ME (1994) Zur Anthropologie der endneolithischen Funde aus Vučedol. In: Die Neandertaler und die angange Europas, Katalog zur Sonderausstellung. Eisenstadt: Burgenlandischen Landesmuseum, pp. 61-78.

Thurzo M (1969) Antropologický rozbor kostrového pohrebiška "Lupka" v Nitre. Ac. Rer. Nat. Mus. Nat. Slov. 15: 77-153.

Todd TW (1920) Age changes in the pubic bone. I: The white male pubis. Am. J. Phys. Anthropol. 3: 285-334.

Todd TW (1921) Age changes in the pubic bone. III: The pubis of the white female. IV: the pubis of the female white-negro hybrid. Am. J. Phys. Anthropol. 4: 1-70.

Vámos K (1973) An anthropological examination of the Avar-Age population at "Szeged-Makkoserdo". Anthr. Közl. 17: 29-39.

Walker PL (1985) Porotic hyperostosis in a marine-dependent California Indian population. Am. J. Phys. Anthropol. 69: 345-354.

Wenger S (1955) Anthropological types of the population of the Great Migration Period at Szentes-Kaján. Ann. HN. 47: 391-410.

Wenger S (1957) Donnees osteométriques sur le material anthropologique de cimetiére d' Alattyán-Tulát, provenant de l' époque avare. Cran. Hung. 2: 1-55.

Wenger S (1968) Data to the anthropology of the Avar Period population of the Transdanubia. Anthropol. Hung. 8: 59-96.

Wenger S (1970) Data to the anthropology of the Early Árpádian Age population of the Balaton area. Anthropol. Hung. *9*: 63-145.

Wenger S (1974) On the anthropological problems of the Avar Age population in the Southern Transdanubia. Anthropol. Hung. *13*: 5-86.

Wenger S (1975) Paleoanthropology of the population deriving from the Avar Period at Fészerlakpuszta (Transdanubia). Anthropol. Hung. *14*: 57-110.

White TD (1978) Early hominid enamel hypoplasia. Am. J. Phys. Anthropol. *49*: 79-83.

Wiercinski A (1971) Zmiany w strukturze antropologicznej ludnosci Wislicy w ostatnim tysiacleciu. Rozpr. Nauk. Zespolu Badan nad Polsk. Sredniow. U.W. i P. W. 181-198.

Wokroj F (1953) Wczesnosredniowieczne czaszki polskie z Ostrowa Lednickiego. Mat. Prace Antrop. *1*: 5-172.

Wokroj F (1971) Zaludnienie Cedyni we wczesnym sredniowieczu w swietle antropologii. Materialy Zachodnopomorskie *17*: 229-296.

www.ingramcontent.com/pod-product-compliance
Lightning Source LLC
Chambersburg PA
CBHW061006030426
42334CB00033B/3383